Sistering

'The stories of sistering that the women of this study tell are gripping and challenging . . . [The book] aims to make sistering more visible, to theorise women's differing experiences of sistering and to begin to develop a language of sistering for the public domain. In achieving all of these aims (and more) in an accessible style that retains complexity of analysis and argument this book makes an important and timely contribution to the sociology of the family, to kinship studies and to debates in feminist politics.' *Sociology*

'This book will be of interest to those doing research on family relationships, and on relations of power between women. In addition, Mauthner offers food for thought to those working on feminist theory and who use sisterhood as a political metaphor. The empirical accounts of familial sisters show that we should not overly mythologize this relationship as an entirely positive one; at the same time, women's conscious efforts to work through or accept differences between them may indeed create a relation that is highly supportive. Mauthner's contribution lies in showing how the relations between women are better captured by the notion of "sistering" – a verb that evokes the on-going effort of creating kinship – rather than taken for granted as a fixed, naturalistic, or essentialistic relation which the noun "sisterhood" too easily implies.' *The Canadian Review of Sociology and Anthropology*

'In Sistering, the use of an auto/biographical approach through in-depth interviewing certainly generates rich, fascinating data which enables the complex nature of sistering and the four sistering discourses to emerge. . . . This book is an excellent read, discussing complex ideas, highlighting both the joy and pain involved in sistering, whilst being written in a language which is accessible. . . . It is a book which is very thought provoking and accessible to anyone interested in feminist discussion of female relationships, and also of interest to undergraduates, postgraduates and academics concerned with Sociology and Female Relationships or Women's/Gender Studies.' *International Journal of Social Research Methodology*

'Sistering is a fascinating, intricate and intriguing account of a particular set of female relationships that have rarely been studied and articulated in public.' *Gender and Education*

Sistering
Power and Change in Female Relationships

Melanie L. Mauthner

Faculty of Social Sciences
The Open University

With a Foreword by Jeffrey Weeks

First published in hardback 2002
First published in paperback 2005 by
PALGRAVE MACMILLAN
Houndmills, Basingstoke, Hampshire RG21 6XS and
175 Fifth Avenue, New York, N. Y. 10010
Companies and representatives throughout the world

PALGRAVE MACMILLAN is the global academic imprint of the Palgrave Macmillan division of St. Martin's Press, LLC and of Palgrave Macmillan Ltd. Macmillan® is a registered trademark in the United States, United Kingdom and other countries. Palgrave is a registered trademark in the European Union and other countries.

ISBN 13: 978-0-333-80080-5 hardback
ISBN 10: 0-333-80080-X hardback
ISBN 13: 978-1-4039-4125-1 paperback
ISBN 10: 1-4039-4125-4 paperback

This book is printed on paper suitable for recycling and made from fully managed and sustained forest sources.

A catalogue record for this book is available from the British Library.

Library of Congress Cataloging-in-Publication Data

Mauthner, Melanie L., 1964-
 Sistering : power and change in female relationships/ Melanie L. Mauthner.
 p.cm.
 Includes bibliographical references and index.
 ISBN 0333-80080-X
  1. Sisters. 2. Sisters--Family relationships. 3. Women--Psychology. I.
 Title.
 BF723.S43 M385 2002
 396.875--dc21
                                                                          2002072320

        10   9   8   7   6   5   4   3   2   1
        14 13 12 11 10 09 08 07 06 05

        Printed and bound in Great Britain by
        Antony Rowe Ltd, Chippenham and Eastbourne

In memory of my mother and her sister who both died a decade and a half ago – in memory of their lives, their bond and their inspiration

Contents

List of Tables and Figures

Acknowledgements

The women whose sistering experiences lie at the heart of this book gave generously of their time: their emotions and reflections shaped my argument. I am immensely grateful to them for sharing their lives and their insights with me.

Many colleagues, friends and kin made this book possible. Janet Holland supervised the doctoral dissertation on which it is based and taught me how to combine rigour and passion in qualitative research. Valerie Hey's intellectual energy and gift for friendship sustained me at all times. I also learned a great deal from Ann Oakley at the Social Science Research Unit, Institute of Education; she trained me in a range of methodologies and encouraged me to explore sisters' relationships.

Many people helped me to produce this book. Eva Garmarnikov, Mary Maynard, David Scott and Liz Stanley helped to clarify a number of key issues. Special thanks are due to Elina Lahelma, Virginia Morrow and Adam Steinhouse, who read through the entire final draft; and to Julia Mackenzie and Rachel Thomson, who commented on key chapters. Thanks to Diana Leonard, Sue Sharpe, Jo VanEvery and Susan Williams for their advice on turning a thesis into a book; and to Claire Higgins and Amanda Nicholas who transcribed the interviews. Members of the Women's Workshop on Qualitative Family/Household Research at South Bank University and colleagues at the Institute of Education, Southampton and Reading University Sociology Departments provided stimulating and testing audiences for the presentation of my ideas.

I appreciate the financial support of the AL Charitable Trust, the British Sociological Association, the Social Science Research Unit and other funds at the Institute of Education, University of London.

For their friendship, humour and nurture I would like to thank Bruce Currie, my brother Hugo Mauthner, Fenella Morris, Clare Mortimer and Anita Schrader. My sister Natasha Mauthner provided guidance through every step of this project. My father's concern and generosity have been inestimable. For his sustaining presence, I am grateful to Adam Steinhouse: his encouragement to begin, affection and patience throughout, and space to complete.

Foreword

If 'family' is what we do rather than some thing we simply belong to, an activity rather than a given, then how we do it matters. As we recognise more fully that family life is not so much declining but changing, perhaps radically, so we can begin to understand the complexity of family meanings and relationships. On the whole social scientists have broadly focused on relations between spouses/partners, and between adults/parents and children. But that scarcely exhausts our involvement with family. A growing literature is documenting the close overlap in many situations of family and friendship, so we can begin to understand the emergence of patterns of 'friends as family'. We are also increasingly aware of the significance of sibling relations. But in the case of relationships between brothers and sisters, brothers and brothers, sisters and sisters the temptation is always to confine them to the realm of the given and taken for granted, the domain of nature rather than social relations. Despite the iconic significance attributed to sisterhood in modern feminism, the familial origin and reality of that aspiration has been little studied. Melanie Mauthner's sensitive and subtle study of sistering, informed by feminist theory, challenges all that. What she rightly describes as a marginalised and neglected aspect of family life is brought fully within the scope of the sociological gaze, and in the process she convincingly demonstrates that doing sisterhood, sistering, matters.

Avoiding romanticisation and idealisation of the bonds between sisters, Melanie Mauthner nevertheless illuminates them in distinctive colours. The four discourses that emerge from the interviews that form the core of the research – best friendship, companionship (close and distant), and the positioned and shifting positions – provide a flexible typology which propel the exploration of sistering. At the same time, the book feeds into other research, which explores the micropolitics of family life, and the complex ways in which gender and subjectivity are shaped through the play of power in everyday relationships. The strategies of power and the resistances they evoke can be traced in the quotidian interactions between sisters, which remind us that in the ordinary and mundane lie the seedbeds of the wider relations of society. Sisterhood, like all social relations, has to be constructed from delicate strands whose fate is not predetermined by ideologies of the family, but woven in the push and pull, give and take, trial and error, of material life.

The biographical material used in the book vividly illustrates all this. Sisters speak with honesty and frankness, and a sort of everyday eloquence about their experiences as they confront the necessity of negotiating sibling bonds in the situations they find themselves in, making their own histories, but not always in the circumstances they would have freely chosen. Sisterly relations, it appears, are both structured, in a variety of ways, and flexible, ritualised, but open to change, potentially restrictive, but often empowering, demanding at times, but potentially supportive in transitions and fateful moments. There are successful relationships and failed relationships, and a host in between which veer between the extremes. Sisterly life does not depend on a hidden teleology. It has to be worked at.

That fact, however, is what gives sistering its strength. Relationships that are worked at are relations that can work. Successful sistering is a prolonged process, an achievement not a given. But as Melanie Mauthner abundantly demonstrates, when sisterhood is achieved, it can play a critical role in the organisation of personal identity and in the development of unique forms of intimacy. Not the least of the achievements of this book is that we can understand more clearly than ever before how that process works, and at the same time in the rich texture of the testimonies of sisters we can also feel the pains and pleasures of the experience of sistering.

Jeffrey Weeks
London South Bank University

Introduction

> My deepest-held habit was assuming that differences between Rose and me were just on the surface, that beneath, beyond all that, we were more than twinlike, that somehow we were each other's real selves, together forever on this thousand acres
>
> (Smiley 1991: 307)

Ginny, the protagonist of Jane Smiley's *A Thousand Acres*, ponders over the difficulty of reconciling some of her differences with her sister Rose. Beneath the veneer of her sistering bond, she realises that her image of their entwined selves is a fantasy. Her reflections capture several of the questions addressed in this book. What is sistering and what are women's experiences of it? What factors affect sistering and how does it change over time? This book argues that sistering among girls and women constitutes as significant a part of female experience as mothering or daughtering. Sistering influences the way that gender identity is formed as we grow up. As McNay (2000: 156) writes: 'For gender sociologists, the family constitutes the most important micro-level institution.' This book explores sistering as part of a feminist re-examination of kinship ties[1] broader than mother–daughter, father–daughter, mother–son or father–son relationships. My interest lies in sistering for its own sake, rather than as a by-product of family life or parenting.

This book fills a gap in our understanding of sistering – a common female experience – by focusing on its complexity – exploring its tensions and conflict, the ambivalences of the sister relationship as well as its nurturing aspect. This complexity, I suggest, is one reason for its neglect. The book puts primary sibling relationships on the map. I propose a framework rooted in caring and power relations in intimate relationships for exploring these tensions. This framework draws on various strands of fem-

1

inist theory, including standpoint and post-structuralist, and expands on them, combining these with an auto/biographical approach. This sociological project reveals how femininity is influenced by structures of family intimacy, and it also contributes to empirical analyses of subjectivity.

The book provides new knowledge about a widespread yet socially invisible aspect of girls' and women's lives. It argues that their experiences of caring and being cared for, and of changing positions of power as sisters in their families of origin, reveal many assumptions, which our culture identifies as part of femininity. By femininity, I mean 'the process through which women are gendered and become specific sorts of women', as Skeggs (1997: 98) writes. My definition includes age, stage of life and caring roles.[2] Sistering takes shape through everyday manifestations of femininity, much as girls and women as daughters, mothers and wives are expected to care for their significant others and often subsume their own needs in the process. Unsurprisingly perhaps, yet previously undocumented, these expectations are also played out between sisters. Sistering forms, in all its complexity, a key part of the way that femininity is socially constructed in Western industrialised culture. The caring work and power relationships we find in sistering mirror parallel processes in mothering and daughtering which play a significant role in producing femininity.

As women's usually unspoken, expectations of their sisters, fluctuate from girlhood to womanhood, their experiences of sistering evolve. The book argues that, on the one hand, sistering changes under the influence of factors external to the sister relationship, such as life events: motherhood, marriage, divorce or death. On the other hand, sistering evolves according to internal factors, such as shifting power relations – varying levels of control and autonomy – and changing subjectivity. My definition of subjectivity draws on Chris Weedon (1987: 32), who writes: ' "Subjectivity" is used to refer to the conscious and unconscious thoughts and emotions of the individual, her sense of herself and her ways of understanding her relation to the world.' The book forms part of a sociological and post-structural project rather than a psychological or psychoanalytic one. It explores the role of caring and power relations in the lives of girls and women growing up as sisters, rather than the impact of birth order, the age gap or rivalry. Its focus is the social dimension of sistering between women, as opposed to the sistering of men or brothering.

The sociological relevance of sistering

Sistering in the context of family relationships both fashions our gender identity and is influenced by our changing subjectivity. Who we are and how we change affect equally our experiences of sistering. As Morgan (1996: 73) writes: 'The notion that it is the family and family relationships that construct gender identities is very widespread.' Gender is a complex social construction with multiple dimensions which bear on the dynamics of families (Thorne 1992). At the individual level, multiple forms of femininity are central to the shaping of identity. The process of acquiring identity connects the dynamics of gender with the ongoing life of families, even though gendered identities are also learned in other sites outside domestic cultures. Gender, central to the organisation of households and caring, takes shape through different conceptions of sistering. Feminists argue that the specifics of daily family living, allocation of tasks, giving and receiving of nurturance, conflicts and decisions cannot be understood without attention to structures of age and gender. As Wetherell (1995: 251) explains: 'The reproduction of gender identity involves complex and contradictory emotions, desires and motives . . . '

Yet more visible by their absence, sister relationships remain marginalised as a topic of social, political and even sociological interest. Why then study sistering? What can we learn from this neglected aspect of family life? How and why is this a socially and sociologically relevant relationship and female experience? Sistering, this book argues, as a common feature of many women's lives, rather than the exceptional and famous sisters represented in the media, deserves more attention. One reason for exploring sistering is that it is a widespread female tie which forms a central part of women's experiences of family life. These experiences suggest that, from girlhood to womanhood, sistering can be supportive and nurturing as well as beset by conflict and tensions. By studying a range of experiences we can see how what we live through, as individual events, are very familiar to other women and their sisters. The book illustrates how an aspect of women's lives that is overlooked can also be very complex, and this may partly explain its social neglect.

A second reason for studying sistering is to explore the nature of this complexity by documenting detailed processes of change to do with circumstances and individual agency. The way that women's bonds with their sisters evolve over the decades reveals how personal ties are maintained and socially constructed rather than biologically given. Rarely do sisters experience continuity in all aspects of their relationships from their teenage to their adult years. The way that sistering changes at the micro-level from closeness to distance, or dependence to independence, reflects other transitions in girls' and women's lives which are linked to key events such as moving home or school, making or losing girlfriends and boyfriends, starting work, leaving home, motherhood, divorce and bereavement.

Third, a detailed investigation of sistering sheds light on current trans-formations in intimate ties. In the context of the dissolution of the nuclear family, relationships with significant others beyond parents, partners or children are assuming more importance in people's lives. Ties other than these ones, which are privileged by heterosexuality, such as sibling, grand-parent, aunt, uncle and nibling ties (nephews and nieces [Parkin 1997]) are taking a more prominent place in domestic life. While these transformations are probably exaggerated in practice, as Jamieson (1998) contends, the notion that 'structures of intimacy' (Nelson 1996: 3) are changing is a powerful one.

Furthermore, the notion that choice is influencing private life more and more through the 'ethic of love' in the way that we can actively create kin and fictive kin ties constitutes another aspect of transformations in intimate ties.[3] In creating new living arrangements, to use VanEvery's (1995) term, feminists, lesbians and gay men have challenged the notion of the 'family' and broadened its definition to include same-sex partners and networks of friends. Whether in sistering or in same-sex ties where the 'ethic of love' is perhaps most visible, the absence of specific rules of social conduct for managing intimacy reveals the scope for individuals to fashion their interactions themselves. Changes that occur in sistering can illuminate similar processes in other personal relationships: sistering and same-sex ties share interesting traits. Both are becoming increasingly important in a climate where the unitary model of nuclear households is fragmenting and new family forms and ties based on negotiation are emerging. In this context, sistering can be seen as one of these significant bonds along with lesbian and gay relationships, ties with kin other than parents, and friendships. Attention to sistering can also inform debates about family diversity, 'chosen' and postmodern extended families (VanEvery 1999; Lewin 1993; Stacey 1992; Cheal 1991). There is poten-tially more possibility for negotiation and choice in the maintenance and management of created relationships based on an 'ethic of love'.

Lastly, a detailed examination of sistering allows us to question the nat-uralness of biological ties and our assumptions about their special quali-ties, their intrinsic value or their superior quality over non-biological ties. This type of interrogation helps us to understand how, when we look closely, we see how both biological and non-blood ties such as friendship require maintenance, thought and emotional work. This similarity leads to a contentious idea, which views both friendship and biological ties as socially constructed (Franklin 1997).

Sistering in social context

Sistering is notable for its marginalisation in social and cultural life, mirrored by its absence in family social policy and social research. Marks of visibility appear, however, in popular culture, fiction and politicised forms of sistering such as sisterhood. However, social aspects of sistering as a form of friendship or family bond – such as voluntary nurturing, obligation or responsibility – are invisible in patriarchal society. When these elements are visible in cultural representations, sistering characteristics such as nurturing or rivalry are portrayed as opposites. Moreover, different forms of sistering are individualised and their social significance ignored. In this sense, the notion of 'the social' in the book is restricted to the context of intimate familial ties: my gaze remains firmly on the social in private rather than public life (Edwards and Ribbens 1998). Yet sistering, in intimate life as documented here, is multifaceted and includes both nurturing and conflict. The varying degrees of in/visibility of this hidden female culture are connected to the lack of specific terms with which to refer to these practices of nurturing or caring and conflict or power relations that women experience in their sistering. Indeed, several feminists have puzzled over the different meanings associated with the terms sister, friend and comrade (Brown and Cowman 1999; Lugones and Rosezelle 1995).

From the time I began the research on which this book is based in 1993 sister relationships and sistering were notable by their absence from debates about social and gender transformations and changing family forms. Neither sisters nor siblings feature in government discourse about 'the family' or in family policies (Smart and Neale 1999; Silva and Smart 1999). Sibling ties, however, are becoming an issue of increasing concern in social policy, education and social work where their social relevance is recognised. Sibling ties are taken into account in decisions made about placing children together in schooling and in fostering and adopting families (Mullender 1999).

Recent trends indicate that new family forms challenge the dominance of the nuclear, patriarchal and heterosexual unit in political discourse and family studies (Walby 1990; Leonard and Hood-Williams 1988). Yet new directions in social research that investigate changing family lives bear little resemblance to government thinking about the institution of the family (Smart and Neale 1999). Researchers are exploring the diversity of family experiences among same-sex couples, as well as friendship and parenting, and family migration and labour patterns based around sibling ties. Except for Chamberlain's (1999) work on the role of siblings in patterns of Caribbean family migration, and Song's (1999) study of siblings' contribution to family labour, sisters and siblings are absent from social research.[4] This reflects the marginalised role of sistering in social life. In the domains of social research and political discourse and policy-making, sister relationships, sistering and sisterhood are invisible. Yet this widespread tie features in women's lives from infancy to old age. One explanation for this neglect of sistering, mirrored in its cultural and political marginality, lies in its complex and multifaceted character as personal lived experience.

Researching sistering

Exploring a social tie invisible except to those involved in it presents several challenges. One task is to find a suitable language for describing this private and hidden world. In the interviews, the women and I shared aspects of our experience in a very personal and emotional way. Details about the women who took part in the study appear in Appendix I. One way of talking about sistering is through comparisons with other female ties between best friends, and between mothers and daughters. Another strategy is to review changes and turning-points in the women's lives and relationships. I also brought various ideas to the interviews which I rarely mentioned explicitly unless the women asked me: for example, the feminist dimension of sistering, identity and the way it is influenced by social structures, in this case the family.

These auto/biographical interviews which mesh one woman's narrative with snippets from one (or more) of her sister's lives, evoked happy and painful memories. For most women, the story of their individual trajectory was connected in some way to that of a sister. As Morgan (1996: 77) elucidates: 'There has been a rise of the dominant discourse about the centrality of the interpersonal, understood not simply as the formal linking of two or more people but as the deeper psychological and interpersonal interweaving of two biographies.' I have provided more details about this auto/biographical method and the influence of feminist principles of conducting research in Appendix II. In the interviews, I pursued five themes: first, the different forms that sistering takes and how these are based on sociability, intimacy, care or rivalry. Are they more familial or friend-like? A second theme is how sisters maintain their relationships and what their different patterns of contact are. Third, which factors affect sister ties? While several are relevant, such as age gap, birth order, number of sisters or siblings in the household, stage of life, class, geographical proximity, and ethnicity, I concentrated on age. Another theme

was how sistering changes as women grow older. And finally, what differences and similarities exist between sistering and female friendship?

The poignant sistering stories that the women tell reveal their strong
feelings about what many consider to be an indissoluble bond. While
interest in the importance of sibling ties or 'sibships',[5] including sisters, is
not new, relationships among teenage and adult sisters are less often
examined than other forms of intimacy. Exploring sistering in adolescence and mid-life contributes to our understanding of broader transformations occurring in family relationships and the growing importance of
ties other than parent–child bonds. Here, change is examined through
life-events and moments of transition in auto/biographical narratives.

The book seeks to answer questions about how family ties, in this case
sistering, influence gendered subjectivity. Sistering as one example of
non-nuclear ties reveals how these can be mapped through life-events
and turning-points. This particular analysis of sistering experiences is
based on interviews with women from a variety of cultural and social
backgrounds and informed by sociological and feminist concepts. The 37
women whom I spoke to live in the South-East and Midlands of England
and vary in age from 6 to 50. All but one are heterosexual, half are single;
two-thirds are white, two-thirds are middle-class and one third are
mothers. The make-up of the group reflects the way that I found intervie-
wees willing to take part in the research through my professional and personal networks.

Theorising sistering

Although feminist sociologists have investigated female friendship and
families, there has been little theorising about sistering. The influence of
feminist scholarship on theories of family relationships has been the
most significant change in recent research in family sociology (Morgan
1996; Cheal 1991). Of all the issues raised by feminists, those that bear on
the family are the most controversial (Thorne 1992) – reproduction,
childcare and parenting responsibilities, single and gay parenting, and
new family forms.[6] My theoretical project is to provide an analysis of how
subjectivity is moulded by and shapes sistering through a close examination of caring and power relationships. Kranichfeld (1987), for example,
argues for closer attention to the micro-politics of power in family life.
The book argues for a recognition of the complexities of women's experiences of power within sistering – linked to divisions and differences,
as well as loyalties and similarities – drawing on Janet Holland and
the WRAP (Women, Risk and Aids Project) team's work on power in

heterosexual relationships (Holland *et al.* 1998). My focus is on the different and contradictory strategies adopted by relatively more powerful sisters in order to maintain or assert their power and by relatively more powerless sisters to resist or evade the imposition of power. Indeed, as Morgan (1996: 75) indicates: 'Different and complex mixes of powerfulness and powerlessness, therefore, provide important strands in the construction, and undermining, of gendered identities through family relationships.' I explore the different relational investments that women make in sistering and the strategies they adopt in order to modify these.

My aim is to theorise agency empirically in the context of a female family tie. The conceptual framework stems from the interweaving of feminist standpoint theory, feminist post-structuralism and auto/biographical work in sociology. As part of this theoretical project the book investigates feminine subjectivity empirically and contributes to a feminist sociology of the family and friendship. Not only is there little research on sisters, except for studies looking at sistering among the elderly, there is even less from a sociological perspective. Moreover, few studies consider subjectivity empirically in the context of the family; Lawler's (2000) on mothering and daughtering is a notable exception. Several feminists theorise subjectivity in related contexts such as female friendship in school (Hey 1997), social class and classrooms (Skeggs 1997; Walkerdine 1985) and heterosexual relationships (Hollway 1989).

My interest in sistering comes from personal experience as a sister myself and from reflections after their deaths on my mother's tie with my aunt. Research that I carried out on how people in families talk about health issues revealed parallels between some teenage sisters' experiences and my own.[7] My own sister identity and changing experience of sistering made me curious about the possibility of rewriting family scripts, or the ability, as Rich (1995) says, 'to invent what we desire' in the context of a gendered and subordinating structure – kin ties in nuclear and extended families. My mother's bond with her sister and her dynamic female friendships heightened my awareness of women's 'multiple selves' as mothers, wives, girlfriends *and* sisters. Yet their identities as sister and friend, which clearly sustained them in their daily lives, seemed less visible than their caring roles as wives and mothers. Circumstances that make some feminine selves more dominant than others and that shape and change sister identities over time lie at the heart of this book. The parallels and differences between women's personal sistering experiences and political collective sisterhood in the women's movement also intrigued me. What connections exist between social female ties and political sorority? I return to this at the end of the book.

Sistering discourses and practices

This book is part of a larger project, in sociology and women's studies, to contribute to feminist research on the richness of female experience and the complexity of theorising one specific aspect of gender identity. One way to describe a hidden culture is through women's own words. Ways of thinking and understanding sistering can be summarised in discourses which include material aspects of doing sistering or the actual practices of sistering (Morgan 1999). Morgan (1996: 11) defines family practices as 'a set of ideas about parenthood, marriage and kinship and accompanying expectations and obligations associated with these'. Drawing on feminist and postmodernist discussions, Morgan (1996: 14) argues that 'family practices have a key place in the analysis of a complex and fluid society'. Like Morgan, I am interested in how women actively *do* sistering rather than passively experience it as an institution or structure. Sistering discourses include beliefs, representations, emotions and enacted material practices to do with caring and power dynamics about what it means to be a sister and to sister.[8] Each chapter illustrates several facets of the four sistering discourses, which emerged from the research.

The four sistering discourses are ways of thinking and understanding the different forms that sister relationships can take. They permeate each other and can coexist within one relationship at a single moment or over a period of time. *Best friendship*, for example, is a term several women use when describing their sister ties. It includes a high level of contact, talk, intimacy, reciprocity and emotional closeness. *Companionship* takes two forms: *distant companionship* is associated with low levels of contact, talk, intimacy, reciprocity and emotional closeness; *close companionship* comprises a midway stage between *distant companionship* and *best friendship*.

The *positioned* and *shifting positions* discourses refer to how sisters experience fluctuating power dynamics and their own subjectivities in their relationships. The *positioned* discourse reproduces specific elements of mother–daughter relationships, especially responsibilities associated with what Edelman (1994) calls minimothering, where sisters adopt 'big' and 'little' sister roles of carer and cared for, and where power relations tend to be fixed. Here women can position themselves and be positioned by their sister or other family members into carer or cared-for sister. In the *shifting positions* discourse where role reversals occur, women can alternately adopt dominant, dominated or more equal positions of power. These two discourses contradict and yet coexist within *best friendship* or *companionship*. Thus, two companionate or best friend sisters may also experience other dimensions of their relationship as positioned or as part of a role reversal, with shifting positions.

When sisters talk about their lives, they describe two types of factors that affect the way that their relationships change over the decades. On the one hand, they highlight key transitions and life-events, such as leaving home, starting work and becoming a mother, bereavement or getting married, which alter their sister tie. Different patterns surface in their changing relationships to do with increasing distance or closeness, separation or intimacy, dependence or independence. The women also mention the role of their own evolving subjectivity in influencing their sister ties. Some women seize the initiative themselves to alter aspects of their sister relationship, for example to help out in situations of crisis or, on the contrary, to withdraw and attend to their own careers or families of creation. Both of these external and internal factors – transitions and life-events, on the one hand, and changing subjectivity, on the other – contribute to sisters' changing relationships.

Changing subjectivity

The concept of changing subjectivity is key to the whole book. By subjectivity, I mean women's rational and emotional sense of their own identity rooted in their experiences of and reflections about sistering, as well as the meanings they give these. Their emotions about their sisters, their talks and the silences between them, as much as their beliefs, ideas and insights about their ties, shape their identities as girls and women. My argument is that this is how subjectivity is experienced: through both material elements – emotions, contact patterns, silence and talk – and discursive features – ways of thinking about sistering through language (Griffiths 1995a; Lauretis 1984). In focusing on subjectivity, I am particularly interested in emotions as sources of knowledge and in the links between emotions and language. The complex feelings that many of the sisters recount – positive, negative or ambivalent – were palpable in their choice of words, tears and pauses in the interviews. What is intriguing about the way they recalled their experiences is that some displayed coherent and reflexive narratives, while others explored emerging thoughts. The seamless monologues of Hazel and Phoebe, in chapter 5, offer a stark contrast to Jeanne's or Rowena's attempts, in chapters 4 and 8, to find words adequate to capture difficult moments in their recent past. As they recollected and interpreted key events, they described difficult and contradictory emotions: resolution, acceptance, uncertainty, resignation or impasse.

This brings me to another aspect of subjectivity central to the book: the role of agency in determining the course of sistering. By agency I mean how active the women experience themselves as in framing the conditions of their relationship, how instrumentally and purposefully they decide to act in order to modify patterns in their sistering. Several women in their twenties, such as Chloe and Annabel, Rae and Bukhi, and Suzanne and *Collette*, manage to create more satisfying ties than – Madonna and Roxanne, Rowena and *Grace*, or Clare and *Stella*, all in their thirties and fifties. Sisters' abilities and struggles to resist, accommodate and accept the differences in their relationships reflects changing facets of their subjectivity.

The book illustrates how subjectivity is experienced, theorised and constructed in relationships – a perennial theme in sociology.[9] It explores subjectivity as a notion based in both material and discursive aspects of experience: emotions,[10] talk, silence and power relations as much as the impact of various discourses and beliefs about sisterhood and sistering. The role of talk and language in bridging the gap between experience and knowledge and reflection about lives is significant. One of the book's main aims is to provide a new vocabulary for naming and explaining the tensions and conflicts in sistering, based on women's own words. The book illuminates the shaping of feminine subjectivity and of knowledge from lived experience through auto/biographical narratives.

Outline

Chapter 1 provides a sociological framework for the book. It illustrates one of the difficulties of researching social rather than psychological aspects of sister relationships: sistering is hard to define and connected to both kinship and friendship. Sister ties share many of the characteristics of family relationships and female friendship. Among research on siblings and female friends, the most exciting work that I found for generating new ideas about sistering was feminist research on women's lives and feminine subjectivity. These studies provide a springboard for investigating sistering as a specifically female experience.

Chapter 2 contrasts the distinct contact patterns of *best friendship*, *close* and *distant companionship* through three case studies: Zoë and Sofia's teenage sistering experiences, and those of Lauren and Rowena, both in their late thirties. Chapter 3 sets up an analytical framework for interpreting the women's narratives and exemplifies the four sistering discourses through a case study of Beth and Louise. It outlines the concepts derived from two strands of feminist theory – standpoint and post-structuralist –

that influenced my understanding of the women's narratives. These concepts include power relations, caring/emotions, subjectivity and discourse.

Chapters 4 and 5 illustrate how moves occur out of the *positioned* discourse into the *shifting positions* discourse, prompted by changing subjectivity. The emphasis is on how *internal* change occurs in sistering, prompted by shifting power relations and emotions – in addition to life-events such as motherhood, bereavement and divorce. Chapter 4 presents examples of sisterly mothering connected to the *positioned* discourse through two case studies: Suzanne's and Jeanne's experiences. Chapter 5 offers a detailed case study of the role reversal undergone by Hazel and Phoebe over three decades.

Chapters 6 and 7 reveal the impact of turning-points, such as bereavement, acquisition and loss of friends and lovers, and divorce, on changes that occur in sistering. The focus is on how *external* circumstances trigger change. Two case studies trace the evolution of relationships among women in their thirties and forties. Chapter 6 explores the shift from Leila and *Annar's*[11] *distant companionship* in their teens to *best friendship* in their adult years. Chapter 7 examines the shift in the opposite direction: Madonna and Roxanne's teenage *best friendship* changing to *distant companionship* in their current lives.

Chapter 8 concentrates on how changing subjectivity emerges from within sistering and outside it in other female bonds. In particular, subjectivity is dissected for the way that it is refashioned inside and outside the sister tie, either voluntarily through subjectivity, or involuntarily, through turning-points and life-events. Two *best friendships* are compared, among women in their twenties – Rae and Bukhi, and Chloe and Annabel – who become closer over the years, with two *distant companionships* among women in their thirties and fifties – Rowena and *Grace*, and Clare and *Stella*.

The book concludes with a discussion about the implications of this sociological analysis of sistering for sisterhood and feminist politics and for furthering our appreciation of the social construction of kinship ties. The closing chapter challenges popular beliefs about sisterhood and its symbol as a utopian bond of a community of nurturing women.

1
Sistering and Friendship

> From adolescence onwards, young women have tried to under-
> stand, with one another, the world around them. Female friend-
> ships have taken on enormous significance and prominence . . . .
> For many women, intimate relationships with women friends,
> sisters, aunts and co-workers are a bedrock of stability in their
> lives.
>
> (Orbach and Eichenbaum 1987: 17–18)

One paradox about sistering is that, although it is a widespread female
experience, sistering practices remain largely invisible. Sistering occurs in
the private cultures of female friendship and kin ties. Outside these private cultures, we see occasional public representations of sistering in popular culture and in the political forms of sisterhood (Cartmell and
Whelehan 1998). Another paradox about sistering is the absence of any
specific definition or language with which to describe it. Because sistering
is made up of elements of both kinship and friendship and because of the
overlap between these, thinking about different kinds of friendship sheds
light on the varied forms sistering can take. Friendship provides a rich
metaphor and image for exploring the social dimensions of sistering.
Terms such as sociability, solidarity, intimacy and 'best' friendship used to
describe ties among friends and kin are useful for defining sistering. What
exactly does sistering consist of? Is it more a tie of caring between family
members, such as mothering? Or does it resemble female friendships; a
voluntary bond based on choice rather than duty or obligation? This
chapter draws on studies of various forms of kinship and friendship in
order to develop a range of definitions of sistering. It begins by exploring
how and why sistering is a socially invisible tie as well as a socially diverse
one.

A socially invisible tie

Unlike motherhood, marriage and 'the family' (Clark and Haldane 1990; Rich 1984), relationships between biological sisters lack their own social institutions or representations in the public sphere. This raises difficulties for describing a tie that exists primarily in the private realm of domestic life with no language, public discourse or images of its own (Mason 1989). How do we define a socially invisible personal relationship? Analysis of this dilemma illuminates other invisible ties without their own social institutions – between lesbians and gay men, adopted children and birth parents, step-kin and other family bonds – where among certain cultural groups voluntary negotiation of responsibilities and 'contracting',[1] instead of duty, are becoming the prevailing ethos.[2]

The absence of sistering is evident in the public sphere and in *public knowledges* (Johnson 1986: 287) in general, and in social research in particular. By public sphere, I mean the formal organisations, formalised politics, law, media and academia, and the discourses on high culture and politics that form *public knowledges*. Sistering is under-represented here unlike mothering and the mother-in-law/daughter-in-law tie, for example, which exist through a long tradition of parody (Lawler 2000; Cotterill 1994). There are, however, some exceptions in three specific sites: in child development discourses, cultural representations and feminist politics. Sibling rivalry is addressed in childcare manuals for parents.[3] Images of sistering flourish in the media and popular culture, film and fiction – screen adaptations of Jane Austen's novels are a good illustration of this.[4] Sisterhood has provided a metaphor and political rallying point for women coming together in the nineteenth and twentieth centuries to build communities and campaign for their rights.[5]

Nevertheless these public representations remain marginalised within mainstream culture and fail to provide substantial knowledge of sistering experiences or a language for these as a *lived culture*. Johnson (1986) offers some useful explanations for understanding why this knowledge is not available: power, he says, operates in a way that ignores salient issues for subordinated groups – in this case, women – and privatises the *secrecies of the oppressed*. Moreover, public representations of private forms can distort these when they are male-defined and middle-class; they can also universalise, stigmatise or pathologise. Hence, the lack of public representations of sistering explains the absence of a language with which women can narrate the sistering aspects of their lives. A private language of emotions and power relations exists, however, which sisters use to voice or silence aspects of their relationship.

This absence of public representations is echoed in research where studies in psychology and medicine outnumber sociological work on sisters (O'Connor 1987; Allan 1977a).[6] What little is known concerns psychological rather than social or cultural aspects of sistering, and childhood and old age rather than adolescence and adulthood (Murphy 1992; Lamb and Sutton-Smith 1982). In addition, the sibling bond, or 'sibships', brothers and other family ties between parents and children have all received more attention than sister ties (Sharpe 1994; Apter 1990; Warman 1986). In-law, step-family and gay relationships and family negotiation and communication have also been examined far more than sistering (Dunne 2000; Holland *et al.* 1996; Cotterill 1994; Burgoyne and Clark 1984).

How can this neglect be explained? Sistering remains a taken-for-granted aspect of women's lives compared with their role and identities as mothers, wives, daughters and even mothers/daughters-in-law.[7] Changes in kin ties are little researched apart from transitions in marital relationships and the evolution of notions of family responsibility.[8] Relationships between sisters have been the subject of popular psychology, literature and autobiography rather than sociological enquiry (Farmer 1999; Dowdeswell 1988; Downing 1988; Spender and Spender 1984). While these texts do offer a public sistering language, it is descriptive rather than analytical and focuses on the individual rather than on social aspects of the tie.

There are a number of reasons why sistering remains underexplored compared with other female ties between mothers and daughters and girlfriends. The neglect of private and personal relationships by sociology reflects its traditional concern with public, institutional and structural forms of social life and lack of interest in women's relationships with each other in general (Edwards and Ribbens 1998; O'Connor 1992). In particular, the continuing preoccupation with women's gendered servicing and caring role overshadows other possible identities as friend – a tie where pleasure rather than meeting physical dependency needs may be primary (O'Connor 1992).

Secondly, greater attention has been paid to a critique of romantic love than to an exploration of female friendship, apart from historical accounts and recent studies of married women's and girls' friendships.[9] As Allan (1989) has argued, friendship in general, equally ignored, is like sistering, not institutionalised in our society and difficult to define. There is also the taboo surrounding the underexplored issue of friendship and lesbianism, especially physical intimacy between female friends (Griffin 1994;[10] O'Connor 1992).

A third reason for this neglect is the gap between the idealised and politicised myths of *sisterhood* as solidarity and similarity upheld by the women's movement (Fox-Genovese 1991; Morgan 1984) and women's lived experiences with their sisters. These can include conflict and arouse painful and ambivalent emotions about what is often a sensitive relationship (Sandmaier 1995; Fishel 1994; Mathias 1992). As political ideal, *sisterhood* 'has drawn upon a familial metaphor to evoke an image of non-authoritarian bonding among female peers. It thus sought to retain notions of attachment and loyalty associated with non-contractual family relations' (Fox-Genovese 1991: 15–16). While *sisterhood* has come under scrutiny for ignoring class and race differences between women, part of the strength and appeal of the term as a political rallying-point lies in its vision of collective experience and the creation of new knowledge about previously invisible aspects of women's lives.

The invisibility of sister relationships and sisterhood in the public sphere is reinforced by the presence of institutionalised brotherhood in a number of settings where 'metaphorical bands of brothers, sons, lovers, warriors' roam and are dominant (Hearn 1992: 206). While familial ties between brothers appear to be as little researched as those between sisters, the fraternal ideal of brotherhood and 'mutual concern' prevail in several organisations (Cicirelli 1995; Mendelson 1990; Ervin-Tripp 1989: 184). The role of brotherhood is clearly more visible and significant in a number of areas of political and social life than that of sisterhood.

Men have organised and bonded in patriarchal structures which range from the Army, pubs and clubs, trade unions and traditional male employment sectors to secret political organisations and protest movements. These include the Afrikaner Broederbond and the Irish Revolutionary Brotherhood in the nineteenth century; the elitist, male-only and 'extraordinary brotherhood' of Freemasons and its links with government and the law (Knight 1983: 1); artistic groups such as the Pre-Raphaelite Brotherhood; and brothers and partners in business and industry – in banking, advertising and glass-making.[11] These public patriarchies and masculinities, as Hearn (1992) calls them, are in marked contrast to the private femininities of sistering. The absence of similarly constructed organisations around the notion of sisterhood or sistering, and their hidden practices, ideologies and identities, are highlighted by the prevalence of these masculine 'monocultures' (Hearn 1992: 200).

A socially diverse tie

Another aspect of sistering, which in addition to its invisibility makes it difficult to define, is its social diversity. Like friendship, it is far from being a homogeneous tie and its forms vary according to social differences between women and their relationships. These include differences in sisters' contact patterns, geographical proximity, age and life-stage. I pay more attention to age, life-stage and geographical proximity than to class or ethnicity, as they are the primary structural factors addressed in the study.

Age and life-stage

I explore age differences between sisters from a social perspective in order to move away from the focus in psychology on birth order,[12] sibling rivalry and the age gap. I was curious about the different caring roles or 'positions' adopted by older and younger sisters, which I return to in chapters 3, 4, and 5. Elder sisters' caring responsibility for younger siblings is a recurrent theme in sistering experiences: younger sisters mention their support and nurture as well as their challenge and authority, and the role models they provide (Seginer 1992; Oz and Fine 1991; Bryant 1989; Stoneman *et al.* 1988; 1986; Bates *et al.* 1983). I privileged the less explored decades of girlhood and womanhood because most research on sisters considers childhood and old age.

Some researchers have found that the closer the age gap, the closer the bond; for others, personality and parental relationships are stronger influences on sistering (Dowdeswell 1988; Brody *et al.* 1987a). Adult sisters are closer to each other than brothers, and same-sex pairs closer than siblings are (Pulakos 1987). Sister stories encompassing active childrearing and the empty nest contain more conflict themes than other siblings' accounts (Bedford 1989). In spite of this focus on rivalry and conflict, these dynamics are rarely conceptualised in terms of power relations, except when seen as constructing a social process, such as friendship and bonding (O'Connor 1992; Allan 1989).

The focus in infancy includes birth order, age gap and rivalry (Yeatman and Reifel 1992; Lobato *et al.* 1991) while older sisters' care for younger siblings, sexual abuse and eating disorders are some themes of studies of adolescence.[13] Sibling contact clearly fluctuates over the life-cycle, with sisters closest to each other as teens and at the end of their lives, while greater distance marks adulthood (Drummond 1991; Argyle and Henderson 1985). Sistering remains important during adulthood, however, with conflict as a common theme.

It is only among the elderly that the centrality of women's relationships with siblings and friends is recognised (O'Connor 1992). This attention to the sibling tie as emotional support among elderly women has been mainly sociological, unlike the dominance of psychology in childhood research (Avioli 1986). Here the prime focus has been on caring – sisters caring for their parents and each other.[14] Both strands of caring – parental and sisterly – encompass 'willingness to care' among elderly sisters, a notion seen as the defining trait of kin relationships and also a feminist double-edged sword – a blessing and a bind. Prior to the 1980s there was a tendency to blur the difference between 'emotional caring' and 'practical tending'. This notion of obligation to care for kin is now being challenged in Western society and replaced, in some cultural groups, by the concept of negotiated responsibility (Mason 1996; Finch and Mason 1993; 1990).

Although over three-quarters of older adults have siblings, little is known about the actual and potential support they offer each other (Avioli 1986). Childhood experiences can bind or separate siblings: as they grow up they usually separate geographically and psychologically, yet help out when needed. Contact patterns and changes in living arrangements among the elderly have been explored as sibling contact can take on new meaning in later life. Shared history of lifetime experiences makes this relationship unique in social networks: among siblings with positive relationships contact decreases loneliness (Gold 1987).

While some elder siblings provide considerable support, for others sibling interaction is not related to morale or loneliness. Support at this stage of life depends on both the specific relationship and individual needs (Avioli 1986). Frequency of face-to-face contact is related to gender, marital status, geographic proximity, mutual confiding and considering siblings as close friends (Connidis 1989). Sisters in Connidis's study appeared no more likely than other pairs to be close friends or mutual confidantes despite more frequent contact: thus, the concepts of 'mutual confiding' and of 'greater closeness' are not a given in spite of frequency of contact. Cicirelli (1989) found that older people's well-being depends on closeness or disruption in the sibling bond: closeness to a sister for both men and women is related to less depression. Women's perceptions of conflict and indifference in their sister relationships are related to increased depression. The role of siblings in the support networks of single and childless elderly people shows reciprocity between siblings and cousins (Ikels 1988). Predominant patterns of support, Ikels found, included sister–sister and sister–brother households: geographical proximity accounted for sisters' greater involvement.

Sibling support may be instrumental in facing ageing, potentially providing, next to adult children, older adults with permanent housing (Avioli 1986). In alternative living arrangements to institutionalisation, siblings are more likely to live with a sister than a brother; women to live with sisters; and men with friends (Chappell 1991; Borland 1987). In old age, sibling ties can meet social and emotional needs.

Geographical proximity and class

The effects of geography, class, employment, access to resources, time, money and appropriate meeting places (public and private) for friendship are well documented (O'Connor 1992; Allan 1989). All these factors can facilitate or limit the types of friendships that are possible, and the processes through which they are created (O'Connor 1992). However, class and race differences in female friendship are underexplored (Brown and Cowman 1999; O'Connor 1992). While class trends failed to emerge among O'Connor's (1987) married women's ties with their sisters, mothers and friends, Allan (1977a) found marked class differences in his early study.[15] Although working-class women in O'Connor's (1987) study were more likely than middle-class women to confide in their mothers, it is not clear to what extent class or geographical stability was the crucial variable. Allan (1977a) found that closeness to siblings was likely to be greater among working- than middle-class siblings. Gouldner and Symons Strong (1987), however, found that among their middle-class respondents, some sisters were best friends, especially among the older women.

Anthropologists have examined links between friendship and social structures more than sociologists, who have concentrated more on the individual than the social significance of friendship (Allan 1989; Leyton 1974). While O'Connor (1992; 1987) considers how friendship reproduces both class and marital structures, Hey (1997) presents a complex account of the intersections of class and race in the formation of girls' heterosexual subjectivities in their friendships. Hey illustrates how girls' school friendships were 'coded and were entangled within the densities and intensities of social division' (Hey 1997: 125). In my study, class features in the diverse make-up of the small sample that includes middle- (75 per cent) and working-class (25 per cent) women: given the small number of women I spoke to (37), I privilege specific processes that socially construct sistering – primarily gender and age.

Ethnicity

While we know little about 'what goes on behind closed doors' in the family (Bernardes 1993), we know less about sistering in the lives of distinct ethnic groups. Cultural diversity and family forms (Brannen *et al.* 1994) have been explored, as well as links between group closure in friendship, kinship and ethnicity (Hey 1997; Allan 1990; Shaw 1988; Larson 1982). While black families, women and girls[16] have been studied; the single black family has tended to be pathologised (Phoenix 1991). Notions of the Western family are inadequate to capture the diversity of black and other ethnic minority families and the concept of the 'family' in general has been criticised.[17]

Features of black women's lives highlight racism, employment, the double burden, domestic violence and access to higher education rather than the role of sistering.[18] Sistering in the lives of black girls is also ignored: education, career aspirations, migration and teenage motherhood have dominated.[19] Exceptions include Chamberlain's (1999) research on the role of female kin in Caribbean migration patterns, and work on the support of sisters-in-law following childbirth (Woollett and Dosanjh-Matwala 1990). Another exception concerns the links between the origins of *sisterhood* in the American Civil Rights movement and black women's lives when white women joined their black 'sisters' in fighting racism (Lugones and Rosezelle 1995). However, when second-wave feminists appropriated the term, its roots in the resistance to enslavement were lost. I return to links between sistering and the political implications of *sisterhood* at the end of the book. While the study includes a proportion of working-class and black women, class and ethnicity are not analysed in any depth. The issue of disability likewise is left out.[20] Age and similarities between the women in their experiences as sisters are the primary focus in spite of their distinct class and cultural backgrounds.

A kinship and friendship tie

Socially invisible and heterogeneous, sistering contains elements of both family relationships and female friendship: the caring work of kinship and the apparently voluntary and chosen aspect of friendship. Sociologists have investigated patterns of sociability among sisters from different class backgrounds as well as married women's friendships where sisters are significant (O'Connor 1992, 1987; Oliker 1989; Allan 1977a). These studies of sibling bonds and female friendship form part of the tradition of social network and kinship studies associated with British anthropological work on working-class communities.[21] Anthropologists' interest in kinship is most evident from their concern with how 'patterns of personal relationships sustain dominant social institutions and practices' (Allan 1989: 6).[22]

Allan examines social aspects of friendship while O'Connor highlights processes involved in creating and maintaining friendship. Their work reveals similarities between sibling and friendship ties regarding sociability and emotional support, although siblings are more likely than friends to provide practical help (Wellman 1990). Sociability and support in close sister relationships were important among the elderly women in

Jerrome's (1981) and Hochschild's (1973: 65) research: they reduce 'aloneness . . . [providing] laughter more than comfort, conviviality more than the act of being needed'. Other researchers find that friendships among girls and women, like some mother–daughter relationships, protect and enhance psychological health and contribute to 'nurturing' ties (Hey 1997; Brown and Gilligan 1992).

Research on mothers and daughters, female friends and 'best friendship' where sisters feature as 'best friends'[23] reveal parallels between sistering, mothering, daughtering and best friendship. Mother–daughter studies highlight themes to do with changes in power, interdependence and separation.[24] O'Connor (1987; 1991), for example, who explored the role of kin in married women's friendships, found that for a third of the women in her sample their confidante or person with whom they had a high level of intimate confiding was their sister.

Sibling solidarity and special siblings

Graham Allan's study (1977a) of 41 adult siblings in Essex, including sisters, grew out of earlier kinship studies. Influenced by Young and Willmott (1962), who noted a special tie between siblings nearest in age in large families, Allan's (1979; 1989; 1990) research highlights social aspects of the sibling bond and contributes to theorising sibship, friendship ties and, by extension, sistering. He examines class differences, distinguishes between obligation and choice in kinship and friendship ties, and contrasts the emotional or psychological benefit of friendship with its social utility.

Allan's attempt to define the sibling tie represents a departure from the wealth of research on sibling rivalry and the psychological effects of birth order. His focus on patterns of frequency of interaction between adult siblings, which he termed 'sibling solidarity'[25] or 'informal contact', led him to a far more precise definition than existed previously: 'Sibling interaction generally involves little more than chatting and being friendly on occasion, often in a group setting' (Allan 1977a: 181). Contrasting this type of tie with 'special' or 'best friend' siblings, he found that sibling ties endure and that class, gender and geography are significant in compatible relationships.[26] Working-class siblings had strong ties with one sibling, usually same sex and closest in age: with this 'best friend' sibling the emphasis is on enjoyment rather than chat for the sake of keeping up contact.

When Allan defined sibling relationships as either 'solidarity' or 'best friends' he paved the way for subsequent research on friendship and kinship. His notion of sociability or 'maintaining contact for its own sake' is a key aspect of friendship especially in relation to gender differences (Hays 1988; O'Connor 1987; Fischer 1982). Male friendships tend to be characterised by sociability or shared activities, whereas female friendships tend to be distinguished by intimacy and confiding (O'Connor 1992). When I set out to define sistering, I followed Allan's approach: I explored contact patterns and focused on women's own perceptions of what was *relevant* in their ties.

Distinguishing between obligation and duty, and individual decisions to keep up relationships, is another way of contrasting kin and friendship ties. Yet sistering, sibling and friendship ties all combine elements of both obligation and choice. How useful is the duty/choice idea for thinking about kinship and friendship ties? And are kinship and friendship similar enough that they can be substituted for one another? Finch (1989) and Finch and Mason (1993; 1990) theorise the voluntary aspect of kin relationships, primarily between parents and their adult children: they locate these in a structural context and also consider the individual as an active participant in the construction of that world within their own social setting. Finch is concerned with the 'social meaning which these [kin and other relationships] give to individuals' lives' (Finch 1989: 236). Her work demonstrates the conditional, negotiated and often ill-defined nature of kinship ties. It raises the possibility that friendship like kinship is negotiated with particular expectations about commitment, intimacy, reciprocity or the setting of interaction. Other aspects include time and the level of confidences. Little work of this type, however, has been done on friendship or sistering (O'Connor 1992).

The fact that sister relationships are less institutionalised or regulated than parent–child relationships in Western society (O'Connor 1992; Allan 1989) makes them, like friendship, difficult to define and theorise.[27] This downgrading of relationships that are not of immediate relevance to understanding sexual oppression, Morgan (1996) suggests, is a consequence of the focus on gender, parenting and inequalities in marriage in research on family life. Sister, sibling and other kin ties, and issues of age and generation, have been overlooked. Yet as early as the 1960s, Firth *et al.* (1969) noted that sister ties represented the choice element among kin ties where women could negotiate the type of interaction and quality of contact. I return to this notion of negotiation, which I link to power relations, in chapter 3.

Sistering however, unlike parent/adult–child relationships, requires us to imagine and negotiate all these dimensions of the tie ourselves in similar ways to how we organise our friendships, rather than draw on agreed and socially sanctioned codes of conduct. Similarities between kin ties and friendships can be obscured by generalisations about the obligatory aspect of kin relationships as opposed to the voluntary aspect of friendship (O'Connor 1992: 153). For Allan (1989) the idea that we 'choose' our friends is a myth: social factors such as class, ethnicity and age all help to shape whom our friends are.[28] He questions the idea of personal choice in friendship, stressing the way that it is socially constructed. Similarities between friendship and sistering include intimate confiding and especially the use of the sister idiom to indicate 'fictive kinship' within friendships (O'Connor 1992: 157).

Allan's distinction between 'sibling solidarity' and 'best friend siblings' influenced the terms *companionship* and *best friendship* that I used to describe different types of sistering which are illustrated in case studies in chapter 2. My thinking about sistering was also informed by studies of female friendship and best friendship, which I turn to next.

'Very close relationships' and best friendship

Researchers curious about the role of friendship in girls' and women's lives have investigated it since the mid-1970s. In her London study of married women's friendships, Pat O'Connor (1987) found that for half her sample of 60 lower-middle-class women, their most intimate relationship was with a sister rather than a friend or mother. She explored how women maintain 'very close relationships' based on intimacy and talk. She found that very close sister ties were less based on practical help or ongoing dependency than equally close relationships with mothers were. Ties between very close sisters had a high level of 'primary quality' (O'Connor 1992: 159), defined as intimacy and solidarity more usually associated with friendship. The majority of the women's ties with their sisters had a high level of 'primary quality' compared with half of those ties with mothers that were identified as very close. More than two-thirds of the close sisters enjoyed a high level of intimate confiding compared with less than with one in five of the women's mothers who were identified as very close. O'Connor's use of 'solidarity' to describe intimacy contrasts with Allan's notion of a more distant and sociable tie and reveals the lack of a unified terminology to describe different forms of friendship.

O'Connor's (1987) focus on 'intimate confiding' in 'very close relationships' contributes to theorising friendship through notions of companionship, intimacy, nurturing, attachment and solidarity during marriage and cohabitation.[29] Her analysis of similarities between the content and quality of women's ties with sisters, mothers and friends shows how relevant these terms are for defining both kin and friendship ties. Thus, degrees of 'intimate confiding' or gendered talk rather than kin itself appear as the main distinguishing feature of married women's 'very close relationships'.

The way that women establish and maintain different relationships through contact patterns and 'intimate confiding' reveal the similarities between female friendship and sistering. These also emerge in 'best friendship'. In an American study of married women's friends, Oliker (1989) found that a quarter of the 21 women she spoke to named their sister, rather than their mother or a friend, as their best friend. These sister best friendships closely resembled those with non-kin best friends in terms of mutuality, intimacy, durability and commitment, although Oliker (1989: 78) notes their longer histories and perception as 'eternal'. The idea of mutuality is gendered and more significant in female relationships than in men's, according to Finch and Mason. Women, they say, 'are more likely than men to begin on a path in early adult life where they start to develop sets of reciprocal relationships with kin' (Finch and Mason 1993: 176). Some of the reasons for this development of reciprocity are structural, they suggest, to do with women's greater responsibility for childcare and domestic life and lack of financial independence.

Mutuality and reciprocity, like contact patterns and talk, form another part of the kin work or nurturing labour that kin and friendship ties share. They constitute the maintenance work involved in 'doing' friendship and are valuable notions for conceptualising sistering. Kin work, in contrast with leisure, includes, according to Di Leonardo (1992), several routine activities that we perform in our daily lives in order to keep in touch with significant others. We maintain and create ritual celebrations of cross-household ties through telephone calls, visits and letters. We send presents and cards to kin, organise holiday gatherings, decide to intensify or neglect particular ties, reflect on these ties and imagine alternative images of family life.

The practical and mental work that girls carry out in order to establish reciprocal or 'bitchy' relationships with their friends at school is intricately documented by Valerie Hey (1997). Her analysis of schoolgirl friendship – among middle- and working-class groups of girls aged 11 to 14 – in two London schools is pertinent for understanding sisterly bonds marked by similar tensions and contradictions around heterosexuality, interdependence and power relations. Her ethnography of best friendship, based on the humorous and vicious notes girls send each other in class, shows how they use the safety of these relationships to discuss the social relations of sex. They speculate on potential boyfriends, review past experiences and debate strategies to manage the sexual double standard. Best friendship can be a contradictory process where girls learn that 'accommodation, survival *and* resistance' can take place to the social pressures and discourses of femininity that surround them (Oliker 1989: 170).

Oliker's and Hey's descriptions of the processes of best friendship extend Allan's and O'Connor's notions of 'best friend' sibling and 'very close relationship'. They provide us with another facet of the many forms that personal relationships can take, rooted in contact patterns and talk. Crucially, the way that Hey explores girls' subjectivities in the context of schoolgirl discourses of femininity enabled me to investigate female identity in relation to sistering discourses. The sistering discourses based on different forms of friendship are the focus of the next chapter.

Mothering and changing relationships

Sistering also shares similarities with the caring work of mothering. Sistering and mothering, in more marked ways than friendship perhaps, are each characterised by changing patterns of talk and silence, power relations, autonomy, connection and change over the decades.[30] Among American studies of sisters and siblings, Fishel (1994) compared sister and mother–daughter relationships in terms of connection and independence.[31] And in her study of rivalry and friendship, Mathias (1992) found that the most common feeling among her respondents was ambivalence about their sister relationship – characterised as fluid and changing – at different stages of life.[32] Her focus on emotions, sisters' private language and especially 'the little mother syndrome' (Mathias 1992: 107) alerted me to the significance of sisterly mothering. I describe in more detail the emotional and practical mothering that takes place in some forms of sistering in chapter 4.

Sandmaier (1995) contrasts the sister bond – based on talk, best friendship and its primacy in women's lives – with ties between brothers and siblings.[33] Brothers tend to be more competitive and violent than sisters or sibling pairs (Cicirelli 1982), carry out joint activities and compete for father love.[34] Sandmaier's (1995: 190) reference to marriage as a turning-point in sibling relationships leading to a 'post-marital intimacy gap' also applies to sistering.[35] Thinking about sistering in relation to life-events such as marriage, bereavement or divorce is another fruitful way of finding an appropriate language with which to describe this hidden tie. Vaughan (1987), in her study of how heterosexual relationships end, similarly identifies turning-points as key moments of change in their decline. Chapters 6 and 7 chart these types of change in sistering connected to life-events as the relationships evolve from one form of friendship to another.

Conclusion

Despite the social invisibility of sistering and its neglect in social research, its importance is acknowledged primarily in old age and in its move towards becoming the kin relationship of choice where there is room for negotiation – where contact and the form it takes can be discussed. However, the processes and strategies that sisters use to maintain their relationships including contact patterns and intimacy based on 'talk' or 'shared understandings' are undocumented (O'Connor 1992; Morgan 1990). Kin and friendship ties share more attributes than differences. Both are sustained through emotions and contact and affected by gender, age and geographical proximity. Differences in friendships connected to varying degrees of sociability and shared activities, confiding and mutuality also characterise patterns of *close* and *distant companionship* and *best friendship* in sistering, as we shall see in the next chapter.

2
Buddies and Best Friends

Women's sistering experiences encompass shared pursuits, from talking and socialising together, to discussing emotions, or, on the contrary, keeping silent about specific aspects of their lives. The degrees of intimacy, affection and reciprocity are linked to how often sisters see each other, how near to each other they live and how involved they are in their respective lives. For several sisters whom I spoke to, from teenagers Zoë (17) and Sofia (16), to women in their thirties such as Lauren (37) and Rowena (37), *best friendship* and *companionship* are defining characteristics of their ties. These forms of sistering can permeate each other and are far from fixed. They can coexist within a relationship, with sisters moving from one to the other over time, as we shall see later on in the book. After describing sistering experiences as forms of friendship I then look at women's beliefs about sistering more broadly and ask whether the 'blood' or biological element is really its most distinctive feature. Drawing on examples of sistering among 'fictive kin', where some women establish sisterly solidarity with friends (Nestor 1985), I suggest that discourses of sistering are primarily socially constructed rather than rooted in notions of biological essentialism. To begin with, I turn to the ways in which gendered talk structures different forms of intimacy.

Gendered talk

Talking plays an important role in the maintenance work of personal relationships. The significance of talk for the social construction of different ties is well documented. It is largely through talk that subjectivity and relationships are experienced. Duck's (1991) notion of 'relationshipping' or 'doing' the 'social ideology of intimacy' through talk illustrates how talking maintains social worlds and the discourses within them among friends, sexual partners and kin.[1] Talk among women based on collaboration and intimate confiding creates a private world where relationships are 'managed' (Ribbens and Edwards 1995). Girls' friendships lead to specific conversation styles and verbal skills in which they learn to criticise others in acceptable ways and interpret accurately the speech of other girls (Maltz and Borker 1982). Their collaboration-oriented talk, unlike male competition-oriented talk, establishes distinct gendered interaction styles, which continue among adults (Coates 1993; Tannen 1991).

The accomplishment of gender through talk about emotions, and of these through participation in everyday social practice, is visible in gendered speech patterns (Coates 1996; Coates and Cameron 1988). Female friends discuss certain topics for longer than men do, share information, self-disclose and talk about their feelings (Coates 1993). Coates' (1988a,b) research on women in their 'speech communities' reveals 'cooperativeness' and 'competitiveness' as two distinct styles with 'conversation where speakers work together to produce shared meanings' (Coates 1988b: 118) and the joint working out of a group perspective which takes precedence over individual assertions.[2]

Confiding and reciprocity are key aspects of female friendship talk.[3] Patterns of intimacy and sociability are gendered, with women more likely to have intimate confidantes, be demonstrative and more mutually helpful rather than sharing activities as men do.[4] For women, intimacy involves admitting dependency, sharing problems and being emotionally vulnerable. Some sisters enjoy high levels of intimacy and girls' confiding patterns illustrate their preference for sisters and mothers as confidantes after girlfriends.[5]

Best friendship: 'we get on like a house on fire'

Intimacy and confiding are most prevalent in *best friendships* – according to those sisters I spoke to, who characterised their tie in terms of high levels of contact and emotional closeness. Unlike companionate sisters, 'best friend' sisters used the term *best friend* to describe their sistering experiences. Companionate sisters, however, referred to their relationship as 'not close', 'not as close', 'never close', 'distant' or 'one-sided'. Some companionate sisters did have more contact and were more intimate than others. In order to distinguish between degrees of companionship, I refer to *close* and *distant companionship*. Of the 37 women interviewed, 14 women described a tie of *best friendship* with a sister, 13 one of *close companionship*, and ten one of *distant companionship*.[6]

Best friendship was as likely between teenage sisters and women in their forties as the case studies, in this and other chapters, illustrate. Table 2.1 summarises their contact patterns, which range from daily to weekly and termly according to geographical proximity. *Best friendship* is not dependent on frequency of contact alone. The patterns vary considerably according to changes in the women's lives to do with life-stage and life-events. Whereas Zoë (17) and Sofia (16), Mildred (26) and Frieda (24), live together and have entwined social networks, Revi (21) and Vandana (25), who live in different neighbourhoods in the same city, go to great lengths to phone and see each other. Vandana, who lives with her in-laws, enjoys less freedom than Revi, who lives in her own home. These two have many experiences in common: they arrived in the UK to marry men already working here and gave birth to their first child at a similar time. Other ties, like those between Leila (40) and *Annar* (38), and Hazel (34) and Phoebe (35), where the depth of the bond and understanding between them rather than the frequency of contact determines their *best friendship*, are explored in other chapters. (Background information about the sisters is provided in Appendix I.)

Contact patterns between sisters depend on a number of factors: geographical proximity, marital status and living arrangements. They vary in

Table 2.1:   Best friendship contact patterns

Geographical proximity	Type of contact	Frequency
Sisters who live together		
Zoë (17) and Sofia (16)	Leisure activities, socialising	Daily contact
Mildred (26) and Frieda (24)	Leisure activities, sport, socialising	Daily contact
Sisters who live in same city		
Rae (30) and Bukhi (25)	Socialising, phone calls, childcare	Weekly contact
Revi (21) and Vandana (25)	Phonecalls, cooking	Several times a week
Suzanne (29) and *Collette*[7] (25)	Sport, phone calls	Several times a week
Leila (40) and *Annar* (38)	Socialising, support, see each other with children	Weekly
Sisters who live in different cities		
Chloe (20) and Annabel (20)	Socialising, phone calls, family events, letters	Every three months
Hazel (34) and Phoebe (35)	Family events, phone calls, see each other with children	Fortnightly

frequency and regularity and take different forms: sisters keep in touch by phone, letters and see each other both alone and often with their partners and children. Revi and Vandana, who spoke to me together, emphasised how they enjoy spending time and talking together: 'I like to be with, I like to stay with her [laughs] each other,' Vandana said. Revi highlighted the way that they glance back at their past and the intimacy of their contact: 'We are talking about our life, you know, when we are small.'

Mildred and Frieda

Another pair of sisters, Mildred and Frieda, aged 26 and 24, who lived together described themselves as 'best buddies':

> *Frieda*: . . . I mean Mildred comes up in my conversations the whole time at work everywhere, and it's always like living with her. It's like anyone you live with really. Like if you're living with your best buddy or . . .

> *Mildred*: Is that how you see me now, as a best buddy?

> *Frieda*: Yeah I do, and I mean . . . everyone knows you at work even though they haven't all met you because you just talk about them and . . .

> *Mildred*: Yeah, I talk about you quite a lot as well.

> *Frieda*: I don't do it consciously, I just suppose . . . at the moment because you play a major role in my life, so.

Mildred and Frieda see their relationship as one between 'best friends':

> *Mildred*: At the moment it's very good, I mean . . . you know, we're like best friends in a way and we talk about everything. Have a laugh, I mean, we do quite a lot of things socially as well together.

> *Frieda*: Yeah, yeah, I mean, it's totally different when you're living together because I think um . . . like as I said before, when you're living together you just get on well, it's like living with a best friend you just . . . you take each other for granted really, you don't really . . . I mean, I don't know if . . . if you haven't seen someone for a long time, it's really excellent to see them . . . and you're, I don't know, you just have so much to catch up on but when you're living with someone, whether it be your sister or your best friend you just, I don't know, you see each

other every day and therefore . . . you know . . . I mean we just basically share . . . everything, and we talk about everything. I don't think there isn't anything that I wouldn't . . .

Mildred: Mm. And that's why it's quite nice living with her because you can just, you can just be yourself, you don't have to act, you can relax . . .

They socialise, exercise, eat and cook together, and enjoy their knowledge of each other, shopping and having fun:

Frieda: Yeah . . . and it's really funny because, you know, when you know what the other one is thinking because you know someone so well and you just look at them and you just know exactly what they're thinking.

Mildred: Mm.

Frieda: That's quite funny! And often we'll buy the same things or . . . say exactly the same thing, but I'm sure that's because we're living together as well. It's not telepathy.

Mildred: We already did it once this evening when we said something at exactly the same time, exactly the same thing.

Frieda: We always do that and look at each other and laugh!

Mildred: That's the other thing, that sometimes we laugh and giggle uncontrollably together, I mean not that often, but sometimes when we do, we are just pathetic and everyone, that irritates everyone else.

Their laughter and their talks, their shared activities, constitute key processes through which they experience sistering. They described different styles of talking – bickering, teasing, having a giggle, gossiping, confiding, asking and giving advice and listening. Mildred and Frieda said 'we talk about everything':

Mildred: I mean sometimes, when we've got time we do have, sort of mega-conversations about . . . maybe when we're going somewhere in the car together or something, we do . . . do then have pretty heavy conversations . . . [. . .][8]

Frieda: just having a good chin-wag or whatever.

Interestingly, they talked openly about how Mildred's personality had changed over the years. They could pinpoint the turning-points: leaving the country to travel abroad, breaking up with her boyfriend and starting paid employment. They agreed on this version of events and tended to feel the same way about changes in their relationship. Frieda is the main storyteller:

Mildred: Well she's told me, she's told me that I've changed.

Frieda: Yes, she has definitely. Well I mean, when she was at university she was . . . basically she lived with this guy, you've got to let me speak. And er . . .

MM: [laughs]

Frieda: I mean, I was really good friends with Luke and, you know, we all got on really well and he was a really nice guy, but Mildred was quite, you know, she did what Luke . . . wanted her, you know, [. . .] and basically she just sort of spent most weekends with him and doing whatever he had organised.

Mildred: OK, my life revolved around his for a while.

Frieda: [. . .] this is my theory, and she was really happy. And although she wasn't particularly independent she was . . . I don't know, she was happy with the way things were and then she went off, still seeing Luke at the time and during those two years they actually split up, obviously there was distance between them.

Mildred: when I was travelling.

Frieda: And by the time I got back Mildred had really changed. I mean she was much more independent and sort of, her whole outlook on life had changed . . . I don't know, it's really weird but . . . I mean now . . . she's so much more, she knows her own mind, she's . . . she's extremely independent and she's also quite, I don't know how to put it . . . hyper, whereas before she was really laid back and now she worries about everything, she worries about money and

Mildred: [under her breath] It's true actually

Frieda: . . . . um getting things organised in time, work, everything. She hasn't done enough exercise or something, what she eats, she worries about everything, and it's really weird to see the change. I mean we still get on as well as ever, she's just [a] totally different person in that way. [. . .]

Mildred: Yeah, yeah. I must say I have changed a lot.

Frieda: Mm.

Mildred: Um . . .

Frieda: I'm sure it's because of men, a man.

Mildred: Well, yes but it's also because of . . . starting working and that kind of thing.

Frieda: Yeah.

Mildred assents to and briefly corroborates Frieda's analysis of how she changed and why. The way Frieda highlights both positive and negative changes, Mildred's greater independence and increased anxiety, her former laid-back mode compared to her new frantic mode displays the breadth of Frieda's knowledge of her sister's life.

When best friend sisters spoke to me together they acknowledged discrepancies or disagreements between them. Unlike companionate sisters, they were able to disagree or agree to disagree. Among companions the contradictions remained unspoken in their relationships, but did emerge in the interviews with me. In another joint interview, Zoë (age 17) in a similarly open way recounted her anger at Sofia's (age 16) 'bunking off' from school and her fear that her younger sister's schooling and academic path might suffer from mistakes which she, Zoë, was only too familiar with.

Zoë and Sofia

Zoë (17) described her bond with Sofia (16) as *best friendship*:

Zoë: [. . .] it's like um, you have best friends, yeah, but . . . you know that you've got that secret from your best friend as well, that you can only tell your sister . . . so it's like, it's like a second best friend where you, so, I don't know, she is

MM: So?

Zoë: She is like one of my best friends

They live together, share a bedroom with their younger sister *Gita* (9), and have closely entwined social networks. They recount the pleasures of a night out with friends:

Sofia: We went to a party last night and er

Zoë: It was a good party.

Sofia: it was a wicked party! [laughs]

MM: [laughs]

Sofia: It was one good party and like the boy whose party it was, it was his twenty-first, [. . .] so like this party

Zoë: And I said to her, don't worry.

Sofia: We're going to take you to a good party tonight.

Zoë: We have to let you enjoy your life, you know, have one bit of enjoyment, it's like, she went, she was like, I never danced and I danced and I'm like, I never danced, and I danced.

Sofia: Me, it was like non-stop dancing for half, like we went there about 7. We got there 7, we left at 11.

Zoë: No, not eleven, twelvish, the party it was like non-stop music and dancing for all that time, and so [. . .] [laughs] So, but, you know. We had a really good time, we didn't get off the dance floor for all of it and the music, it was hot, it was really hot! [laughs]

Sofia: Wicked music!

Zoë: So we had a really good time and she was like: Oh, I don't want to go home yet, I don't want to go home! [laughs]

As well as socialising together, they spend a lot of time talking and analysing their lives, which creates intimacy:

Sofia: So it's like, not everything I tell my friends, most things, yeah really most things I do, but everything I do tell her, I have to, I can't keep it in [laughs]. [. . .] Well uh, like I always need somebody to talk to, coming back from school 'n everything, I always need somebody to talk to, you have to tell somebody what is going on, what has just happened to you or something like that and like, and she's like the nearest person, the easiest person to say anything to . . .

This 'telling' and 'girlfriend knowledge' (Hey 1997: 88) are vital ingredients of *best friendship*. However, while there has been a lot of interest in this aspect of talk, less attention has been paid to its role and, I would add, to that of silence, in 'constructing divisions' (Hey 1997: 138). Zoë reflects on how silence coexists with talk in their relationship, and how silence represents another facet of their knowledge of each other:

Zoë: It's like, I know what she's going to say before she's even said it, she's thinking it and I'll just look at her and I'll say, don't even bother, don't even try saying that [laughs] 'cos it's that, we know each other that well. [. . .]

Sofia: You don't have to explain to your sister what's going on.

Zoë: People think that, oh twins have a lot of, kind of, it's like they've got that telepathy but . . . it's with every brother and sister, it depends how close you are, like. Some brothers and sisters they don't even like talk to each other, it's like, there's nothing there but then there's some brothers and sisters that are so close that . . . before they even, before they've done it you know what they gonna do, you know, you know what they're thinking at the time. And like some people are like nah nah nah my sister wouldn't do that and I'll be like, yes my sister would do that [laughs] 'cos you know what, I don't know, it's like . . . it's, it's unexplainable the way . . . you know, we know what we're gonna do, you know. I know what she's gonna do before she's done it, she knows what I'm gonna do before I've done it.

When Zoë talks about knowing what Sofia is going to do, she is displaying her intimate knowledge of her sister. Negative aspects of her own experience of missing school lessons roused strong emotions in her and influenced her protective attitude towards Sofia. These emotions were linked to education. In spite of their closeness, the difference between them lay in the distinct educational paths that they were pursuing. Sofia was studying A-levels and entering the academic route while Zoë, the elder at 17, was pursuing business studies. Zoë described Sofia as the 'brainy' one as they weighed up the merits for Sofia of attending different types of institutions – a Sixth Form or Further Education College – for A-levels:

> *Sofia*: Like, I know myself if I get into a doss mode then that means doss doss doss and I can't concentrate on my work then. And like the Sixth Form has got teachers and they control you, they like, they make you do the work and stuff. Whereas in colleges, it's not so strict, so like if I . . . no, she was even saying it to me as well. If I go Sixth Form I'll work and as well as have a good time whereas if I go um

> *Sofia* and *Zoë*: College, it's all good time.

> *Sofia*: It's all good time.

They discuss the minutiae of their daily lives together, from clothes to decisions regarding their educational careers:

> *Zoë*: But I dunno, I tell my sister everything that happens in College, I tell her, I just like, tell her and come home and say, oh this this happened and she'll like . . . Well, like, we'll tell each other something, we'll tell each other what has happened and like, that other person will give their reaction to it, like . . . . This, you shouldn't be doing this, you should be doing that, this and the other and you like . . . it's like a, it's like, you've got your own opinion but you want a second person's opinion on everything you do. It is, that's what everybody thinks. God, am I doing the right thing? It's like, say you're going out somewhere, no, no, not this dress, the other dress, no not this dress. She's like a second voice, second opinion saying, yeah, you look better in that one. Because you can't decide on what you want, you need somebody to push you to make a choice, yeah, at the end of the day, it's your choice but . . . you need that one extra person and my sister's the best thing there! [laughs]

Zoë's experience of 'dossing' and truanting enabled her to position herself as older and wiser:

> *Zoë*: I was angry I was like, goddamn you! I've done it, I've got∧ ∧, I've messed up badly, I don't want you messing up as well and I was like, no I don't ever want to see you do it, ever again! [. . .] If I ever hear of you bunking again, believe me you ain't going to hear the last of it!

Zoë's positioning as the older protective sister dates back to their early years at nursery together:

> *Zoë*: I remember when we started nursery this little boy used to pick on her all the time, you had to put that big sister act on and say [loudly] you can't touch my little sister!

Zoë's own experience gives rise to anger when Sofia 'bunks off' school, an emotion connected to the fierce loyalty and affection that she feels towards her:

> *Zoë*: It's like some people do it with their mums, they'll phone them up and say this happened mum today and that happened, 'cos when they're in the depressive mood you just need that one person that's going to say, everything's going to be alright. For me, it's my sister, so even if we're living a thousand miles apart I could phone her up and say this and the other and she'll probably say, don't worry about it, everything will be fine, so, you know

Zoë, positioned by her parents and herself as the responsible and protective 'big sister', enjoys this responsibility. Sofia acquiesces to her big sister's advice regarding her choice of A-level subjects: 'If she doesn't approve I can change it, if I don't tell her there's no chance of me changing it'. There is an element of the *shifting positions* discourse in their relationship: Zoë receives fashion advice from Sofia and Sofia experienced puberty and matured physically earlier than Zoë – 'God man, you've got bigger tits than me!'

One aspect of their lives that they discuss with relish is heterosexual desire, boyfriends, sex and marriage. While sex for them is taboo before marriage, they fantasise about 'studs' and enjoy the 'living on the edge' which their curtailed freedom provides. They have an understanding with their parents that they will only get married once they have completed their education. Here they consider the edict about no sex before marriage:

> *Zoë*: Yeah, in a way yeah, when it comes to my parents, you've got to think like that, yeah. But I dunno, sometimes you have that weird 'once upon a time' thought, yeah what would it be like! [laughs]

> *Sofia*: No, but then you say, people are saying, oh the world's going to end so and so,

Sofia and Zoë: Don't want to die a virgin!!! [laugh]

Sofia: And like that's it, no way, no way.

Zoë: There's like different time, different thought, it's quite funny, like one day, I'm saying this that and the other and that does it! We're going out tomorrow, come on, we're going to come back non-virgins [laughs] and things like that, we're just like, really laugh about things like that. But you know, most of the time, yeah, we agree with our parents, yeah, we're brought up, we're just brought up in that kind of way.

Zoë emphasised the importance of talk in their bond tracing the rapprochement between them to the time of *Gita's* birth when Zoë was 8 and Sofia, 7:

Zoë: And like it's better than talking to the brick wall, I talk back [laughs]. No, but since we've been little because like um . . . when my younger sister came, everything went . . . it was like, we got closer then when my younger sister came because well, you know, when she was small my parents paid more attention to her and my sister was born quite late, she's like eight years younger than me, my younger sister, and um because they then started paying more attention to her, then me and her had to get like, a bit more stronger and like . . . sometimes, we'd get into trouble to get a bit of attention but other than that, it's like um. We get closer when there's that, when your parents are thinking, yep this is the little one now [laughs] that's it, and then you think, oh god, well, it's me and you now! [laughs]

When they look ahead, Zoë and Sofia draw links between their talks, contact, emotions and change in their relationship over time:

Sofia: I want to know everything that happens. You think like when you get married everything's going to change . . . you know, you want it to stay the same but you know everything's going to change. The only way you can keep it the same is like . . .

Zoë: If you keep in contact

Sofia: If you keep in contact. [. . .]

Zoë: Yeah, it is different when you get different ages and different stages like we're thinking closeness now at this stage and some people that are in their late twenties are thinking 'God, if I ever see my sister again I'll kill her!' [laughs] Things like that.

Next, *best friendship* is contrasted with *close companionship* where contact, emotions and talk take different forms.

Close companionship: 'we enjoy each other's company'

Close companionship is a less intense bond where sisters still play a pivotal role in social networks but are not the primary confidante. Sisters confide in each other less than best friend sisters, yet share more and see each other more than distant companions. Table 2.2 presents patterns of contact for the thirteen women who had close companionate ties. Their contact varies from those sisters who live in the same city and are part of each other's social networks, such as Eliza and her sisters, and those who live in different areas of the country and see each other on special occasions like Anne and Flora. 'High days and holidays' – Christmas, Easter and birthdays – are often the focus for family gatherings. Sisters and siblings also travel to be together for weddings and funerals. One middle-class woman

Table 2.2:   Close companionship contact patterns

Geographical proximity	Type of contact	Frequency
Sisters who live together		
Hilda (9) and Adrienne (12)	Horse riding, playing, shopping	Daily contact
Eve (18), Celia (16), Amy (13) and Isabel (6)	Family meals, letters to Eve, joking, mothering Isabel	Daily contact
Sisters who live in the same city		
Eliza (38), Alice (36) and Rosemary (30)	Family events, socialising, childcare, sport, shopping, girls' night out, phone calls	Weekly
Madonna (31) and Jeanne[9] (45)	Outings with Jeanne's partner, shopping	Monthly
Sisters who live in different cities		
Anne (38) and Flora (40)	Family events, phone calls, holidays	Monthly
Lauren (37), *Muriel* (36), *Shirley* (34) and *Marie* (30)	Family events, phone calls, childcare, DIY	Every 2–3 months
Leonie (48) and Jeanne (45)	Occasional visits, phonecalls	Every few months

contrasted kinship and friendship ties in terms of the whole 'infrastructure' or 'machinery' that existed in her family ensuring regular contact, in contrast with her ties with her friends where the encounters needed to be set up.

This 'infrastructure' had its advantages and disadvantages. For example, a significant and positive aspect of the sister bond for some was the notion of sisters 'being there' for each other, which Madonna (30) described in the following way:

MM: What does 'being there' look like?

Madonna: It's like a big squidgy cushion! [laughs]

Other advantages of *close companionship* – informality, support, common background and traits, and shared references – were mentioned by Celia (16) and her sisters Eve (18) and Amy (13):

Celia: [. . .] you don't have to keep up a front because they know you much better than your friends do.

Eve: [. . .] with your family, you know they won't let you down, you know they care.

Celia: [. . .] you've got, you know, a lot more in common in that you've had the same upbringing [laughs] [. . .]

Eve: Same things apply, mannerisms and things.

Celia: Exactly. You've experienced the same things, so there's no kind of lack of communication.

Eve: Yeah.

Celia: So you don't have these *double entendres* that you get the wrong end of the stick of [laughs] because you've actually, you know.

MM: Mm.

Celia: You're a part of them. You laughing at me?

Amy: [laughs] I don't know what I'm . . .

Celia: You're laughing at me [laughs] I know that! . . .

Amy: [laughs] [. . .]

Eve: So also we've all had a very sort of family-based upbringing so we're, I'd say all of us were pretty close to our maternal grandparents, well, well our maternal grandmother and paternal grandfather, and um, so we can sort of say, 'Ah, isn't granny a pain!'

Celia: [laughs]

For other sisters like Adrienne (12) and Hilda (9) who live together, this infrastructure can lead to the presence of an almost constant and available companion to play with. As Adrienne said:

Adrienne: If I, if I suddenly . . . want to be babyish again, I just be, I go and play with Hilda, you know. If I'm . . . [. . .] if I'm in a mood, if I want to play offices or something . . . [. . .] You know, I mean, I'd never play offices with my friend, I mean, you know, you don't admit to your friends that you, you want to play offices. I'll go and play with Hilda . . .

Living together also leads to tensions for Hilda and Adrienne around safeguarding their autonomy and managing their sister's moodiness. Although these two know each other's lives intimately, they do not describe themselves as best friends. Each has her own best friend at school.

Another disadvantage of the family 'machinery' is that sisters may end up spending more time together than they desire. One woman, remembering her childhood, recalled bittersweet emotions of admiration and wariness of her older sister who bewitched her with her elaborate fantasies and stories and also expected her to obey instructions and carry out tasks for her. She explained: 'I do remember her once telling me to go and get a broom to clean out some, you know . . . I don't think it was actually her room but it was something close to it . . . and suddenly, saying to myself . . . no, I don't have to do this.'

Among adult sisters, the issue of whether or not they are in a sexual relationship can have a significant influence on the type of *close companionship* they enjoy. Several women with partners and children felt ambivalent about the single status of their sisters: one felt concerned that she rarely saw her sister on her own without her partner. Another aimed to 'steer clear' of the topic of their distinct marital statuses and avoided 'yacking away about the whole kind of mix of, of, of things that happen here' out of 'protective-ness' for her single sister. This silence constituted an important aspect of their tie, a way of avoiding broaching sensitive differences between them. A single woman who wanted a lover and children felt envious and wary of a sister's nuclear set-up, saw her regularly and yet distanced herself from her emotionally by not disclosing her recent membership of a new social club.

Lauren and her sisters

Close companionship can include regular contact patterns with less emo-tional intimacy than *best friendship*, positive elements for some women. Lauren (37), for example, maintained ties of *close companionship* with *Muriel* (36), *Shirley* (34) and *Marie* (30) in spite of geographical distance and changes in their social class positions.[10] This is how she talked about her sisters and her brother Paul (31):

> *Lauren*: They know . . . Well, no, they don't know what's going on, that's not true . . . They know what you're doing on one level, but they wouldn't know intimate details about relationships I have down here. You know, that sort of thing, they'd only know certain things, much more on the surface type thing.

Lauren, the eldest, diverged from the traditional family path: she was the only one among her siblings to have obtained A-levels, entered higher education and landed a job without 'struggling'. And she was also the only one who moved away from the Welsh town where all the others still live.

> *Lauren*: I think it's the rest that makes the bigger difference.

> *MM*: Like?

> *Lauren*: Going to college and moving away from home without mov-ing in with a partner and spent more time on [my] own, whereas my sisters lived at home. One didn't but . . . may as well have done. [. . .] I think it's to do with having that different experience and having dif-ferent expectations really. It's more to do with that. That's why they don't see me as often because I didn't get married . . . you know, I'd just be flitting around doing whatever I wanted to.

Her single status is another difference that marks her out. Although like them she, too, is a parent, they are all married and she remains single. Her single status remains a silenced topic, which she does not discuss with them. Lauren remarked on how, in spite of this social difference between them, her siblings accept her urban, single lifestyle. It has not affected her family contact or led to any distancing. Here she reflects on how her marital difference has been easier for them to accept now that she is a mother, while her silence about her sexual relationships remains a puzzle:

Lauren: They just think, well, she's different. And they just accept it and that's that. They find it a bit normal me having a child than . . . they've got something to latch onto a bit more. And as I say, it wasn't that we didn't get on . . . we just . . . I don't think they resented it, but I think it just . . . . it's probably more of an interest, isn't it, that they didn't know about as well. I'm probably more like them than they realise! [laughs] It's just that they can't see it.

Lauren has more 'common ground' as she says with her friends:

Lauren: I think it's also to do with . . . They've had more similar experiences to you, they left home to go to college, and got work and then they've settled somewhere away from home I think, whereas my sisters didn't do that. They left school, got a job near home, got married . . . moved in with . . . the person they got married to and had kids.

Despite the differences between them, Lauren is very involved with her siblings' lives and maintains regular contact, travelling to see them and organising visits when her son Ryan (age 3) stays with them while she works.

Lauren: They are very important, but it's not on a day-to-day basis. And not important in your daily lives like other people but they are . . . they are a support network but it's a different sort of support. Things like I mean, *Muriel*, has come down here and looked after Ryan. She'll come down, when she's not working and looks after him for three or four days when I've been at work . . . he goes up and stays with her.

MM: By himself?

Lauren: Yes. Go up for two weeks, a week.

MM: Without you?

Lauren: Yes.

MM: So, he obviously knows them.

Lauren: Oh, he knows them really well. He's . . . yes . . . he stays at my mum's . . .

As a single parent, Lauren's siblings form a vital part of her social network. As the eldest, she looked after them while her parents worked, and felt 'different' even then. She and *Muriel* passed the 11+ exam and attended an all-girls' school, yet only she pursued her education. It was her mother who encouraged her to study outside Wales, rather than Lauren wanting to leave. Lauren's commitment to her sister ties is clear: they enhance and ease her life, rather than being a source of upheaval:

> *Lauren*: I think they're important relationships. It's just . . . from looking for things and how they've changed and they've changed because I think of fairly normal reasons; nothing . . . there's not been a major trauma that's caused any changes and the relationships themselves haven't caused major traumas.

Reflecting further on change in these ties over the years, she highlighted what she and her sisters have in common rather than their differences:

> *Lauren*: I don't think they have changed a lot, I think . . . they reached a point and they've stayed, we are more equal than we were in that they . . . I can talk to *Marie* now about things I wouldn't have talked to . . . when I was there because we're all . . . we've all got . . . a house to run and children to look after and a job to do and that sort of thing, so your age is sort of . . . you come closer in age, in a way, as you get older . . . the age difference was much bigger when I was there . . . so that has changed, but the actual relationship, I don't think probably, has changed a lot.

Lauren's companionate bonds with her sisters are important to her, though not on a daily basis. They have a familiar, round the corner tie in spite of geographical distance. They have little intimate knowledge of her, unlike her best friend Sylvia, for Lauren only reveals what she wants them to know.

> *Lauren*: Sylvia would know most things about, say, relationships with men that I have or whatever, whereas they wouldn't . . . they would see it much more on a public level than . . . I wouldn't sit down and

discuss things with . . . and it's partly because there's no point to a large extent because they're not around

Here Lauren distinguishes between the private and the public within sistering. Furthermore, she presents selected details of her life to her siblings: 'If they only see you every three months, they only see what's presented at that point,' Lauren said. This image of women selecting material for disclosure in their personal lives mirrors a similar process that took place in the interviews.

Distant companionship: 'we weren't a sort of buddy team'

Compared to *best friendship* and *close companionship*, *distant companionship* is marked by lower levels of contact among sisters who live together or apart. Table 2.3 summarises the contact patterns of the ten women whose sister ties were characterised by *distant companionship*.

Distant companions experience the least contact, affinity, talk and emotional 'in-depthness' to use Leonie's word, or rapport. In some cases, the age gap contributes to distance: Judith (16) and Nicole (10), Beth (27) and

Table 2.3: Distant companionship contact patterns

Geographical proximity	Type of contact	Frequency
Sisters who live together		
Judith (16) and Nicole (10)	Cinema outings, window- shopping	Daily
Sisters who live in different cities		
Beth (27) and Louise (22)	Family events, holidays, occasional visits, phone calls	Every few months
Jeanne (45) and Roxanne[11] (39)	Family events	Twice a year
Madonna (31) and Roxanne (39)	Family events, phone calls, occasional visits	Every two months
Leonie (48) and Madonna (31)	Family events, phone calls	Monthly
Leonie (48) and Roxanne (39)	Family events, phone calls	Monthly
Rowena (37) and *Grace* (34)	Occasional visits, phone calls	Every few months
Carmen (47) and *Rita* (33)	Family events, phone calls, no physical contact	Every few months
Clare (50) and *Stella* (52)	Family events, no physical contact	Every two months

Louise (22), and Carmen (47), 14 years older than her sister *Rita*, all mentioned it as a significant factor. For Rowena (37) and *Grace* (34) competition between them as teenagers and geographical distance in their adult lives have led to irregular contact. Similarly, Clare (50) and *Stella* (52) rarely see each other partly because, in Clare's words, they are not close, partly they never were. Moreover, the family silence around Clare's disability led her to distance herself from her sister and mother. And for Roxanne (39) and Jeanne (45), an unresolved rift between them as twenty-somethings and the subsequent communication breakdown has led to their estrangement.

Other factors leading to negative distancing, in contrast with the positive distancing that Lauren experiences with her sisters, include the lack of reciprocity or support during moments of trauma or transition – endings and beginnings of sexual relationships, or medical operations, for example. One woman gave a vivid illustration of her one-way relationship with her sister: ' . . . . by telling me her problem, we got close, we got close. But as close as, it was more or less a one-sided relationship. She talked to me and I gave advice. But it wasn't a closeness that I tell her my problems, she tells me her problems.' Another woman described how let down she felt after a difficult surgical intervention: 'The whole thing was a devastating experience. And my sister just wasn't there at all for me, my sister [. . .], she was out of the country at the time and when she got back she had heard what had happened, I mean she'd heard that I was [operated on] and then she'd heard through her [children] that I'd had an [operation] and she didn't ring or anything to see how I was and I was just utterly devastated by that when I knew that she'd been in touch with my brother . . . '.

Rowena and Grace

Rowena and *Grace's* relationship illuminates salient facets of *distant companionship*. Rowena (37) and *Grace* (34) are in touch and maintain contact, yet are not very involved in each other's lives. *Grace* has worked in Alaska for the last decade and Rowena in England: their contact is infrequent. The distance between them is geographical and emotional:

> *Rowena*: I don't actually rely upon her on a day-to-day basis. I mean, when you're talking about, you know . . . friendships, with women, friendships, you know, when I have problems in my life, I don't go and ring her up to talk about them. [. . .] It isn't just the distance. It's something more . . .

Rowena traces the origins of her feelings to girlhood when she felt envious of *Grace*:

> *Rowena*: As a family I don't think we were ever particularly closely knit. I didn't, I think I saw my sister as a competitor rather than as a friend. [. . .] I look at this picture and I see myself at five as rather . . . tense, with a forced smile and rather skinny with a scab on my nose and there's my little sister, er . . . looking pretty with curly hair and a round face and a nice smile.

Her envy turned into jealousy: she always felt jealous of *Grace*'s looks, boyfriends and 'self-sufficiency'. At the end of the interview Rowena searched for a recent photograph of *Grace* that she could not find: instead she brought out a family album of their teenage years:

> *Rowena*: there she is, sweet with curly hair, I was always jealous because she had curly hair and I had straight hair as well. [. . .] I was at home when she was born and it's reported that I drew all over the walls with lipstick or wax crayon or something, so it was a very sort of major jealousy reaction there . . . .

The sisters went to school together, but led separate lives outside and inside the home:

> *Rowena*: We had a long thin bedroom and we used to have it divided by a bookcase, so it was very much a divide as opposed to a muck in together and share. It was very much her part and my part.

Their relationship was one of competitiveness: *Grace* was the cheerful, plump, pretty one who took after their 'scientific' father. Now, as adults, the pattern has remained similar partly owing to *Grace*'s decision to live abroad. Another difference between them is their marital status: Rowena is married with three children and *Grace* is cohabiting.

Rowena went to visit *Grace* once in Alaska soon after she had relocated there and earlier in the year *Grace* had come to the UK on holiday. This most recent visit turned out to be more emotional for Rowena than she expected:

> *Rowena*: We were just chatting and just as she went, I broke down and said . . . I really miss you and it was something I hadn't realised . . . it sort of came out spontaneously and I had a good old weep and a hug

with her and . . . yeah, so I thought about it since because it very much surprised me, that reaction because I'd never had . . . had that much closeness. I rarely ring her, I never write to her, I think I must have written about once in the whole nine years she's been away.

The distance is a key factor in their relationship which has led Rowena to form close ties with other women especially Aysha (age 31), a North American cousin. Over the years, Rowena bonded with Aysha, spending a summer with her when Rowena was 18 and Aysha later visited Rowena for several months when she was in her early twenties. Aysha now lives in Europe and they see each other more regularly. During a recent crisis in Rowena's life when she had an operation, she turned to her cousin for support. She did not ring her sister, or even tell her about it. About Aysha, she says:

> *Rowena*: she lived with us but she's very much more . . . you know, she'll talk about emotions and we've had sort of much longer and deeper conversations than I ever had with my sister. [. . .] I've adopted her as a sister . . .

Reflecting on her relationship with *Grace*, Rowena says 'we are not very meshed': she would like more contact with her and suspects that they will when *Grace* has children. Her description of her bond with *Grace* summarises *distant companionship*: 'the last ten years have been . . . . work, career-building, career progression, relationship, children . . . the lot, you know, and those are the years I haven't shared with my sister.' Her sadness was palpable in her voice, sadness about not knowing *Grace* very well.

Is blood thicker than water?

Rowena's comment 'I've adopted her as a sister' about her younger cousin Aysha touches on the possibility of sororal ties with other women – kin and girlfriends. Before exploring these other sisterly bonds also known as 'fictive kin' I want to consider a myth about sisters and ask whether 'blood is thicker than water'. Some women themselves hinted at the myth. When Rowena said about Grace, 'That's the connection that we have is that we're children of the same parents and we haven't necessarily got so many connections meshed between us', she emphasised how, although related, they are not enmeshed in each other's lives. I want to look more closely at the biological aspect of the sister tie to see how it influenced the women's general beliefs about sistering, before contrasting these beliefs with their actual lived experience.

The myth about sisters that 'blood is thicker than water' suggests that the loyalty of the biological bond is stronger than other non-kin ties. Its positive aspect is the belief that kin will 'come through' in times of hardship: this notion of 'being there' was represented in Madonna's image of a 'big squidgy cushion'. This view was corroborated, as we saw earlier in the chapter, by teenagers Celia (16), Eve (18) and Amy (13) in their description of the advantages of sister ties – understanding, common traits and shared experience. Hilda and Adrienne mentioned, on the other hand, the negative aspect of the biological tie, the difficulty of shrugging it off. The fact that providing support and 'being there' are not always borne out in practice surfaced in many narratives, especially in relation to personal trauma, in the case of an operation (for Rowena and Roxanne) or the end of a sexual relationship. Clare's (50) disappointment with her sister *Stella's* (52) reaction to her break-up with her long-term partner reflects the more difficult reality of lived relationships in practice. Their *distant companionship* epitomises the disappointment felt when 'sisters don't come through'. Clare recounts the upsetting episode of this split when neither her sister, brother nor cousin Joan (45), who was also her best friend at the time, rang her up. Clare felt let down:

> *Clare*: And then my mother was saying, 'Oh, you know, blood is thicker than water and your family is always here'. And so I said, well, where were the family?

As she reflects on her experience she is led to reconsider the unrealistic expectations implicit in the myth: in order to explain its failings, she hints at the differences that can exist between biologically related women who do not necessarily share a friendship based tie. Although bitter, her tone is one of acceptance:

> *Clare*: I think we put too much on the idea of sisters. [. . .] You're bound to get a mish-mash of genes so, if they're not the sort of people who will make natural friends of each other . . . then why should they? And just because they're sisters, it's as though they would do it almost to strangers or sort of people who wouldn't . . . be that different.

The experience of 'sistering' belies the ideal of loyalty suggested by the myth that can fall short of desires and expectations in moments of crisis, as Clare discovered. It can also be oppressive, as Hilda's and Adrienne's comments below indicate. What Clare, Hilda and Adrienne, in spite of the decades between them, have in common, in their eyes, is a tie marked more by companionship than friendship. One of the issues they consider is the difference between having a sister and having a friend. They contrast the element of choice in friendship with that of biology in kin ties. Feeling 'joined at the hip' is one of the disadvantages of having a sister:

> *Adrienne*: A sister, a sister you have to live with all the time. A friend you can just see when you want.
>
> *Hilda*: You tend to find out their bad habits and stuff.
>
> *Adrienne*: Yeah.
>
> *Hilda*: An' I mean with a friend you don't kind of have those awful kind of fights with each other and stuff. And um . . .
>
> *Adrienne*: With a friend you have to be more tactful to . . .
>
> *Hilda*: Yeah.
>
> *Adrienne*: . . . because you can't say 'Oh you're just such a little prat', you know, and go away. If you do that to your friend, you'd say, 'Could you please', you know.

This point about the inability to end this tie, unlike other non-biological bonds is echoed by Leila (40):

> *Leila*: [. . .] why shouldn't work go into a relationship with a sister? But we just take it for granted because it's a blood bond and like, you'll always be a sister, while a partner can say, well, I am out. A sister can never say, I'm out, can she? Completely taken for granted. [. . .] and yet you really have to work on it . . . to fulfil the best you can or get the best out of it.

Moreover, Leila's emphasis on 'work' in the context of the sister tie hints at its social construction rather than its being a 'natural' bond.

Sistering: beliefs and experience

Several sisters invoked a notion of fundamental and indissoluble links at some point in the history of their relationship. These beliefs illuminate ideas about the unique characteristics of sister relations. Some women held contradictory ideas about minimum standards and the ideal relationship – as both a family tie and a friendship, something given as well as created not simply relying on the existence of blood ties. Bukhi (age 25), Rae (age 30) and Annabel (age 20) said:

Bukhi: If it's your sister, you've grown up with them and you know more or less what their family background is, so it's better in a way, I mean if you can be good friends with them, I think I'd rather be good friends with my sister than just have a best friend.

Rae: [. . .] Whereas Bukhi I feel . . . um I feel sort of related to her. Just all those niggly things and the difficulties, that I mean to me that's, er, it's like with me and Jake. It's family, it, it's a . . . because I've always thought that you, that your family don't have to be, for me family's not your mum and dad and your brother and sister, it's, it's those people that affect your life on a regular, on a regular basis. I mean, I suppose I'm thinking of a good family, that's, that's what you want from family and I would definitely say that Bukhi is a, is a solid family member, welcome family member, in spite of all the bad things that I feel have happened.

Annabel: I mean family is quite a strong, well it is, it's very strong, I know it's very important to all of us [. . .]

For other women the myth of the blood connection and loyalty was borne out by experience. This could be owing to the *best friendship* that some of them enjoyed such as: Mildred (26) and Frieda (24) who lived together, or Leila (41) and *Annar* (39). An important aspect of Mildred and Frieda's tie, and of the myth of 'blood is thicker than water', was their 'buddiness', which we saw earlier. In their early twenties, while both working and travelling abroad, they were parted for two years and missed each other. Then their tie was put to the test when an accident led Frieda to fear for Mildred's life: Mildred severely injured herself, had a blackout and fell into a coma. For Frieda, it was a traumatic experience:

Frieda: I thought she was dying. Took me ages to try and sort of erase it from my memory. I couldn't sleep for ages afterwards. . . .

Mildred and Frieda's bond clearly corresponds to the ideal and the myth of caring, reciprocal ties between sisters. In contrast with Clare's tie with *Stella*, during an unexpected event, an accident, the notion of 'being there' was enacted, linked to the idea of dependability. Mildred and Frieda's view of friendship and kinship stems from their experience: sisters offer a unique form of friendship that ties with friends cannot emulate. The biological foundation of this view forms a central part of the 'blood is thicker than water' belief, which I want to demystify. Just as the looser ties of companionate relationships challenge the inherent link between biology and loyalty, so does the prevalence of other 'sisterly' bonds with non-kin in women's lives.

Fictive kin: other sisterly bonds

Several women highlighted the way that 'sisterly' bonds that they enjoyed with cousins, sisters-in-law and girlfriends became substitutes for sister relationships. Carmen (47), who formed an intimate bond with her now deceased sister-in-law Ellen (42), said: 'I was more closer to her than I was to my sister. With her, I, we, I could talk anything, from . . . headache, period, and men, so it didn't matter. But to my sister I can't talk liberally.' In contrast with her *distant companionship* with her sister *Rita* (33), her tie with Ellen, who married one of Carmen's brothers, became over the years a *best friendship*. Carmen's possessiveness and longing for Ellen were reminiscent of those of a lover:

> *Carmen*: Something I never tell, I, I even went, before they closed the coffin, I want to be the last one to kiss her . . . you know . . . because it, I felt possessive, I didn't want anybody to be the last one . . . It's terrible, I didn't want even my brother to be the last one to, you know. I wanted to be the last one to say good-bye . . . . It's very, very odd, very very odd, but . . .

She struggles to compare the intensity of her emotions for Ellen with her feelings for Moira, her friend and neighbour:

> *Carmen*: I haven't let anybody get that close, like Moira, my friend, we are very friendly, she's there every day, she's there for me, I'm here for her. She's here almost, she live here, ∧ I'm very close to her. But, uh, emotionally, I haven't . . . we are close physically, but I haven't let myself feel like that emotionally towards her. [. . .] We are very close as friends, but, uh, if something will happen to her, I'll get very upset, but

I haven't let myself develop an emotional, uh, emotionally, uh . . . close tack, uh. We are very very friendly an' I, I don't know how to explain it. It's just that, uh . . . well if Moira goes back to Scotland next week, I'll miss her, but I won't feel like, I will look like, she's, if she's going, probably she's looking for something better for herself. But . . . . I won't feel, I will miss her, but I won't feel like a longing of her presence.

Carmen's feelings for Ellen, her sister-in-law, shed light on the way that ties that are not based on biology can take on sistering qualities. This phenomenon, in the case of non-kin, is described as 'fictive families' or 'going for kin' (Stack 1974; Giallombardo 1966). These expressions suggest that aspects of the sister bond can be replicated with other women and that strength of emotional feeling is socially constructed rather than biologically founded.

This does not discount the influences and importance of the biological connection both in terms of a shared history regarding the natal family and in relation to health concerns where hereditary factors are relevant (Downing 2001). One woman said:

I tend to think of my sisters now as more like, um, you know, adult, adult, discreet adult friends with whom I have a, a more or less close relationship. I mean clearly there are, there are sort of, you know, all sorts of bonds of history and you know having a whole cast of family in common [laughs] sort of thing.

What I am stressing here, however, is the contradictory aspect of a biological tie whose qualities are both invoked and yet decried for their oppressiveness. As one woman said: 'sisters are very strange relationships to have with, they've almost got to be there for you in a way that friends don't have to [. . .] they've got to stand by you'. Moreover, in practice, in both the private realm of personal relationships and in the public sphere of the politics of feminism, reality often falls far short of the ideal.

For women like Mildred and Frieda, their belief that 'blood is thicker than water' is based on the connections experienced in their sistering owing to circumstances, emotions and, implicitly, the biological aspect of their tie. For others, like Clare or Carmen, the myth of reciprocal caring based on a blood tie is not borne out by experience, and they enjoy sororal relationships with other women – sisters-in-law, cousins. The sister relationship is what you make of it – 'the relationship we have or not is down to us,' one woman said. Some women referred to the influence of feminism in the way they thought about their friendships and their sister ties.

One woman said: 'I try and sort of extend the sort of sisterly feelings which I have towards other women, because I think that's how, what, how I should be, I try and do that to my own sisters, although I don't necessarily agree with their lifestyles or what they're doing.' And another woman said the opposite: 'I don't let things like, er, sisterhood, or big big labels like sisterhood or malehood or, actually come between me and somebody I like, you know.'

So for some women, the myth that 'blood is thicker than water' was borne out by their sistering experiences. For others, their experiences did not match up to their expectations and they felt let down by the myth. Feminist notions of female camaraderie influenced some women in their sistering and friendship ties. The positive elements of friendship would seem to be the scope for intimacy, founded on trust and communication, and the breathing space it allows without the intense expectations associated with sistering.

This is how one woman in her thirties explained the differences between sistering and friendship:

> [. . .] the way that you sulk or misbehave with a sister which you just would not get away with and which you, you, which, you know, you would not get away with, with a friend. Um, but and I, I think that's the difference, isn't it, that with friends you kind of, they're relationships which are built on trust and communication. That's not, that's not the same with sisters. They're kind of, they're developed through years of being flung in the same place and quite often to get noticed in a big sort of family situation, you have to kind of sulk or misbehave in order to get noticed, rather than just say, 'I'm not feeling good about this at the moment. Can we have a chat about that?' You kind of, because I mean, it's just, it's the, the old and obvious thing of the fact that they will always be there. Um, you know if you don't get sorted, if you don't get it sorted out this week with a friend it's something which can, which can develop into something unpleasant. You know with a sister it's like well, if you don't get it sorted out this week, you'll, you'll be on the phone to them next month and say well you were in a bad mood, what was that all about?

Perhaps the key point about fictive kin, and other sisterly bonds or friends who become surrogate sisters, is that their intimacy is connected not necessarily to less intense emotions, as we saw in the case of Carmen, but to less intense expectations, expectations that can be negotiated rather than assumed. Salient features that mark out the similarities and differences between sistering and friendship include:

contact patterns, talk and silence and the way emotions shape our changing sense of ourselves.

While playing a similar role in constructing and maintaining interpersonal bonds among kin and friends, responsibilities[12] and expectations vary tremendously in different types of sister ties. These responsibilities and expectations about caring, reciprocity and loyalty, whether implicit or explicit, take on distinct meanings in each relationship. Their intensity and how implicit or explicit they are varies according to specific sistering ties. Thus for distant companions such as Clare and *Stella*, Rowena and *Grace*, or Carmen and *Rita*, not only does the 'blood is thicker than water' myth seem remote from their lived experience. Moreover the few expectations which they do hold about sisters being there for each other at crucial moments are not realised. For sister best friends like Mildred and Frieda; close companions and fictive kin, Carmen and Ellen, in contrast, their experience with specific women comes far closer to the ideal of sororal solidarity. Living up to the myth in these women's lives is less connected to the biological aspects of female bonds and more to particular types of tie – *distant* or *close companionship*, and *best friendship*. While kin benefit from 'a ready-made context where responsibilities can develop' (Finch and Mason 1993: 169) as well as commitments, thus hinting at the distinctiveness of kin bonds, these women's experiences indicate that in practice these are easier to negotiate in close rather than distant sister relationships.

Conclusion

Talking between sisters, silencing certain topics, contact and emotions constitute the 'practices' that make up *best friendship* and *companionship* in sistering (Morgan 1996: 188–9). Sisters use a range of strategies in order to sustain, enjoy and manage their relationships. Mildred and Frieda, Zoë and Sofia, Hilda and Adrienne, Lauren and her sisters, and Rowena and *Grace*, all experience sistering based on distinct patterns of contact, talk, silence and emotions, linked to their age, geography and marital status. One difference between *best friendship, close* and *distant companionship* is that women tend to feel positive about their best friendships, because of or in spite of their 'emotional intensity' and especially because of their 'reflection of a self confirmed as 'normal' since the face that smiles back is our friend/ourself' (Hey 1997: 88). Hey (1997: 136) suggests that 'what is invested in friendship practices is the attempt to inscribe the subject into a position which suppresses or directs desire and difference'. Women's feelings can be more ambivalent regarding *close* and *distant companionship*. Lauren feels satisfied with her ties of *close companionship*, Jeanne would like more contact with Madonna, and Alice would prefer greater intimacy with her sisters. Rowena feels sad about her *distant companionship* with *Grace*, whereas Carmen and Clare have accepted the distance between them and their sisters.

Asking whether blood is always thicker than water uncovers assumptions about the myth of sororal bonding as well as gaps between ideals and lived experience. Demystifying the importance of the 'blood' tie suggests that sistering is socially constructed. Parallels between practices and meanings of sistering and friendship reveal that sisterly solidarity (Nestor 1985) can be just as present in kin as in non-kin bonds.

Patterns of *best friendship* and *companionship* offer partial definitions of sistering. Another way of understanding sistering is to look at the caring work that sisters carry out in their relationships, the power relations between them and how these all shape their changing sense of self or subjectivity. The next chapter complements the picture by examining different forms of caring and power relationships in sisters' ties.

3
Power Relationships

In chapter 2 we looked at aspects of sisters' relationships connected to affection, bonding, intimacy and talk, as well as silence and distance. This chapter focuses on problematic facets of caring, such as tensions and differences between sisters. One way of understanding conflict and difficulties in these relationships is through the idea of power, especially discourses of power. Several women described their sistering through changes in power and interdependence between themselves as sisters, and as daughters in relation to their mothers. This dimension of female ties, surprisingly, has hardly been explored. The first part of this chapter outlines concepts employed in the rest of the book: the *positioned* discourse and the *shifting positions* discourse through a case study of Beth and Louise's *distant companionship*. The first section traces how I formulated the four sistering discourses: the two discourses of power in addition to *companionship* and *best friendship* described in chapter 2. In the next two sections Beth's (27) and Louise's (22) narratives illustrate the pattern of motherly caring that Beth, the elder, adopted towards her sister and Louise's reflections on being the 'little sister'. Their memories reveal how they exchanged roles more in relation to their mother and their daughtering than in relation to their sistering. Their tie, like that of other sisters in the following chapters, is one where the pattern of caring they experience in their twenties remains set and has changed little since their girlhoods: Beth still figures as the 'boss', the one 'in charge', even though she and Louise contemplate alternatives.

The second half of the chapter moves on to examine these notions of control and domination in caring work in greater detail. A central concern of the chapter is to reveal the multifaceted aspects of power: entwined with caring responsibilities, oppressive and regulating, as well as liberating in the form of individual action and autonomy, and thus an instrument of change. I define my use of the term power relations before considering two key sites where power is located: in caring practices of family life and in discourses of femininity. Following on from these caring and regulating dimensions of power, I concentrate on its potential as a source of agency and emancipation. In the final section I turn to the role of subjectivity and agency in sister relationships: as a further site where power is located and as a tool for transforming sistering.

Sistering discourses

The case studies in chapter 2 illustrate a range of friendship discourses and practices based on different degrees of shared activities and talking. Beth's and Louise's accounts of their sistering, which I present next, reveal discourses of power in sister relationships: the *positioned* discourse and the *shifting positions* discourse. First, I retrace the steps that I took in formulating the four sistering discourses. When I first read the women's narratives I detected three different ways of talking about sistering: as a distant tie, as a strong bond and as best friendship. 'Strong bond but not best friends' was the most prevalent description. However, the terms 'distant' and 'best friend' were not subtle enough to capture the women's varied understandings of 'distant' and 'friendly', nor their complex feelings – distant and sad, or distant and content about one-sided relationships, for example. These early categorisations reflect the difficulties of finding suitable words for characterising sistering. I summarise the process of analysing the interviews in Appendix II: Method and Methodology. Only when I studied and compared the women's experiences in detail did I devise four more specific categories based on talk, emotions and power relations:

1. Motherly: care and responsibility, protective, one-sided, duty.
2. Friendship (i): 'she's there for me', 'I'm there for her', friendly, not emotionally close, voluntary (not duty).
3. Friendship (ii): mutual, give and take, listening, voluntary (not duty), emotionally close.
4. Best friendship: friendship (ii) + longing for her presence + physical affection + possessiveness

However these experimental discourses remain problematic: is the fact that they can be applied to both kin and friends a strength or a weakness? One limitation stems from trying to apply them to personal relationships – trying to define and fix these ties in time when they are in constant flux and difficult to pin down. Nor do they adequately capture contradictory emotions, changes in power balances or tensions around loyalty. Equally they do not encompass unresolved aspects of relationships, which some women with distant ties felt negative or unhappy about.

Nevertheless, these provisional categories contain salient themes: emotions (care, longing, possessiveness), talk (listening), changing relationships (motherly, voluntary) and different types of tie (friendship, best friendship). They include all the elements of the final four discourses in an embryonic form. The motherly category, with its notions of care, responsibility and protectiveness, evolved into the *positioned* discourse. The different forms of friendship developed into the *close* and *distant companionship* discourse; and *best friendship* remained intact. The *shifting positions* discourse incorporates ideas of mutuality and 'give-and-take' where role reversals occur. These discourses permeate each other and coexist within relationships as sisters move from one to the other at a single moment in time or over years, as illustrated in the following chapters.

The *positioned* discourse

The *positioned* discourse reproduces specific elements of mother–daughter relationships documented in studies on mothering as experience, institution and discourse.[1] In 'minimothering' sisters adopt 'big' and 'little' sister roles of carer and cared for, and power relations tend to be hegemonic or fixed.[2] Women can position themselves and be positioned as 'minimother' (Edelman 1994) by their sister or other family members into carer or cared for. While minimothering is formed in a specific gendered context – the family – at the same time it clearly emerges from women's passionate or sometimes dutiful investment, to use Hollway's (1989) term, in motherly sistering. Some women in effect actively embrace minimothering with all its tensions and contradictions. What is interesting about this type of caring is the way that it shapes women's subjectivities, something I return to towards the end of the chapter.

The minimother/child positions and elaboration of the *positioned* discourse extend ideas about gendered caring work. Adkins and Leonard (1993), who examine daughters' domestic work in households, draw links between girls' family work and the production of gender and class in relation to schooling and educational opportunities. Edelman's notion of minimothering, Mathias's (1992) 'little mother syndrome' and Adkins and Leonard's concept of family work highlight material circumstances in which gendered caring practices emerge. Specific expectations regarding caring obligations, or what O'Connor (1992: 153) calls 'willingness to care', exist in kin ties that shape femininity, such as mothering and daughtering. What is complex about sistering is that the exact nature of these expectations and obligations is unspecified, much less prescribed. Sisters themselves, however, can define these aspects of their roles and responsibilities and negotiate appropriate forms between them. This is more likely to occur when sisters swap caring roles and shift positions, as we shall see in subsequent chapters.

Minimothering in the *positioned discourse* encompasses pleasures and constraints as revealed in Beth (27) and Louise's (22) *distant companionship*. Each of them, at several months' interval, described their relationship as distant:

> *Beth*: I probably wouldn't phone her just to see how she was. And we really wouldn't, there'd probably be a reason for it . . . yeah, I wouldn't just phone her up for a chat, I don't think. [. . .] With my sister I wouldn't think of her, I don't see her as I see my friends. I'm not as close to her as I'm close to, you know, most of my friends, but I'd never, well I'm probably quite protective of her, I guess.

> *Louise*: I think we sort of get on with each other, we always nearly sort of have done. And I think because we've never really sort of been that intimate with each other er . . . never really discussed anything really, really personal, I don't think . . . er . . . and because we live so far apart, we don't really, I suppose we talk to each other, you know, sort of on the phone throughout the year, mainly to discuss, you know, I'm coming down here or something, I need to stop over on my way to somewhere else, usually about my mum's birthday or something, and arranging a present or whatever, that kind of thing.

They recounted how in their family Beth became a minimother from a young age, looking after her two younger siblings as her mother worked outside the home. In this sense, her mother *positioned* her as carer and domestic worker:

> *Beth*: . . . . I see myself in some ways as being separate from my brother and sister because I was sort of, I had to look after them and my mum worked and she had a lot of problems with my dad over working and so I sort of, and he felt that she couldn't look after the house and work at the same time so I kind of took over her role in the house from quite an early age. I mean, I was probably, I was in primary school.

And here is Louise's account:

> *Louise*: Beth looked after us a lot and stuff like that, she was the eldest child and she looked after the two of us, so she was round us a lot and, er . . . . I don't know, she always seemed to be the boss or whatever, I suppose in that way that she was left in charge.

The sisters' references to Beth's role as the 'boss' who 'took over', 'looked after' and was 'left in charge' reflect the material practice of mothering in which she was involved. Beth also remembers the emotional dimension to this caring work with ambivalence, for she was positioned as her mother's emotional confidante:

> *Beth*: I spent most of my time just listening to her problems, and things about my dad and whatever, and um she still expects that. It's like this one-way thing and I find that very difficult now. And that's one of the reasons I didn't go home for a long time. I kind of, when I got aware and actually realised, you know, hey God, you know, this isn't on, really. It's sort of like a role reversal, I think, in a lot of ways.

She hints at how she, as daughter, and her mother have swapped places in a sense, regarding the emotional aspect of mothering. Examples of this type of mothering between sisters feature in more detail in the next chapter. Moreover, Beth positions *herself* as responsible for and protective of Louise. She seems to recognise her own 'investment' in the minimother role, in a way that is reminiscent of women's and men's investments in positioning themselves in different sexuality discourses (Hollway 1989). As Beth says of Louise: 'I'm not as close to her as I'm close to, you know, most of my friends, but I'd never well I'm probably quite protective of her, I guess.'

Beth's positioning by her mother as carer and emotional confidante and by herself as 'protector' of Louise operates at two levels: in relation to her younger siblings and in relation to her mother. Beth draws links between this positioning as carer and emotional confidante and tensions in her relationship with her mother. After leaving home, she attempts to name this process to her mother in order to resist it. Her strategy is problematic and leads to conflict: as a result, mother and daughter have little contact. However, a different situation emerges between the two sisters. Beth's positioning as carer and protector changes slightly when she leaves home to study. This brings us to the discourse of reciprocity, to do with the way that these subject positions can change within a relationship.

The *shifting positions* discourse

The *shifting positions* discourse captures moments in relationships when role reversals occur, illustrating the post-structuralist notion of power as fluctuating rather than fixed. Women alternately adopt dominant, dominated or more equal positions of power. They can negotiate different caring responsibilities with their sisters and transcend social differences between them. Finch and Mason (1993), in their study of material and emotional exchange among kin, including sisters, stress how family members negotiate reciprocity and responsibility, thereby allowing for the possibility of agency in these interactions. Through giving and receiving material and emotional services, sisters can exchange caring roles.

In this discourse, women can experience different subject positions. In their study of how women teachers become school administrators, Bloom and Munro (1995) examine how they struggle with the contradictory expectations made of them as women, as teachers and as professionals, moving into positions of authority which they do not necessarily seek, eager 'to theorise the subject as a "site of identity production" (Gilmore 1994: 14) which recognises the subject as constructed at the nexus of multiple subject positions'. Bloom and Munro (1995: 99) document how these conflicting subject positions constitute identity. Examples of these tensions between different and coexisting subject positions are present in Beth and Louise's *distant companionship*.

When Beth reflects on her minimother positioning she highlights how, to some extent, this role inevitably diminished when she left home in her late teens to go to university. At this moment, her mother positioned Louise as her emotional confidante. Eventually, the sisters discussed this and Beth outlines how this led to greater contact between them:

> *Beth*: . . . we sort of talk about um about my mum because my mum and dad were sort of splitting up and mum had been really depressed and it was sort of um mum trying to, I think she [Louise] was sort of, had to take on this role that I'd had, and um, so I suppose we do talk a lot more now and we kind of have the, and we have the same point of view on things, I suppose. And, but I think yeah, yeah, so I suppose it has got better, it has got better when I think about it, um.

Beth's remarks about 'it getting better' summarise some of the changes in their relationship, leading to more closeness in their adult years. Louise echoes these changes when she considers the limitations of the little sister position and the possibility of moving away from this aspect of the *positioned* discourse by *shifting positions*:

MM: I mean you said, you know, she called you the little sister. Do you think that can . . . it's possible to grow out of that, of being the little . . . ?

Louise: Yes, I think . . . yes, I think, I sort of did really, and I think that's maybe why there was a strain when Beth left that . . . the relationship I suppose was changing and . . . I wasn't sort of looking to her and she wasn't sort of . . . guiding me as her little sister anymore either, so I suppose I wasn't so cute anyway [laughs] . . . er . . . yeah, I think maybe that's one of the reasons why it's a bit more strained.

MM: So when do you think that happened? Or started to happen?

Louise: I suppose when Beth left, to go to university this would be '85/86. It would be about then. I think when she came back from Africa she'd stopped treating me so much like a little sister.

Beth's departure from home for university and travel abroad marked a turning-point – the end for Louise of Beth treating and 'guiding' her as a little sister – even if Beth admits to her continuing feelings of protectiveness towards Louise. Their relationship does not suggest a role reversal, although Beth and Louise exchanged places to some extent in relation to their mother. Louise did not become Beth's big sister in the way *Collette* (25) and Suzanne (29), and Hazel (34) and Phoebe (35), swapped positions, as we shall see in chapters 4 and 5. Nevertheless, they shifted positions in relation to their mother and to each other, as indicated by Louise's claim that Beth no longer treats her as a little sister.

Interestingly, Beth and Louise both feel ambivalent about wanting and not wanting more closeness. While they agree on the distance between them, Louise seems more satisfied with this state than Beth. Beth fears that it may be 'nice', but it may be 'awful'; Louise values her privacy. What is striking is the similarity of the words that they use in their separate interviews: 'I don't (really) sort of regret' and 'it would be nice'.

Beth: In some ways because I haven't, um, had much to do with Louise, I, it sort of makes me really wonder why I haven't, and um, I don't sort of regret it in any way but I think it would be nice to have quite, it would be nice to have a sort of, a close, I think it would be nice, but maybe it wouldn't, it may be awful.

Louise: . . . maybe it would [be] nicer to have more of an intimate relationship but I'm not sure I want it. I think maybe it would be nice but at the same time I do like my privacy, definitely. I don't really sort of regret that [the] relationship . . . isn't really, you know, intimate . . . er . . . . I don't know really, I don't really have sort of, any regrets . . . I'm quite happy with the way things are generally.

Another example of the distance between them concerns *doting* in relation to the big/little sister dynamic. Beth seems slightly naive about her *position* as the big sister and its impact on Louise. Louise, however, appears very aware of her *position* as the little sister and feels ambivalent about the tensions, benefits and disadvantages around remaining a little sister or experimenting with the *shifting positions* discourse.

Beth: . . . I don't think she'd ever, she's not the sort of person that would ever come, she's not the sort of person that would sort of, I can't imagine her ever looking up to anybody in particular or you know, don't know. What do you reckon [addressing her brother Colin]? And kind of holding either of us as a sort of big brother or big sister kind of. She'd never dote after us, you know like, but no, she's kind of too . . .

Louise: . . . I still sort of feel that she is my big sister and that what she does is important and what she says to me is important. I suppose in some ways I'd like her not to be quite so important to me, in some ways . . . and yet, at the same time, I like having someone there that I can ask sort of things of, or I can look to and think, maybe that's alright, maybe it isn't, but . . . I don't know, really.

Beth and Louise's *distant companionship* exemplifies the different positions of power that sisters are placed in, and adopt, as well as the extent to which they can negotiate reciprocity in their ties. Beth and Louise accept the status quo in their relationship – its ambivalences and uncertainties. Reciprocity hardly features in their sistering. Other sisters like best friends Rae (30) and Bukhi (25), or twins Chloe (20) and Annabel (20) however, described in chapter 8, actively opt to mould their relationship into one of reciprocal ties. Fundamental in this process is the sense they have of their own subjectivity and agency. Before I explain how I theorise sisters' subjectivity, I want to clarify my use of the term power.

Theorising power

While power relations may be more difficult to identify than friendship patterns, they constitute a significant part of sisters' experiences. Several of the women whom I spoke to made explicit references to changing power dynamics in their relationships. They used the word themselves without any prompting or else synonyms such as 'boss', 'in charge' or 'in control' as we have seen. Beth's and Louise's references tell us something about the form power relations take among sisters. These power dynamics between women and their sisters, as will become clear in the rest of the book, stem from differences in their ages, positions in the family, educational trajectories, and marital and mothering statuses. My question is: how do power relations shape sistering and, in particular, feminine subjectivity?

Power, generally understood as inequality based on a dichotomy of domination and subordination, is a contested concept in the history of sociological thought. A traditional view assumes that individuals either possess power or are subjected to it and are therefore powerless. However there is disagreement about its origins, forms and meanings, and this assumption has been superseded by the idea that individuals are more, or less, powerful depending on a range of factors and contexts. Consequently, there is no single definition of power. Nevertheless, this traditional understanding of power relations is unhelpful for exploring ties between sisters, who can be both powerful and powerless. Focusing on power relations allows me to theorise differences between sisters as well as the process of change that occurs in their relationships. My notion of power is influenced by Antonio Gramsci's idea of hegemony – positions of leadership formed through resistance, compromise and accommodation. I understand power as diffuse and shifting, in contrast with earlier modernist notions of power relations as unitary and fixed.

Power relations in the private realm of family ties emerge in multiple sites. In the context of sistering, power is located in four sites much like those that Holland and her colleagues (1998) identify in their study of young women's and men's experiences of heterosexual relationships. The first site relates to structured, institutionalised power relations and corresponds to the institution of the heterosexual family (Delphy and Leonard 1992). I return to this site of family power relations in the next section. The second site where power comes alive is in enacted practices and experiences. In sisters' lives, this manifests itself through their contact patterns, talking, caring and emotions, joys and conflict, as the case studies of Zoë and Sofia, Mildred and Frieda, Lauren and her sisters, and Rowena and *Grace* in chapter 2 illustrate.

The third site where power is present is in specific sistering discourses, at the level of ideas and ways of thinking about sistering, such as *best friendship*, *companionship*, the *shifting positions* and the *positioned* discourses. These are illustrated through the case study of Beth and Louise and incorporate the practices described in chapter 2. Lastly, power is located in individual agency and action. This form of power enables women consciously to modify the way they think about and manage their sistering thus allowing them to adopt more powerful, less powerful or reciprocal positions. The rest of this chapter focuses on each of these sites where power is located in more detail – except for the second site of enacted practices covered in the last chapter. Next I examine sistering in the context of family power relations before considering two further significant sites of power: discourses and subjectivity and agency.

Power relations in the family

Institutionalised power relations in families form the background for this investigation of power between women, a less researched area than its heterosexual counterpart (Holland *et al.* 1996). Gendered power relations visible in the caring work, which women either perform or resist carrying out for their kin, structure domestic life. Notions of appropriate feminine and masculine behaviour to do with caring and being cared for underlie conventional households. The expectation to care forms an intrinsic part of femininity. This kin work can be forced on girls and women by mothers, fathers and siblings who expect daughters to nurture, look after and even mother their sisters. Yet some women like Beth actively decide to care for and oversee the welfare of their sisters. Do sisters care for each other from a sense of duty or, as friends do, because they want to, or both?

In the context of these institutionalised power relations, how can sisters be empowered to resist these pressures to be caring? Feminists researching femininity highlight the need for women to resist various pressures and expectations in their lives, if they are to be empowered (Holland *et al.* 1998; McRobbie 1991). Empowerment refers to 'a collective project which shifts the balance of power between women and men throughout society. [It] remains a contested process and we recognise the categories of empowerment that we have used as unstable' (Holland *et al.* 1991b: 24). The tensions and contradictions involved can make empowerment an ambivalent and shifting project, at times desirable but also, difficult. This is equally true of sistering. Brown and Gilligan (1992), for example, who studied girls' emotional health, call for 'political resistance' in order to challenge the social construction of femininity, motherhood and sexuality, which structures girls' and women's lives.[3] Girls who they defined as 'political resisters' often had close relationships with their mothers. Interestingly, a notion central to their idea of 'resistance' is gendered talk. I return to female resistance in the final section.

Discourses of femininity

Power also manifests itself at the level of ideas and ways of thinking about different forms of sistering. After setting out what I mean by 'discourse' I summarise the way that Liz Frazer formulated discourses of femininity in her research on schoolgirls. Her study provided a springboard for my own in the way that she favoured the term 'discourse' over that of 'ideology' to capture girls' involvement and struggles over meanings of femininity. My use of the term discourse interweaves both power relations and language in relation to friendship and familial ties (Jones 1993; Weedon 1987) and draws on the work of Michel Foucault, Wendy Hollway (1989; 1984) and Liz Frazer (1988a; b). Feminist theory has seized on ideas from Foucault's and Derrida's post-structuralism and Lacanian psychoanalysis to expand knowledge about language and desire (Maynard 1995; 1993).[4] While some feminists have criticised this cultural turn (Maynard 1995; Jackson 1992), several ideas such as 'discourse' are useful for thinking about caring and power in sistering. Although they are often used interchangeably, I use the term 'post-structuralism' rather than 'postmodernism', in order to distinguish between the work of postmodernist writers such as Lacan, Lyotard and Baudrillard and the post-structuralism of Derrida and Foucault, which has been far more influential in feminist theory (Maynard 1995).

While discourse is a difficult term to define, there are four identifiable strands in *discourse analysis* (Potter and Wetherell 1994). One strand is primarily linguistic and concerns conversation analysis in specific settings. A second is psychological, to do with discourse processes in relation to recall and understanding. The third strand stems from the sociology of science and scientists' construction of their work as rational. The fourth strand has most influenced feminist researchers and is most relevant for exploring sistering. It draws on continental social philosophy, cultural analysis, semiology and history, especially in Michel Foucault's work. Social scientists 'have tried to show how institutions, practices and even the individual human subject itself can be understood as produced through the workings of a set of discourses' (Potter and Wetherell 1994: 47). In this sense, discourses are ways of 'representing – a particular kind of knowledge about a topic' (Hall 1992: 291). They are also ways of 'thinking and talking about the world which are informed and directed by the play of power [creating and setting] limits to the "truths" by which we live and understand the world' (Holland 1996: 24).

Feminists researching discourses of femininity and heterosexuality such as Frazer and Hollway work with the Foucauldian concept of discourse. According to Foucault (1980; 1977; 1972), a discourse can be produced by many individuals in different institutional settings – including families – and constructs positions where individuals become the subject of that discourse (Hall 1992). The four sistering discourses, for example, can become dominant, overlapping and contradictory. Moreover, power dynamics and knowledge about these are embedded in discourse through the production of subjects and objects 'as the self is not coherent, but is positioned and positions in multiple, shifting discourses' (Francis 1996: 16). Weedon, writing from a Foucauldian perspective, summarises the links between these concepts: 'Power is a relation. It inheres in difference and is a dynamic of control and lack of control between discourses and the subjects, constituted by discourses, who are their agents. Power is exercised within discourses in the ways in which they constitute and govern individual subjects' (Weedon 1987: 113).

Foucault's conception questions the distinctions between thought and action, language and practice (Hall 1992). From this perspective, subjectivity is constructed through language and talk as well as through material structures and social experiences. Relationships, emotions and what Lauretis (1984: 182–3) calls 'habits' and 'practices' construct these experiences. Hollway's (1989) four competing discourses for understanding heterosexuality, such as the male sexual drive discourse, encompass practices like emotions as well as agency. For Hollway the *investment* that men and women have in certain positions rather than others sheds light on why we become positioned, or let ourselves be positioned, in damaging discourses. Miller (1990) echoes Hollway's idea of *investment* when she explores the seductions and desires that we succumb to and yet feel ambivalent about.

Frazer's studies (1988a; b) of femininity helpfully grapple with the notion of discourse in a material and empirical way. She examines schoolgirls' institutionalised ways of talking and the role of these in constructing experience. Her work is useful for understanding how sisters position each other in contradictory ways. Frazer found that girls' varied discourses about class, gender, race and their social world depend on their access to different institutionalised discourse registers.[5] These registers enable girls to frame their experience, but can also constrain their analysis of it. Her work illuminates the pressures and constraints of girlhood, especially girls' attempts to resist 'dominant meanings' or contested ideas as well as their negotiation through different practices and accounts (Frazer 1988a: 190).

Frazer's girls identify dominant meanings of gender and social forces propelling them in certain directions, which they are determined to resist using a multiplicity of conceptions of femininity, switching between them according to context. Their contrasting definitions reflect elements of opposite discourse registers which girls employ, resist or reject according to conventions and notions of appropriateness. Discourse registers are visible, limited to specific institutions and social groups, include the public and institutionalised, and allow for a plurality of registers. Crucially, they enable the reintroduction of agency and highlight the way that meaning is produced, perpetuated and struggled over overtly.[6]

Frazer's work reveals how girls' struggles with dominant meanings occur at the level of discourse and also take a material form regarding their classed position. Although discourse analysis is criticised for the attention paid to language at the expense of an analysis of material power (Francis 1996), in Frazer's (1998a; b) and Hey's (1997) studies of girls, material forces such as class and gendered power relations retain a strong presence. In relation to sistering, material features manifest themselves through age differences, contact, talking, power and caring practices. The four sistering discourses, like Frazer's discourses of femininity, are rooted in these material forces. My way of understanding sistering is through power relations and discourses rather than structures.

Next, I turn to the last site where power relations appear: the level of subjectivity and action.

Subjectivity and agency

Women's agency is the process of autonomous motivation and action, which enables them to struggle over, contest, take over and sometimes alter meanings and patterns in their sistering. I understand the feminine self as an active agent able to 'resist' certain subordinating practices and discourses – caring and power relations in the family, for example. Agency forms a central element of gendered subjectivity which feminists are theorising (McNay 2000). Subjectivity refers to our sense of personal identity 'produced within the discourses in which it is positioned and positions itself' (Griffiths 1995a: 227). Lauretis (1984: 159) defines it as what one 'perceives and comprehends as subjective', an 'on-going construction not a fixed point of departure or arrival from which one then interacts with the world' (Lauretis 1984: 159). By subjectivity I mean:

the ways in which a person gives meaning to themselves, others and the world [. . .]. It is characterised by tensions and instability because it is constituted through discourses, which are often in contradiction to one another. (Davies and Banks 1992: 2)

My definition stems from post-structuralist work on the subject. Henriques *et al.*'s (1984: 203) deconstruction of the 'subject-as-agent' allows an understanding of the subject as a *position* within a particular discourse. The power/knowledge relations that produce a subject position imply that there is no necessary coherence to the multiple sites where subject positions are produced, and these positions themselves might be contradictory.

> the subject itself is the effect of a production, caught in the mutually constitutive web of social practices, discourses and subjectivity; its reality is the tissue of social relations. (Henriques *et al.* 1984: 117)

These varied positionings correspond to a multiplicity of subjectivities in women's lives – as workers, consumers, daughters, mothers and sisters. Henriques *et al.* call for the need to specify the different *practices* in which different subject positions and power relations are played out. My definition of subjectivity includes the practices of gendered talk and caring. They also stress the significance of experiences of having more or less power in different social practices, or the experience of contradictions in subjective positionings or 'contradictory subjectivity' (Henriques *et al.* 1984: 118). This approach starts from a triad of power, knowledge and subject in place of the traditional society/individual dualism.

Teresa de Lauretis (1984) and Louisa Alcoff (1988) expand these ideas on the deconstruction of the subject in order to reinstate the presence of agency. Lauretis's sophisticated notion of subjectivity is linked to experience and agency, which Alcoff combines with the concept of *positionality*. Positionality includes the different ways in which women are positioned and position themselves in a network of relations, based on economic, cultural and political conditions (Alcoff 1988). As Flax (1990) and Maynard (1995) argue, the self, subject and subjectivity are changing and made up of desires and emotions, yet retain consistent elements – for example, the ability to think rationally. Thus subjectivity can embrace agency and an ability to act on and in the social world; hence Maynard's (1995: 274) term 'agentic subjectivity'.

Several feminists explore the construction of feminine subjectivity through discourses of domination and power in schooling, the family and sexuality (Holland *et al.* 1998; Rossiter 1994). Hey's (1997) ethnography of girls' friendships echoes Frazer's (1988a) account of the coexistence of contradictory forces and practices in girls' ability to reflect on and conceptualise their experience.[7] Hey found that girls' best friendships can be both positive and negative, encompassing nurturing aspects and 'bitchiness', especially girls' surveillance and controlling of each other.[8] Other researchers consider how girls can occupy shifting positions of power in terms of subject/object and active/passive positions in dominant discourses of femininity and heterosexuality in the construction of their own subjectivity (Jones 1993; Walkerdine 1990).

These investigations reveal simultaneous processes of acceptance and resistance of dominant discourses by 'the subject', which contribute a social and structural dimension to the relational psychologists' work.[9] As Epstein, who also uses the term 'active agent', explains:

> we may occupy positions within different and contradictory discourses, being at one and the same time, in positions of relative power and relative powerlessness. [. . .] power is not always wielded through coercion, but often through discursive practices which people, as active agents within these practices either consent to or resist. (Epstein 1993: 13)

Feminists' contribution to post-structuralism brought two shifts in feminist theory. The first is the move away from positioning women as a group oppressed by a single system or structure (patriarchy): this opens up a space for resistance, struggle, action and agency or 'contradictory relations' (Maynard 1995: 271). The second is the move away from focusing on oppression alone to looking at the unevenness of power; especially the way that women and girls 'are variously positioned in specific contexts' – whether classrooms or families (Maynard 1995: 271). Walkerdine (1994; 1990) and Hey's (1997) work in and on the margins of school highlights girls' multiple and fragmented positions in and outside the classroom, thereby transcending reified explanations which polarise agency and structure.

Is sistering, then, a 'liberating' or 'entrenching' force regarding the social construction of femininity? This question concerns the contradictory role of sistering in women's lives. How can women, as sisters, redefine and reconstruct their sense of identity or subjectivity? What possibilities for change exist within the power structures of the family? How can sisters exchange the subject positions that they find themselves in? The implications of a decentred active subject, fragmented, pluralistic and continually changing is that it opens up sites for 'rewriting' family scripts. My definition of subjectivity includes lived experience and narrative accounts of lives created through language or talk.[10] Language and, in some cases, silence play a key role in constructing and deconstructing what often appear to be fixed roles and relationships between sisters in families. By experience I mean 'a complex of habits' and 'practices' (Lauretis 1984: 182–3), 'strings of interactions' (Duck and Perlman 1985: 5), between sisters such as contact patterns, caring, emotions and conflict. These practices and events, as we saw in the last chapter, include making plans, writing letters, telephoning, buying presents and providing meals. This form of emotional or 'relational work' (Doucet 1993; Ayres 1983) can contribute to the creation of a dyadic culture with its own rituals, pet names and private language.[11] In sistering, talk/language and silence can open up or close options for modifying subjectivities and relationships. My definition also incorporates the ideas of change and positionality. By change I mean that subjectivity is both active and shifting, constructing and reconstructing itself through a process of 'reflective practice'.[12] As Alcoff (1988: 425) explains:

> The key component of Lauretis's formulation is the dynamic she poses at the heart of subjectivity: a fluid interaction in constant motion and open to alteration by self-analysing practice.

Lauretis's (1986) notion of the agency of the subject is constituted within an historical process of consciousness which forms individual identity. This internal process coexists with an external one. Subjectivity is simultaneously exposed to external social influences where it becomes positioned by other discourses and individuals:

> Self and identity, in other words, are always grasped and understood within a particular discursive configuration. Consciousness, therefore, is never fixed, never attained once and for all, because discursive boundaries change with historical conditions. (Lauretis 1986: 8)

Alcoff (1988) uses the term *position* to refer to gender as a place from which to act politically. She understands women's position as relative rather than fixed, changing in a historical and cultural context within a network of relations:

> Therefore, the concept of positionality includes two points: first, as already stated, that the concept of woman is a relational term identifiable only within a (constantly moving) context; but second, that the position that women find themselves in can be actively utilised (rather than transcended) as a location for the construction of meaning, a place from where meaning is constructed, rather than simply the place were a meaning can be *discovered* (the meaning of femaleness). (Alcoff 1988: 434)

Alcoff's notion of subjectivity as positionality includes the idea of both agency and of specific location in multiple discourses. It implies that women can position themselves and be positioned in different ways in a number of contexts and relationships and even within the same relationship. The following chapters illustrate this through examples of the different 'positions' older and younger sisters adopt in their relationships.[13]

Another consequence of defining subjectivity in terms of change and positionality is that it allows for a more complex analysis of the interaction between women as subjects and broader social structures than the notion of 'resistance'. Resistance initially seemed a useful concept for theorising subjectivity and reflecting on the structural effects of sistering. Many feminists examine resistance to the social construction of femininity and feminine sexuality in the context of friendship, well-being and sexual empowerment.[14] Pressure to be a 'good girl' or a 'nice girl'[15] can contribute to 'healthy resistance' in their pre-teens when girls can speak their minds (Rogers 1993: 265); to 'political resistance' when girls 'disagree openly' (Brown and Gilligan 1993: 17); and to 'psychological resistance' when they are pressured to silence their feelings. Processes of resistance illuminate psychological aspects of teenage girls' experiences, especially the link between talk and emotional well-being or connectedness (Gilligan *et al.* 1990). 'Resistance' helps to map changes in girls' subjectivity at a time of transition in their lives when it might not be such a transparent process.[16] The problem is that it suggests a fairly monolithic engagement between subject and society.

In contrast to the relational psychologists' work, post-structuralist analyses of the contradictory aspects of heterosexual feminine subjectivities offer interpretations more embedded in the hegemonic cultural and social practices that form the backdrop of girls' and women's lives. Changing and positioned subjectivity[17] rather than 'resistance' reflects many of the contradictory aspects of women's experiences as subjects in relationships which can be experienced as *both* liberating and entrenching and as fluctuating between connectedness and separateness (Edwards 1993).

Conclusion

The case study of Beth and Louise highlights other facets of caring in sister relationships than the friendship discourses and practices of *best friendship, close* and *distant companionship* set out in chapter 2. In their narratives we see how power relationships are played out through minimothering and experiments with role swapping. One aim of this chapter has been to show how power relations can be fixed, as in the *positioned* discourse, or open to negotiation and potentially changeable, as in the *shifting positions* discourse. This understanding of power relations implies that these take many forms and emerge in a range of sites. These include: the institution-alised setting of family caring responsibilities shaped by age and gender; the enacted practices of emotions, talk and contact patterns documented in chapter 2; the discourses of sistering illustrated through Beth and Louise's narratives; and subjectivity and agency as sources of action and change, exemplified through several case studies in chapter 8.

Another aim of the chapter has been to provide working definitions of key terms that I use in chapters 4–8. In the rest of the book I focus on dif-ferent sisters' relationships, taking in the ideas of friendship, caring, intim-acy and talk on the one hand, and conflict, tensions and power differences on the other. The next chapter considers motherly sistering in more detail through two case studies of the *positioned* discourse displayed in Suzanne and Jeanne's experiences. In chapter 5, Hazel and Phoebe's emotional narratives of their shifting positions over several decades are scrutinised. Chapters 6 and 7 highlight the impact of life-events on sister-ing. Analysing sistering in terms of *best friendship, companionship* and the *positioned* and *shifting positions* discourses does not imply that these are the only forms that sistering can take. Other readings would lead to differ-ent interpretations.

4
Motherly Sistering

How do some forms of sistering resemble mothering rather than friendship? What form does the mothering work, which often burdens elder sisters and working-class young women with younger siblings, take (Watson 1997; Adkins and Leonard 1993)? In this chapter, Suzanne's (29) experiences of mothering and being mothered by her younger sister *Collette* (25) are contrasted with Jeanne's (45) and her sisters'. These two case studies of caring responsibilities reveal a central difference between sistering and friendship. Sisters' experiences of mothering work, a specific attribute of femininity, combine with their gendered location in the institution of the family: family power relations make it difficult to renegotiate caring roles (Delphy and Leonard 1992). Aspects of sistering as a familial tie are much more complicated to negotiate than friendship.

Mothering work

Although Edelman (1994: 139) employs the term 'minimother' to refer to the caring work carried out by daughters for kin (mainly siblings and fathers) in the context of mother-loss and bereavement, minimothering extends to other contexts. Beth (27), as we saw, and Hazel (34) in the next chapter, talk about mothering their mothers. Suzanne (30) mentions her 'big sisterly bit coming out . . . ' vis-à-vis *Collette* (25). Annabel (20), in chapter 8, talks about 'being bossy' towards her twin Chloe (20). Zoë (17) is aware of her protectiveness or tendency to tell Sofia (16) 'what to do', and Vandana (25) insists on paying for her younger sister Revi (21) when they go out shopping. Positive attributes of minimothering include caring and nurturing, protectiveness and responsibility for a sister or sibling. Negative aspects include bossiness, the tendency to be domineering and directive, and the concentration of responsibility, which can be oppressive to *both* sisters.

Motherly sistering is not usually embraced from choice. On the contrary, it tends to result from circumstances beyond girls' and women's control. It is characterised by hegemonic or unequal power relations similar to those that Hey (1997: 84) identifies in racialised heterosexuality where girls take up dominating positions regarding other girls. Even though women are often compelled to sister in a motherly fashion, once they recognise this discourse, it is rarely easy for them to detach themselves from it. Women such as Beth (27) and Jeanne can even feel ambivalent about abandoning this positioning. Through their agentic subjectivity, however, they have the potential to discard the 'big' or 'little' positioning. Beth sees a way out of the *positioned* discourse and yet remains there. Madonna (31), in chapter 7, who flirts with shedding this old skin, jokes about the comforts of hanging on to her 'kid sister' positioning. Younger sisters such as Madonna can also position themselves as 'big sister'. In a counter-example, Rowena (37) in chapter 8 rejects her positioning as eldest and 'big' sister with *Grace* (34): growing up, she did not have a 'leading relationship' with her; she says that she did not hold her hand to cross the road.

This discourse maps the way that women become subjects or objects (Walkerdine 1994; Hall 1992) through adopting 'subordinate and dominant positions of power' (Hey 1997: 92). This is a discourse of femininity, of emotional and practical mothering and caring, in which women as sisters can be highly 'invested' (Hollway 1989) and which they often do enjoy because of the responsibility that comes with it. Zoë (17) and Phoebe (35) talk about the pleasures of being positioned as the older, responsible sister. 'Big' and 'little' sisters experience mothering and being mothered both positively and negatively.

Minimother and baby mother

Suzanne (30) and *Collette's* (25) transition from girlhood to womanhood, and from *distant companionship* to *best friendship*, happened partly through changing circumstances – teenage motherhood and leaving home – and partly through a shift in their tie from the *positioned* to the *shifting positions* discourse. Their story falls into two parts. The first corresponds to their teenage years of *distant companionship* which intensified when a rift occurred and *Collette* left home: the sisters did not speak to each other for two months. In the second phase, they became best friends as adults in their twenties. The transition between the two phases occurred when their father died and *Collette* became a teenage mother.

Another life-time ago

As teenagers, Suzanne's mother did not encourage the sisters to be close: 'If we'd been too close she would have felt we was maybe ganging up against her,' Suzanne says. They were opposites: Suzanne was tidy and aloof, *Collette* messy and unruly. Suzanne ignored her and 'our paths did not cross that much':

> *Suzanne*: I was neat and tidy, she was really messy and she'd take my clothes out of the wardrobe, wear 'em, trash 'em, throw 'em on the floor and that would be, we would have a lot of arguments about that kind of thing. I don't know if that's quite a sisterly sort of, quite a general thing that drives sisters mad, um, but no we never, we never really talked.

> *Suzanne*: [. . .] from the few things she's said, she's always wanted me to really take a lot of interest in her but I was off doing whatever I wanted to do and sort of, and, and never really had much interest in her at all. Occasionally, you know, I'd sort of stop what I was doing and she'd be going out and I'd say, 'Oh shall I do your hair for you?' or 'Shall I help you with?' I started putting make-up on her and, er, she said like she used to really enjoy that. She liked getting the attention off of me in that way.

Suzanne's explanation for the distance between them as teenagers, on the basis of her talks with *Collette*, concerns privacy in connection with their early sexual relationships:

> *Suzanne*: She says that she always felt that I was like this second mother, I was her second mother figure and she didn't want me to, I think probably what she was doing in her life, that at that time she, she, she knows I would have disapproved of it and that's probably why she never told me what was going on in her life.

Both sisters had abortions – Suzanne at 16, *Collette* at 12 and a half – which were not discussed in the family: at the time, each was unaware of the other's experience. Sexuality in their household was denied, even though the sisters and their mother were all sexually active. Regarding their current sexual relationships, *Collette* knows that Suzanne disapproves of her boyfriend. Suzanne's own partner gives the sisters a lot of space to conduct their relationship.

Changing relationships

When *Collette* became a mother at the age of 14, the sisters grew closer as Suzanne became involved in supporting *Collette* during her pregnancy. *Collette* gave birth to a son Tristan (now aged 10) and continued to live at home with Suzanne and their mother. Her teenage motherhood coincided with another life-event – the death of their father – although this did not affect the sisters' relationship. Their parents were divorced, but Suzanne ponders over the possible link between their bereavement and *Collette*'s decision to continue with the pregnancy rather than have an abortion. However, she can only speculate because 'we've never gone back that far really and, and sat down'. This is a silence in their tie.

When Tristan was two, 'the whole set-up of the family just got all blown out of the window'. Suzanne and her mother had taken over the care of the baby and policed *Collette*'s mothering skills. At the same time, they felt resentful of this responsibility and frustrated with *Collette* leading the life of a teenager rather than that of a mother. The tension in the household increased until it ended in a big fight between the sisters: *Collette* left home at 17 with her son. The sisters did not talk to each other for two months. Collette returned home for a short time while waiting to be rehoused and, since then, the sisters have become best friends. Suzanne summarises these events, from *Collette* giving birth to the change it brought about in their relationship:

> Suzanne: . . . that really put a big wedge between us really I suppose, although I was really happy that she was having a baby, for selfish reasons, just because I wanted a baby in the house. Um, it brought us closer in a way, she sort of um seemed to need me as a sister. She hadn't before, she was quite an independent sort of, we was quite separate in our lives, we wasn't close at all.

Collette's departure from the family home represented a crucial moment of change in Suzanne's eyes:

> Suzanne: . . . after she'd sort of threw a few punches and been quite aggressive [laughs] I left the house, went over to my grandmother's house, just to get away from the situation, let her cool down. Um, I was gone for about half an hour and when I come back she'd gone and she'd taken Tristan with her in the middle of the night and that was really a big turning-point in our lives because she then left and she never come back.

Looking back to changes in their relationship, Suzanne pinpoints the key moment:

> *Suzanne*: I really felt that she should have said, she should have apologised, but she never did really, until now. She can see that she was, she was wrong. I think up until then she always felt, really felt that I was in the wrong. And sort of from there, our relationship started to change and we start, I don't know, I don't know why really, um, but it did. You know she, she did come back home for a few months before she got a permanent accommodation.

The big bossy sister

Suzanne herself delves into some of the patterns in her relationship with *Collette* during their teenage years. At school, in the home and after the birth of *Collette*'s son, Suzanne was 'domineering' and 'bossy' and positioned as the 'big' sister. This dated back to girlhood:

> *Suzanne*: I was quite protective over her in school when she started. Um, I used to go and check that she was OK at lunchtime or you know, and let her sort of tag along with me. Um, that was it really, and after school we'd just sort of go our own ways.

This extract shows how the *positioned* discourse can include elements of caring, responsibility, protectiveness *and* distancing. Part of the distancing stems from the additional power bestowed on the sister positioned as the 'big' sister. This is in marked contrast with the *shifting positions* discourse where power oscillates between individuals rather than remaining firmly located with the same person over a long period of time. Suzanne evokes an era when she was in control, assigned to the mothering role and 'took over':

> *Suzanne*: I'd always been [the] domineering older sister, really, really bossy, always telling her what to do. My mum and dad were divorced so we was left on our, my mum used to work full-time, so we was, we was left on our own a lot when we was younger and *Collette* says that she feels that I was her second mum. I really took over the position of mum. I stuck, you know, I was the one who taught her how to do her shoe laces up and I, because I'm that way anyway and, I suppose, and being put in that situation, I did completely take over.

Suzanne's reference to 'being put in that situation' echoes Phoebe's (35) narrative in the next chapter, about becoming a minimother in order to help her mother who was raising a family single-handed.

One form that Suzanne's big sister positioning took was overseeing *Collette*'s mothering skills. This, compounded by her allegiance to their own mother, meant that *Collette* in effect had two women 'policing' her (Hey 1997: 58):

> *Suzanne*: I kind of really appreciate now how hard it was for her as well, you know, being, being that young, wanting to be a good mum, wanting to be, do everything right for her son and having these two, you know, me as a sister and her mum, completely taking over her life and saying like, do this for him, and do that, and I'm saying, you know, shouldn't you be giving him this to eat and shouldn't you be giving that?

A shift occurred with *Collette*'s flight from the family household: 'I suppose when she left she made [. . .] she made a stand saying this is me'. This marked a change in their relationship. Reflecting on their past, Suzanne distinguishes between the personality element of the dynamic they were in and the structural context. She also muses implicitly on the effect of their changed circumstances on the friendship they enjoy as adults. Significant, for Suzanne, is the role of talk in their current rapport:

> *Suzanne*: [. . .] It seems the older that we get the more we talk about things and the more that we, and the closer we've become, the more we realise that we are[n't] what we see as youngsters, what we see in each other as youngsters wasn't really there, you know it was maybe the situation that we was living in.
>
> *MM*: Like, can you think of an example then?
>
> *Suzanne*: Um, not really, no. I mean it, it's just . . . maybe the kind of person that she always thought I was, I'm not.
>
> *MM*: You, you mean like the, the domineering one or?
>
> *Suzanne*: Yeah, yeah. Yeah, the relationship's taken on a completely different, um, you know, just a, a completely different, different aspect. I'm, I don't domineer her anymore, you know, I'm not that domineering sister anymore. I'm just a friend, you know.

Suzanne's trajectory, her shedding of her old bossy self, illustrates the way that it is possible to move out of the *positioned* discourse. Power itself differs in each discourse, fixed and hegemonic in the *positioned* discourse, fluid and shifting in the *shifting positions* discourse, and women can potentially leave one and enter another: in practice, however, this is not a given. Suzanne characterises the changing power relations between them in the past and present through her term *level*:

> *Suzanne*: we wasn't on the same level because I always felt that I was responsible for her, you know, she had to do what I said.

Describing their current bond, however, she says 'we're really on the same level' and the shift from the *positioned* to the *shifting positions* discourse 'has made a more honest sort of an open relationship'. Furthermore, as adults, they have experienced a role-reversal of their situation as teenagers when *Collette* was a mother at home creating havoc in the household by acting like a teenager and going out. The conflict arose when responsibility for caring for the baby was offloaded onto Suzanne and her mother.

As adults, the sisters appreciate their bond after turbulent teenage years:

> *Suzanne*: She knows I love her and think that she's really wonderful anyway no matter what she does ... [...] It doesn't matter what she does in her life, whether, whether, it's the kind of thing that I would do or whether I really approve of it, I still love her and I'm always, we're always going to get on and sort of like each other, even though we might not do exactly what the other thinks is right.

As best friends, they ask each other for advice about emotional and practical matters:

> *Suzanne*: We seem to be able to know really what's going on with the other person and what they really need and what they really want. [...] So we seem to take time out of our lives to be together. We seem to need to do that I think. Um, pop up for a coffee. [...] She is my best friend, yeah.

Roles reversed

Following girlhoods dominated by the *positioned* discourse, now in their twenties they are living through a period marked by the *shifting positions* discourse. Compared with theirs teens when Suzanne was free and autonomous, and *Collette* a mother with responsibilities, Suzanne is currently the mother tied to the home and *Collette*, working outside the home, the more independent sister. *Collette*, with an older child, is also the more experienced mother advising her older sister on child-rearing and education:

> *Suzanne*: I wasn't 100 per cent sure about, you know, um, and then I was asking, because she's got a son that's been through, you know. It, the roles reversed a little bit because she's got the elder son [. . .] You know, so I can, and I said to her, you know, what do you think, and she was really positive, very positive and very definite that I should keep Juliet [her daughter age five] where she was and not bring her, sort of send her to school in this area, really.

Suzanne vividly elaborates on the changes:

> *Suzanne*: Really our whole roles have been reversed because when Tristan was young she was at home and I was out working and doing what I wanted to do and buying the clothes and now Tristan's older, she's, I'm the one that's at home now and she's the one that's out at work and she's got her, well, sort of independence! [laughs] I mean she's working with my mum, so that's been quite fraught at times [clears throat] but, um, in that respect, from our younger years, our roles have reversed. But I'm now the one that's at home and she goes to work and she's more independent than I am.

She compares past and present:

> *Suzanne*: Whereas maybe, when we was younger she would come to me and say, Oh Suzanne what shall I wear and what, um, would you help me, you know, pick some clothes, would you do some make-up for me, can I wear this? Now there's been times when I've gone down to her and I've said, Have you got anything I can wear? and, and, um, you know, where she's done the fitness training, she's quite knowledgeable on that sort of score, so I could go to her and say, and like when she helped me out after I had Juliet and said, you know, start going to the gym, come with me, do this. Yeah.

However, as Suzanne is well aware, she has not completely left behind her big sister positioning. When they talk about their menfolk, *Collette* knows that Suzanne disapproves of her boyfriend. Suzanne comments wryly and with humour:

> *Suzanne*: I just don't think that he is right for her. Um, but that's probably just my big sisterly bit coming out! [laughs] I want the best for my little sister! I don't know.

Looking back

Reflecting back, Suzanne pinpoints a factor that kept them close – going through an emotional and difficult experience together:

> *Suzanne*: I was very involved with Tristan because of the fact that he lived with us I think, from a baby. That's what made, that's what made us, maybe it tore us apart in the beginning but it, it's since been one of the factors that has kept us close because we was all there.

Moreover, Suzanne notes the influence of her mother during the crisis period with *Collette*, when she took on her views about mothering and baby-care. At the same time, Suzanne's mother used her as an intermediary to talk to *Collette* on her behalf. Suzanne's perception has changed now that she, too, is a mother. She can see that their difficulties as teenagers owed less to their personalities and more to 'the situation that we was living in'. Also, her mother 'never encouraged us to be close'. She is determined not to let her mother set her own two daughters against each other. Like Rowena, also a mother of two daughters, Suzanne wants to avoid 'history repeating itself'. Echoing other sisters, she spoke critically of the role that mothers could play in distancing daughters from each other. In the next section, Jeanne's experiences exemplify positive and negative aspects of motherly sistering.

Escape from motherland

This case study sketches Jeanne's family background before exploring links between her notions of 'mothering' and 'being mothered'. Unlike Suzanne, Jeanne feels awkward about both of these positions. As the second daughter in a family of seven siblings, Jeanne (45) was both positioned and positioned herself as a 'big sister'. She relates to her three sisters in different ways: she enjoys *close companionships* with Leonie (48) and Madonna (31) and feels ambivalent about her *distant companionship* with Roxanne (39) (see Figure 4.1). She sees Madonna the most as they live in the same town.

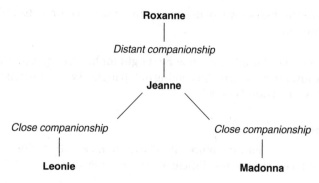

Figure 4.1   Jeanne's sister relationships

Girlhood

Whereas Jeanne as a girl was 'foul' to Leonie the eldest and resented her, she now sees her as a 'semi-mother figure', a family provider of stability unlike their own mother. Her most difficult relationship is with Roxanne, in spite of her affection for her. The gulf between them dates back to their teens when Jeanne, six years older than Roxanne, took advantage of her age and patronised her. The rift occurred when Roxanne returned from college: 'We fell out; she wasn't prepared to listen to my clap-trap'. Jeanne admits that nowadays she 'feels threatened by her dynamism and intellect'. Jeanne and Roxanne have little contact: they do not send each other birthday cards and see each other at 'family do's' only. Jeanne feels closest to Madonna: they are more like equals and friends. They see each other mostly with Thomas, Jeanne's new partner, an arrangement Jeanne feels unhappy with. She has several girlfriends. When she divorced she told her sisters after the event. Roxanne and Jeanne's separate narratives reveal how they agree on its history. This information provides a context for understanding Jeanne's comments. In order to preserve the anonymity of some facets of this set of sisters, I present Jeanne's story in isolation from her sisters' tales. I return to Madonna and Roxanne's tie in chapter 7.

Jeanne talked about her own subjectivity in detail such as not wanting to mother or be mothered by her sisters, about the way she creates distance and sets boundaries between them and herself, and her feelings of guilt about this, which she sees as a slightly negative process. Jeanne appears happy with her relationships with Leonie and Madonna, although she would prefer a more independent tie with Madonna. She is less happy with her relationship with Roxanne. She talked in a reflective manner, with little prompting, in a questioning monologue.

In relation to all her concerns about 'mothering' and 'being mothered' she mentions her son Dylan (13), whom she notes ironically is the only person she wants to mother, although at his age, he resists being mothered. Then there is her mother, who like her son requires mothering and unlike him wants to be mothered. Jeanne's words suggest that she is grappling with several 'subject positions' that feel more or less un/comfortable.

Babies and bottles

Jeanne's narrative illustrates a feminine subjectivity struggling with and resisting positive and negative aspects of mothering. Jeanne seems adamantly opposed to 'mothering' and 'being mothered' in any form. Mothering for Jeanne has at least two meanings: 'always being there' in the way Leonie, the eldest, holds their family together since the death of their father, a role which their mother resists taking on herself. It also denotes her parenting role regarding her son. Of Leonie's mothering and minimother positioning, she says:

> *Jeanne*: . . . She's not a mother figure because that's to er, give her too much responsibility but she's um, she provides that, that certain sort of stability, um to our family, which I don't think our mother was able to do. So I see her as, um very independent, very caring, very together sort of person who makes very few demands of me, she does make some but not many, um, but who is always there for me, in the way that a mother would be really.

In a sense, both Leonie and Madonna in their positions as eldest and youngest sisters, provide Jeanne with examples of what she is attempting to avoid in her sistering – the 'big' minimother position, on the one hand, and the 'baby' sister position on the other. Jeanne explains:

> *Jeanne*: Madonna, when she was younger was just this adored little girl, and she was adored. Because we all had the chance really to, to practise all those, [laughs] all those dreadful mothering skills that we'd been witnessing! [laughs] And from that early age really, you know, we were going to be, um, better at it. We were all going to be better at it, um, than our mother had been.

Jeanne is explicit about not wanting to be either 'mothered' as Madonna was, or mother her sisters, as Leonie did:

Jeanne: I know that I hold back with certain things and it's to do with this, um, the fact it, it's to do with the way that we were mothered and that our mother has required us to mother her, um, and has not been that sort of emotional support that, that you should have. And as I say, I'm exploring at the moment the fact that I, I think that I don't press Madonna, for instance over certain things that I know are worrying her. Um, or tell her certain things that are worrying me because, um, I think on the surface, it's because I don't want to burden her, because that isn't her role, I don't want to force her into the role of mother for me, but more worryingly for me, I think I also keep some distance because I don't want them to force me into the role of mother for them.

Jeanne represents the two alternative roles clearly:

Jeanne: I certainly don't want to force them into the role of mothering me, I know I don't want that. Um, but more interestingly, something that's come out recently is that I think I don't want them to put me in that role either. I don't want, want to mother them because, um, because I, I feel I, I don't know, I, I think because I feel so strongly that I don't want to mother people except the person that I am a mother to, which is my son, who incidentally [laughs] wants nothing to do with me because he's 13! [laughs]

Another problematic 'mothering' association for Jeanne stems from her tense relationship with Roxanne, whom she once patronised. In this sense she negatively positioned herself as a mother. Jeanne lucidly and eloquently notes the power relations between them from which their tie has never recovered:

Jeanne: I was insufferably patronising to her and, and just adopted this sort of role of mother, but it was the role that my mother played with her, but I sort of used the fact that I was closer to her than my mother to impose exactly the same sort of things on her as my mother was trying to do. Oh, horrible. And I think, um, I mean I don't know, I think those years possibly irretrievably damaged that relationship really and she went off to college and we have never been close. You know, there were nights when she was still at home and I was home from college or before I'd gone off to college even, when we would lay in bed and talk and there was no basis for talking as equals. Um I, I was just patronising and dictating to her and telling her how to live her life and it must have been awful for her. She must have hated me! [laughs]

Jeanne links the way that she positioned herself as big patronising sister to her wish for Roxanne not to repeat her own mistakes. As a result, Jeanne 'tried to control her'. Roxanne rebelled and they became distant, which Jeanne feels sad about.

Supermother

A further negative dimension of mothering for Jeanne is the way it involves experiencing her sisters' painful emotions. She contrasts this with her female friendships where some degree of detachment enables her to 'switch off' in a way that she cannot do with her sisters:

> *Jeanne*: I don't want to burden and worry them. To go back to it, I think something that's coming out, um, in my life is that, that, that the possibility that if I expect that [care] from them, they might perhaps expect the same from me and I don't know whether I have it to give. And yet, it's there for friends because, er, I can switch off from friends. I mean, I can care very deeply for them and their pain and their anxiety. It is, it is great, I mean I can feel it greatly but, but it never brings me down. I'm always separate from it. Whereas my sisters' pain I am not separate from it, so their pain is my pain to a greater or lesser extent.

Mothering for Jeanne embodies caring and protectiveness expressed by not burdening others with personal emotional troubles. It suggests the idea of a one-way relationship where one person is providing all the emotional support for another. She says:

> *Jeanne*: With women friends, only one or two, but with one or two I would just, um . . . . tell them exactly what my misery was and I find that very hard to do with my sisters if there is a misery. I find that very hard to do with my sisters and I don't think it's, I don't think it's protecting me that, I think it starts off as protecting them, that if I tell them, I'm saying to you, I'm saying to them, give me all the support. See I have this ideal notion of a mother and it is that, that is the person who I would have done that with as a younger person and would still be able to do it.

Jeanne's 'ideal mother' delivers total support and nurturing – this supermother, however, rarely exists in this form. One interpretation of Jeanne's image is that it stems from its absence in her girlhood, owing to her mother's 'inadequate' mothering. Jeanne's 'supermother' fantasy explains her desire to move away from the *positioned* discourse in her sister ties: except for her tie with Roxanne where she remains locked in a situation determined by past conflict which positioned Jeanne as 'big' sister and Roxanne as 'little' sister. Roxanne rebelled against this positioning and Jeanne admits not having the time, confidence or energy to address and repair this tie in order to transform it. While Jeanne remarks about the research process that 'it is in talking that you see things more clearly', she does not want to talk to Roxanne.

Nevertheless, Jeanne recognises the central issues and options. The hold of the 'ideal mother' myth leads her to comment wryly: 'I still chase the goal of the perfect relationship and, er, still try and be the perfect mother and, you know, superwoman really.' As a result, she distances herself from her sisters although with Madonna, who in her words makes few demands of her, they do hug and cry together. Jeanne's tie with Madonna contains an element of 'equality' and *shifting positions* which marks it out from her other sister ties. This appears to be her only sister tie with a degree of intimacy. And yet the distance that she experiences there, also puzzles her:

> *Jeanne*: I have this feeling that it is much stronger and, um, and more approaching whatever a good relationship is but still, there is distance between us which um, would not be there with say, my closest female friends. I do still hold back and I feel that she does as well.

Distance has negative overtones for Jeanne: perhaps she cannot imagine its positive aspects in 'a good relationship'. Distance becomes a mechanism for protecting herself from closeness and from her fear of 'not coping' if she gets too stuck in: 'I think that's still where the distance comes, that, that I think that, if I get in just too close, I won't be able to cope.' Implicitly, she attributes a negative meaning to her distancing tendency. One reason might be her ambivalence towards distance: 'I do, I regret that, that I am so, that I do create a distance between myself and the people that I care for and I don't fully understand why I do it or how'. She does not have even a slightly positive reading of this distancing process. However, Edwards' (1993) research on mature women students' integration of education with family life suggests positive aspects, for some, of keeping certain aspects of their lives separate. Her typology of connection, separation and mixing connections and separations of education and family offers a positive reading of the process of 'cutting off' (Edwards' 1993: 130) for women between their separate identities.

Sistering and mothering

How do these notions of 'mothering', 'being mothered', 'supermother' and negative aspects of distance relate to the *positioned* and *shifting posi-*

tions discourses? One answer is to look at the *shifting positions* element of Jeanne's bond with Madonna, when Jeanne says 'I feel more like we are equals really'. An example of equality between them is Madonna's ability to disagree with Jeanne assertively by voicing her dissatisfaction with aspects of their tie, which Jeanne sees as a strength:

> *Jeanne*: On the one hand, I felt awful because I felt that she was very justified in what she was saying and, on the other hand, I felt, er, very pleased really, that she'd been able to say that because I think it's a, a breakthrough, I think it's a step forward for me.

Here, 'breakthrough' can be connected to moving out of the *positioned* discourse by having someone, Madonna, take her to task when Jeanne locates herself there. As a result, their relationship contains a whisper of *shifting positions* although it seems that, for Jeanne, the fact they see each other as a threesome with her partner, and seldom at that, is something that she feels unhappy about. Jeanne's narrative sheds light on how meanings of 'mothering' are embedded in and construct the *positioned* discourse. It also reveals linguistic difficulties of defining 'sistering', Hazel's term, without drawing on images of 'mothering' and 'being mothered'.

Conclusion

Suzanne's and Jeanne's experiences and reflections on 'mothering' and 'being mothered' show how caring, emotions and power relations are interwoven in sistering. Each case study revealed changing forms of power dynamics over the years between Suzanne and *Collette*, and Jeanne and her sisters Roxanne and Madonna. These examples raise pertinent questions about the link between mothering and friendship. If hegemonic relationships of dominance and subordination fluctuate in minimothering, to what extent does the *positioned discourse* constitute a friendship discourse? If we view friendship as based on mutuality and equitable exchange, then it does not qualify. However, this discourse also contains other positive caring elements associated with friendship.

If we view mothering and friendship on a continuum of caring informed by different expectations and power dynamics, then the *positioned* discourse becomes less antithetical to friendship than we first imagined. Friendship, as I mentioned in studies cited in chapter 1, is not immune from power imbalances. Nevertheless Jeanne's portrait of her friends as individuals she can 'tell them exactly what my misery was', care for and remain 'separate from' offers one view of differences between friendship and sistering. In addition, if the *positioned* discourse coexists alongside the *shifting positions* discourse or even within it, then, as relationships fluctuate, it would appear, potentially, to incorporate certain friendship traits. The crucial element consists of the reversal or 'exchanging positions' (Lather 1988: 577) in order to dislodge entrenched power relations and positions. In the next chapter Hazel and Phoebe analyse this process in great detail.

5
Kindred Spirits

Hazel (34) and Phoebe's (35) relationship, like Suzanne and *Collette*'s, takes a dramatic turn during their girlhood and adolescence. When their father dies, their mother brings them up, with their two siblings, as a single parent. Many caring responsibilities fall upon Phoebe as the eldest and she becomes a minimother. It is only in their thirties that they start to talk about their varied mothering experiences, their children, their mother and each other. In their adult lives they enjoy a more reciprocal tie with elements of *close companionship* and *best friendship*. Although they have little in common and neither would describe the other as their best friend, they maintain regular contact, feel close and have a profound understanding of each other.

Hazel and Phoebe's awareness of power dynamics in their tie is one of the most explicit among the case studies, similar to Roxanne and Madonna's described in chapter 7. This chapter traces the events that influence the shifts in power between them over the years. Some moments of change are circumstantial resulting from life-events: their upbringing by their lone mother, the deaths of their step-father and half-sister *Denise* (19), the dissolution of Phoebe's best girl/friendship, and Hazel's depression. Others stem from the different ways in which they act on their knowledge, insights and experience in order to modify their tie and become kindred spirits. Like Suzanne and *Collette*, Hazel and Phoebe successfully move out of the *positioned* discourse. This is in marked contrast with Jeanne who contemplates that option and decides not to, thereby remaining positioned as 'big' sister, which she feels ambivalent about.

Rebel with a cause and Miss Goody Two Shoes

Hazel and Phoebe's understanding of the evolution of their tie is based on first, the emotional impact of the changing structure of their family on their girlhoods and, second, the individual 'agentic' change (Maynard 1995: 274) they each engaged in. For Hazel, the rebel, it meant 'breaking out' of the unclever 'wild' girl mould she had been cast in and instead voicing her emotions to her mother and sister. For Phoebe, the dutiful daughter, this change manifested itself in her becoming more 'self-preservatory' and less 'other-directed'. What is remarkable about their narratives is their reflexivity about the changes that their tie has undergone: each discloses *and* simultaneously analyses key events in their lives. The crucial change occurred when they shifted positions and agreed openly that Hazel is now Phoebe's 'big sister'. Their separate stories reveal their shared feelings about their tie and their narratives match. They spoke to me independently as Hazel confirms in her comment about contacting Phoebe about the study:

> *Hazel*: I'll give Phoebe a ring and I shall explain to her and I'll say to her you know, actually what I'll say to her, I . . . I'm not telling you anything I've said because it's . . . you know, if you're going to do [it], it's got to come from you.

Girlhood

Girlhood was a time when the sisters were extreme opposites. Phoebe, or Miss Goody Two Shoes, protected her mother and mothered her younger siblings. Here, Phoebe's mothering picks up where Jeanne's resistance to it left off. Hazel and *Denise* were the rebellious 'bad girls' whom their mother found difficult to manage, Phoebe was the 'good girl'. Hazel felt rejected by their self-employed mother, who had little time for her. In young Phoebe's eyes, Hazel was the cause of 'a little bit of madness and chaos in the family home' through her 'irresponsible' behaviour – breaking things. The sisters' distinct personalities led Hazel to comment sarcastically:

> *Hazel*: Phoebe was always the clever one, Phoebe and Oliver [half-brother] were the academics. *Denise* and I were full of personality; it was almost like a consolation prize . . . this personality!

Hazel and Phoebe were also opposites at school, with Phoebe the more assiduous and obedient one, and Hazel, the one who questioned authority. They attended separate schools and had different friends. They did little together which led their mother to describe them as 'not a close family'. Hazel reflects on this assessment:

Hazel: We weren't, in my mum's opinion we weren't close. Divide and conquer. If you tell a child constantly enough, you're not close to your brother, and there's this constant doubting: 'Well, I feel close enough but you say I'm not'. And how close can you get? Unless you're walking round inside somebody else's skin you can only get so close and as brothers and sisters and mums and all that business, you are supposed to let go to a degree and go off, you're supposed to.

Hazel's words encompass the power relations embedded in the institution of the family when she talks about 'divide and conquer', a language of planning and strategy. Her emphasis on 'to let go' captures the distancing process in family ties about which Jeanne feels so ambivalent – a practice she recognised and yet felt negative and uncomfortable about. Phoebe's 'goodness' plagued Hazel into her twenties when she began to contemplate the possibility of change regarding their location in the *positioned* discourse. The seeds of Hazel's changing subjectivity that emerged when she was in her thirties can be glimpsed here when she says:

Hazel: I was standing out in the garden thinking, I'm never going to be as good as Phoebe, I was about 27, 28 . . . and I'm never going to be as good as Phoebe. Said who, I mean looking back now, said who . . . ? At the end of the day I sometimes wonder if people will be as good as me, you know! [laughs]

Minimothering

Growing up, Phoebe was positioned as a minimother. When the girls' stepfather died (Hazel was 7 and Phoebe 8), Phoebe's role as 'carer boss control', in Hazel's words, increased: she was the responsible daughter assisting her mother during difficult times. Hazel resented being compared to Phoebe – 'the first person we compete with is our sister, then our mother'. Phoebe is aware of how Hazel must have experienced her:

Phoebe: [. . .] There were lots of things that I did, I mean, I mean I must have been nauseating, you know I never got into trouble, I would rush up and ask to rub the blackboard for you, Miss, at school.

Phoebe was constructed as the second mother – a source of emotional support for their mother who ran a business single-handed and relied on her. Hazel resented Phoebe's role of protector and controller. Phoebe was closer to their mother than Hazel was:

Hazel: She's a lot closer to my mum than I am, but I think that's probably because my mum has had to rely on her for emotional and practical support. [. . .] You had this 8-year-old child suddenly being trained as mum number two basically [. . . mainly in] emotional protection and care.

Turning-points

Their girlhood ended, at the age of 7 and 8, with the death of their stepfather. Phoebe recalls their individual reactions to this trauma:

Phoebe: When our father died there were all sorts of confusing things happening which obviously she couldn't deal with, she couldn't cope with but her reaction to them was different to mine. We dealt with them in different ways and it caused conflict between us because I was always seen to be The Goody Two Shoes who would be helpful and, um, I mean poor old Hazel just ended up getting into trouble all the time. But obviously it was her way of, of crying out for some help and support.

As adults they have combed through the past and compared their interpretations of events surrounding this bereavement, concerning decisions made without their involvement:

Phoebe: When we've discussed this later on we both agree that obviously it was done for our best, in our best interest, but we both feel that really we should have been much more part of the family scene.

Another source of turmoil occurred with their half-sister *Denise*'s death at 19 when Hazel and Phoebe were in their mid-twenties. Hazel recounted her tragic death (for ethical reasons, not revealed here). This second bereavement profoundly influenced the sisters' relationship. Each reverted to type and adopted their familiar roles: 'That was it; it was . . . everyone rallied to protect Mum. So then . . . Phoebe became the child again that was in control; I became the child again that was . . . rebelling.' Yet at the same time, after years of confrontation and resentment, the sisters rallied in the aftermath of *Denise*'s death:

Hazel: Phoebe and I were actually now dealing with . . . we were actually dealing with something together for the first time. We both had control because my mum had none, she was grief-stricken and she didn't have any control so we actually united; at that point I would say, was the first time we dealt with a situation as a team as opposed to fighting against it.

Denise's death provoked a shift. It indicated the early signs of the end of the dominance of the *positioned* discourse, which had previously characterised their tie. This discourse was only to be fully dislodged when the sisters reached their thirties.

Piggy in the middle

Recollecting the past, Phoebe sees herself positioned as intermediary between her mother and Hazel. Growing up as minimother to her siblings and mother, Phoebe backed her mother in situations of conflict. She contrasts her interpretation of events as a girl and daughter and as an adult mother in a description of one of her mother's suicide attempts:

> *Phoebe*: Hazel used to, [sighs] again, used to wreak havoc by, I don't know, just rushing about madly and shouting and, and just generally attention-seeking, um, and because I wasn't like that, it caused conflict between us and I don't know if I, I, understood at the time why she was doing it but I, I understood why she was behaving that way; but I didn't think it was appropriate because I could understand my mum's point of view. So I was constantly torn between what Hazel was doing, why Hazel was doing it and then, on the other hand, the reaction that it was having on my mother and therefore I was, I was very much torn between the two of them and, rightly or wrongly, I tended to want to protect my mother more. Which is quite strange really because when you think about it, [it] should be your mother protecting you. Now as a mother I can see that, but at the time, I didn't see, I just saw Hazel as being a nuisance and a pest and inconsiderate. I didn't see her as being thoughtful and therefore I, I became angry with her to try and protect my mum, which is quite strange.

Phoebe reflects on this intermediary position between mother and sister and how her loyalty was tested in spite of her:

> *Phoebe*: I think one of the nice things that's happened, that's a huge relief to me, is that my mum and Hazel have come to understand one another and I think that was, looking back, that was one of the difficulties I had, because I was constantly this piggy in the middle. My mum would make comments about how Hazel was behaving, Hazel would make comments about how my mum had reacted to something, and I

was almost, well I was torn between my allegiances, you know there certainly were times when I wanted to say to my mum 'Butt out, that's Hazel's decision'. On the other hand there would be times when I'd say, 'Well yes, Mummy you're quite right she has done such', and, and it was always this, I, and again I, I mean that was very destructive for the relationship that Hazel and I had because she was, well, aware of that happening.

Changing relationships and subjectivities

Interestingly, the sisters interpret the past in the light of life-events and circumstances of their girlhood influenced by bereavement, and their changing subjectivities in reaction to these. Both these elements, what I call 'changing relationships' and 'changing subjectivities', structure their understanding of their ties in the past and present. Phoebe's snapshot of their adolescence summarises the intersection of unexpected life events with femininity:

> *Phoebe*: There was a lot happening really for us to deal with, as well as just the basic things as having greasy hair and spots and boyfriends who don't love you anymore and things like that! [laughs] [. . .] Because of the circumstances of the way our lives were, added pressures and strains were put on us.

Their teens coincided with upheaval marked by parental and sibling bereavement and attempted suicide. Hazel's version of this family fragility and maternal vulnerability and mental ill health is summed up by the phrase: 'it was all circumstantial not self . . . '. Her comment indicates her awareness of unpredictable tragic events versus her own agency even though she does use these terms.

This context of changing relationships and especially the *positioned* discourse impinged on the sisters' individual subjectivities. When Phoebe looks at her girlhood critically, she observes her positioning as 'good Phoebe'. Almost trapped within that discourse she notes how difficult it was for her gradually changing subjectivity to emerge:

> *Phoebe*: At the time I revelled in it, I'm ashamed to say, it was my glory, I was good Phoebe. Everyone told me how wonderful I was all the time and for years and years and years I was good Phoebe, to the point that even if I wanted to not be good I couldn't, because I'd be letting everybody down. I couldn't actually be me.

Significantly, she describes her own pleasure and investment in the *positioned* discourse, reminiscent of Hollway's (1989) account of individuals who cling to harmful discourses which they feel ambivalent about relinquishing. Phoebe traces her changing subjectivity in an analytical and reflexive manner:

> *Phoebe*: I was almost stuck in this groove but, but certainly for those years, I did, you know, I realise now that I, it was a role I quite happily got myself into. I mean, I enjoyed being good, and I do now, I don't, excuse me, I'm not given to being horrible to people, um, it, it's, I get a buzz out of being nice, I mean if I do somebody a good turn it, it makes me feel good. I mean I think that's, I recognise that in myself. But, um, it was quite difficult because there were some very very difficult times when my mum had, um, a couple a nervous breakdowns between, in our sort of early, middle teens and, um, basically I mothered her, it, that's how I, how I see it. [. . .] I ended up protecting her [. . .].

Eventually, Phoebe's halo faded:

> *Phoebe*: I've certainly said to my mum and I, I reiterate it over and over again, is that I know I have faults, I mean I'm. As a young person I wandered around with my shining halo and I know that it's fallen off, you know, I don't, I don't walk about with a halo.

Phoebe was placed by circumstances in a position where she ended up caring for her mother. Gradually, she accepted Hazel's recent mothering of her. Phoebe's experience of mothering her mother and eventually of being mothered by Hazel contrasts sharply with Jeanne's. Jeanne both vehemently rejects any attempts by her sisters to mother her and remains ill at ease with the activity of 'mothering' except regarding her son.

Breaking out

As Phoebe's halo faded and she moved out of the *positioned* discourse, similarly Hazel, too, broke out of the 'little sister' positioning. Hazel's 'breaking out' initially followed a period of depression in her thirties. After her recovery she voiced her feelings of resentment to her mother and sister. The catalyst for Hazel's 'breaking out' was a family row. The row also marked the end of the minimothering phase of their sistering and the early days of greater reciprocity between them. After documenting their conflict and emotions the case study examines the role reversal which ensued.

The row, which sparked off the eventual role-reversal, occurred at a family gathering. During an exchange between Hazel, her partner and Phoebe about a TV programme which Hazel's partner alleged that he had not been allowed to watch Hazel flared up at him and soon the two sisters were in conflict. Hazel recalls her emotions of resentment let loose:

> *Hazel*: It was this . . . big sister interference just once too often and it was just sort of . . . head swung round and, who bloody asked you whether you were joking or otherwise! Perhaps you should keep your sodding jokes to yourself . . . ! And it was . . . that was it! Once the gates opened it was . . . there's this big sister again, what the hell do you think you're doing, do you think I'm [in]capable of solving a relationship problem! Oh well, you deal with it Phoebe, you've always dealt with my problems so aptly and I'll let you get on with it, shall I? Shall I just sit in a chair and go comatose and then you can run my life for me?

Hazel's outburst was paramount for her. It marked the moment when she set the record straight about her family's perception of her as a young girl – as not clever:

> *Hazel*: To actually have said to them about three, four years ago whenever this big row was, I'm not as thick as two short planks, you've labelled me all wrongly all my life, you don't know me at all and watch . . . and then you get this realisation, well, I don't know me that well, I don't know what I'm capable of, or what I'm not.

The forcefulness of Hazel's words corresponds to her decision to return to study following early unhappy school experiences. She aspired to an 'emotional healing type of job be it sort of child psychology'.

Hazel's auto/biographical monologue traces the apogee of her resentment when she ruptured the patterns of the *positioned* discourse. The impact of her emotional explosion for her tie with Phoebe was far-reaching: when she seized this opportunity to present her perspective this event ultimately led to a role reversal. She recounts her shift from a position of silence to a more verbal mode and describes changing power relations through the term 'control':

> *Hazel*: [You] go through life resenting everything Hazel um . . . that actually carried on up until about three years ago this . . . er . . . 'I know better than you' sort of attitude and sort of, I suppose resenting it

for long enough and keeping quiet about it long enough, there was an absolute almighty family row er . . . . where I laid all my cards on the table and everyone stood there, sort of gob-smacked, I suppose would describe it quite well . . . And I got a phone call and everything sort of reversed. Not where I have control and all the business for Phoebe but where Phoebe accepts that I am an *autonomous* person and I don't need her control and I don't need her standards and I don't need . . . She's constantly, as a child she was brought up and expected to help control the little ones.

The word 'autonomous' captures precisely what is absent in Roxanne and Madonna's flirtation with the *shifting positions* discourse: the ability to see the other as independent and separate which I return to in chapter 7. For Hazel and Phoebe, gradual recognition and acceptance of their differences and autonomy paved the way for a successful move for their sistering from the *positioned* into the *shifting positions* discourse.

Hazel's narrative highlights the importance of silence, talk and language – Smith's 'verbal bodies of acknowledged knowledge'[1] – in this case the impact of trading her silence for words. Language is the medium through which we shape our narratives of self and give meaning to our experiences. Hazel says: 'And I wouldn't speak to any of them, I thought . . . you, it's all been said . . . I don't love you any of the less because I've said it, in actual fact it's probably easier now because you've been told'. Hazel reflects on her changed behaviour – from her usual silence to outspokenness: 'I'd given up smoking at the time as well, which is actually probably why it all came out, because normally I'd light a fag up and I'd think yep, so what . . . you know, button it and hold it'. Her awareness of respecting silence in specific situations reveals her narrative reflexivity, which I return to below. Hazel's idea of closeness, unlike her mother's which is associated with contact and shared activities, is linked to monitoring emotions and judging appropriate silence:

> *Hazel*: People tend to think of closeness in a way of what you are able to say to somebody, I tend to think of closeness can sometimes be what you're not prepared to lay on them . . . like guilt trips or . . . you know, there's certain things you don't say to people because you're close, you know.

Hazel's narrative develops through a language of emotions about scope for openness and silences in families. Her outburst can be interpreted as a rebellion against familial patterns from girlhood when Phoebe withheld her emotions to protect and nurture their mother. While Hazel's depression was the catalyst for her breaking out of the 'little sister' position in which she had been cast in the *positioned* discourse, it also marked the start for Phoebe of a move away from her minimothering 'big sister' role to a position of 'self-preservation'.

Self-preservation

Phoebe's changing subjectivity emerged in relation to specific events in her own life and Hazel's. During Hazel's depression, Phoebe was involved in moving house, recovering from the dissolution of her tie with her oldest female best friend and supporting her husband through a difficult period of his own. She found herself pulling away from Hazel's traumas to channel her energy elsewhere and protect herself:

> *Phoebe*: About that time [moving house] Hazel was very, very depressed and, um, I couldn't, I couldn't help her. I felt really awful, I mean I'd, I'd phone but I couldn't be there for her, it was, um, it was almost as if at that point I'd just had enough of dealing with things and it was, and I felt totally, totally awful about it, um, and it was from then on I suppose really, that I began to get less and less involved with the dramas, um, it was almost, I suppose, a protective thing for me. [. . .] I was just emotionally drained. [. . .] I just didn't want to be involved in any more hurt and pain. It wasn't my hurt and pain; it was her hurt and pain.

Jeanne also talked about the anguish of feeling another's pain and her wish to distance herself from this emotion. Phoebe managed this demanding period hardly asking Hazel for support: she kept in touch with her, but maintained a distance from Hazel's depression. She also kept Hazel at arm's length from her own life, deciding not to rely on her: 'I used to phone her up in floods of tears but I tend to, I tend probably to keep things more to myself . . . at times like that I, I tend to keep my own counsel.'

This phase of distancing herself from events in Hazel's life and becoming more self-oriented marked a break with Phoebe's past mothering and caring role. In her early thirties she redirected herself towards her 'family of procreation' (Parkin 1997: 30):

> *Phoebe*: I had to start beginning to be a bit self-preservatory for my own, well not sanity, I mean that's too dire, but, but for my own sense of well-being. I had to begin to focus on what was happening in my

young family, my children, my husband, my home and to the exclusion at times of them and certainly, even, you know, with respect to, you know, minor crises.

Part of Phoebe's changing subjectivity involved her growing awareness of her capacities and acceptance of her limitations:

Phoebe: I think I've actually begun to like myself again lately and to realise that I know, you know, I have limitations and there is, there is a point at which I can give no more and I've begun to realise that there's no shame in that . . .

Phoebe's detailed account of pulling away from Hazel reflects the difficulties of moving out of her location in the *positioned* discourse.

During Hazel's depression, her brother and mother stepped in to help her. Yet, Phoebe found this a complex process giving rise to emotions of 'betrayal':

Phoebe: It's as if I've put the shutters down and, and that's what I meant about being, betraying Hazel at a time when perhaps she did, could have done with a bit more support from me. I mean, I think she was, I think she was all right and I think, probably, she was so depressed, she didn't notice I didn't go, at least that's what I'm hoping.

Phoebe's narrative of distancing reflects her own version of events rather than a jointly produced account with Hazel. The presence or absence of language for developing knowledge is significant for creating a shared story. Phoebe *has* the knowledge, only she has not exchanged or compared it with Hazel's version:

MM: And so how did that affect your relationship with Hazel if you were sort of withdrawing a little bit?

Phoebe: I don't know, I don't know because on, we don't really, we haven't really discussed that period in very much detail because I, I still find it, I mean there were all sorts of things happening in my life as well as hers, so it's not a period I'm quite ready to get too deep into about with her.

Phoebe's words also show where biography – an account of the other and of relationship – ends and auto/biography – the life-history of the self – begins, as well as how enmeshed and separate they are. Phoebe's wish to secure her privacy stands out: in a sense, Phoebe acknowledges her changing subjectivity but is not yet willing to go into the finer details of it with her sister.

Role-reversal

Hazel and Phoebe's awareness of the circumstances of their youth extends to their heightened reflexivity about their relationship in the present – though not every stage of the past. This realisation is reflected in Phoebe's words: 'I think now that we're actually all of us able to basically get on with our lives, it's given us time to calm down and reflect on, on what's gone on.' In their early thirties, the big argument led to a turn-about when they decided almost 'officially' to swap roles and 'shift positions'. From being positioned as minimother, Phoebe shed her 'big sister' role and shifted positions with Hazel:

> *Phoebe*: We've decided this year that she's going to be my big sister for a little. Why? Because I, I find the sense of responsibility to her, it's just been a bit overwhelming! [laughs] So we've swapped roles for a little while! [laughs]

And Hazel corroborates this when she says:

> *Hazel*: This birthday I got a birthday card from my 'little sister', not physically or age-wise but . . . sort of . . .

An early instance of *shifting positions* happened at school when Hazel, age 12, acted as 'big sister' in order to protect Phoebe, age 13, from a girl who was bullying her.

The process they went through to make explicit their decision for Hazel to be 'big sister' seems to concern changing subjectivity. One example is Phoebe's account of Hazel's ability to accept criticism more easily than she does. The significant aspects of this reflexive process are emotion, contact and language – feelings and verbalising them. Following their pattern of phone contact and encounters in moments of crisis in their twenties, in their thirties they opt for a different strategy. As twenty-somethings they went through a phase when Hazel rang Phoebe, who listened, at all hours:

> *Phoebe*: I must have been about 21, something like that, and she'd phone me up at, there was this period, it sort of seemed to go on for

months, at 4 o'clock in the morning, the telephone would ring and it would be Hazel in floods of tears, needing to talk. Or I'd have to dive up there. My mum, I know, many occasions, used to jump in the car and go up there and just rescue whatever emotional crisis was happening and there was all that happening and so we were always there for each other. [. . .] I wouldn't have not have done it. I mean, she was my sister and she needed to talk and, um, I mean if anyone was to put her down and, I know the same happened from her point of view, if anyone were to make a personal attack on me, um, we would defend one another, it was, it was really quite interesting [. . .] she was very very loyal to me.

In their thirties, they both began to question the *positioned* discourse and how it located them regarding each other and their mother. Hazel recounts a conversation with Phoebe about one of Phoebe's disputes with their mother:

Hazel: I mean she [Phoebe] actually said in the end, she said, I've never actually grown up have I, I've always been . . . too busy being *big sister* to actually do the rest, and I said: well, it's not so much that, your biggest problem is . . . and I think it's a lot of families' failing, that you think that the love that we all have is so fragile, you think you can't have the row, you can't have the blazing argument, you mustn't say that to Mummy, she might get upset, how could you say that to each other, you know, there was all this . . . all those things.

Hazel questioned the impact of the *positioned* discourse on Phoebe and in turn assumed 'big sister' responsibility by telling her to live her own life:

Hazel: Although I resent the responsibility not being shared, I resent her having had the burden of it all whereas it was always taken that I just wanted the responsibility. But when we actually had this big row and we did get talking and I actually said – look, it's like this . . . you're 33 now, or whatever she was at the time, you have to live your life.

A large part of their struggle to move out of the *positioned* discourse involved their relationships with their mother. Phoebe still found herself as an adult in the difficult situation she had experienced since girlhood of mothering her. Hazel still resented being compared to Phoebe, as she had been as a girl, and perceived negatively. Part of Hazel's transformation into 'big sister' entailed supporting Phoebe's recasting of her tie with her mother. In effect, Hazel helped Phoebe to view her daughter–mother relationship in a new light. Hazel was instrumental in backing Phoebe's attempts to break away from their mother to 'live her own life'. Hazel is slightly dismissive of Phoebe's lack of perspective and knowledge of their mother. Her disapproval is tangible when she says: 'I actually looked at Phoebe and said . . . "Oh, you don't know her as well as you think you do!" And she said, "No, I don't." My sister was so busy looking after my mum, she never got to actually know her.' Hazel encouraged Phoebe's autonomy:

> *Hazel*: The more assertive you are in your ability to make a decision and carry it through, the more ready she [mother] is to accept you as a fully grown person.

Hazel's relationship with Phoebe is complex. Regarding their current lives, Hazel urges her to free herself from her mother's hold – to be her own person. Regarding their past, she feels resentful of the responsibility and power – Hazel uses the term 'control' – bestowed on Phoebe as minimother. To Hazel's consternation, Phoebe did not aspire to be located in the *positioned* discourse and as the holder of so much power, constantly rendered Hazel invisible, positioning her as incompetent. While Phoebe confesses that she would have been happy to share it, Hazel however did not necessarily want that – she just thought it unfair for Phoebe to 'have the burden' of responsibility. While Phoebe had not considered this, Hazel's concern was that Phoebe could not live her life on her own terms.

Hazel describes the changing dynamic between them in relation to their shifting power positions through the theme of their mother's will. The will anecdote symbolises all of Hazel's resentment.

> *Hazel*: She actually phoned up, she said . . . 'Oh, the will's in a brown envelope under the . . . ' and I got a bit more information of . . . I said, 'I'm not bloody bothered where the will is anymore to be honest with you! It was just a point that I wanted to make – you always had the control, you always had the responsibility.' She said . . . 'I never wanted it'. I said, 'I never wanted you to have it'. She said . . . 'but I wouldn't have minded sharing it with you'. I said, 'Oh hang on a minute, I'm not saying I wanted it, I'm just saying I didn't think it was right that you had it!' She said, 'I never thought of it like that. I never thought you thought Mummy is putting too much on Phoebe.' I said, 'Of course she was, you never ever lived your own life!'

A shift seems to have occurred in the triangle between sisters and mother, who is no longer the one doing the 'manipulating', to use Hazel's word:

> *Hazel*: And Phoebe went 'Oh . . . I've been going through life thinking I had to do all the changing'. I said, 'For Christ' sake Phoebe, manipulate! She does!' [laughs] And it was and now it's a lot healthier.

Hazel's comment refers to a situation where Hazel had been loving to their mother, after Phoebe had just had an argument with their mother – and Phoebe realised that she did not always have to protect and manage their mother's feelings. Regarding this issue of managing the feelings of significant others, Hazel summarises her new approach, displaying in the process elements of her changing subjectivity:

> *Hazel*: I actually can make myself not feel awful because somebody else is having a bad time in life, it's not my job to make them happy. That's their job and my mum feels that it's everybody's job to make everybody happy.

Companions or best friends?

Tracing transitions in Hazel and Phoebe's bond from girlhoods marked by the *positioned* discourse to womanhood where they have moved into the *shifting positions* discourse reveals changes over the decades. Their sistering has evolved from *distant companionship* to a form of *best friendship*. Phoebe explains the costs of caring for and 'managing' her mother's emotions:

> *Phoebe*: We missed out on being able to be good friends and happy together: Hazel and I, and myself, because we were always or I, certainly was, always so busy trying to keep Mummy sane and happy and as worry-free as possible.

Phoebe reflects on her bond with Hazel in spite of the conflict and distance. Theirs is a relationship with elements of both *close companionship* and *best friendship*:

> *Phoebe*: From quite an early age Hazel learnt to, to, um, dislike me really for just the way I was. And I disliked her because she was, she didn't achieve, and because she was a nuisance and because she caused chaos and it, it was just much like that throughout her childhood and yet all the time even, I mean it sounds awful saying all this, but, all the time underneath all that there was this togetherness, there was this, it

didn't matter what each of us did, we'd always love each other. It was always there, it didn't need to be said, I mean we say it a lot now as we've got older because it's important to say these things but obviously as children, you don't, you don't understand the necessity to say all these things.

Phoebe summarises the *best friendship* element that was prominent when they were in their twenties: 'If she picked up the phone I'd have been there for her, it was that sort of relationship'. And in their current lives:

> *Phoebe*: Hazel and I love each other but we don't have a lot in common. [. . .] Hazel and I, although we're as different as chalk and cheese in many many respects, we have a, a more deep-seated affection for each other.

Hazel's loyalty for Phoebe is matched by Phoebe's appreciation for Hazel:

> *Phoebe*: I think as a result of the life we've had, I mean she is just the most incredible person, and I'm just so proud of her and hopefully she likes me a little bit now, you know, er! [laughs]

Although they have little in common – Phoebe has more in common with her friends – their bond is an intimate one:

> *Phoebe*: I love her quite unconditionally, I love her for exactly who she is. I don't, I wouldn't, I wouldn't change her and I think that's the nice thing, that we've both come to, as we've got older that probably, we were, certainly I would have loved to have changed her. I'd loved to have swapped her at times, [laughs] but I certainly would have loved to have changed her! I found her incredibly embarrassing when I was younger because she was so loud-mouthed and so cocky and so, and I wasn't like that at all. But I mean, I wouldn't change her now, I mean like, she's just very nice. [laughs] But this has all come about lately. That's what I meant when I said earlier it's difficult, it's difficult to look back and remember how things were and how I used to feel about things because my attitude towards my sister has changed so much, um. I've begun, I suppose what I've begun to do is look at her as a person and not take on board quite so much what other people are telling me about her, i.e. my mum, and just look at her for who I think she is. Make my own decisions about her and my own, come to my own conclusions about her.

Contrasting past and present Phoebe reflects on their changing relationship when she says, 'But this has all come about lately'. In their thirties they have come to accept, enjoy and appreciate each other:

> *Phoebe*: It's a sort of [a] period of acceptance now that's come together for both of us, and therefore it's nice because when we are together it's, it is much more relaxed. She hasn't got to try and be me and I haven't got to try and be her. We haven't got to alter each other in any way; we can just be together and enjoy the time that we have together for, for who we are. That's just about it! [laughs]

Phoebe described their tie as continually changing. They listen to and understand each other, recognise and more readily accept their differences. Their relationship is calmer now than during their girlhood turmoil. They feel strongly connected, and always did, despite conflict and painful emotions. They can understand their past through reflecting on experience, including emotions, and living their current lives with greater awareness than previously. Part of this understanding coincides with their abandonment of old positionings of carer and cared for and experimenting with a role reversal. Changes in their sistering partly took place through emotions and from talking together.

Emotions and knowledge

Hazel and Phoebe's narratives reflect the role of talking and listening in developing new interpretations of relationships. Phoebe considers the role of talk and experience:

> *Phoebe*: So much has happened in our family that we are able to talk, sometimes we talk too much. I think sometimes, sometimes we just don't get on with it, if you see what I mean, we spend far too much time being reflective and um, discussing the issues but on the other hand I can see the huge benefits because I think now, um, it does mean that if we do have a grievance, it might take us a little while to get to that point, but we can actually discuss it, um, and see the other person's point of view. We, I think, I think we've learnt to listen to each other, isn't it, that's the thing, isn't it, it's, rather than talking, it's actually learning to listen to each other and to actually take on board the fact that what the other person is saying might not necessarily be right or wrong but it is their point of view, it is, it's valid to them.

A recent part of their talk is their ability to air and listen to grievances. In recounting the past, Phoebe draws the researcher into her mode of talking and analysing relationships:

> *Phoebe*: It's actually quite strange in some way to um, go back over stuff that's gone on in the past because of late, i.e. the last year or two um, it's been in the box and the lid's been closing on it and it's quite strange to have it peeking out again, so, um, if you could just counsel me out of this now so I can get on with the rest of my day! [laughs] No, I'll be fine.

Her evocative metaphor of the closed box opening during the interview evokes Paul D's anguish when he takes the rusty lid off 'that tobacco tin buried in his chest where a red heart used to be' and lays bare his past to Sethe in Toni Morrison's (1987: 72) *Beloved*. Recalling the past self-critically is difficult:

> *Phoebe*: I've tried to move on from that now because I need to function and get on with my day-to-day existence.

Hazel's account of understanding her past is similarly graphic. She compares the process to that of reassembling jigsaw pieces:

> *Hazel*: I actually sort of took all the pieces while I was down and laid them all out on the carpet and put them all back together where they were supposed to be in the first place . . . and then you start realising that, that shouldn't have been there in the first place, it should have been . . . like a puzzle.
>
> *MM*: So how did you do all that then, how did you . . . ?
>
> *Hazel*: Painfully, [laughs] painfully! I looked at them, I looked at me, I looked at how another . . . always how another person would see it, how a fly on the wall would see it and then.

Analysing her life has been a drawn-out process, which she carried out prior to the interview:

> *Hazel*: I've had all these conversations with myself, I've actually sat down and . . . there's . . . it would only bother me like, if suddenly, like I said to you earlier, some people must have realisations in a conversa-

tion like this, I'm not going to have any because my realisation's going to be a very slow and gradual one because I have to do all the analysis first [. . .]. I have to work to understand me and life and how I fit in.

Hazel displays her self-knowledge of her skills and insights into her past, including her depression:

Hazel: Like I suppose that's why I'm analytical: if I know why I'm down, then I don't mind being depressed. Because I can solve something which will lift the depression and Phoebe's actually . . . I think sort of taken a lot of that on board.

She reflects on changes in Phoebe:

Hazel: Phoebe was always trying to please, whereas now she's not as much, well she is, but she's trying to please herself a bit more.

A key way in which Hazel has gained her knowledge about her life including sistering is through emotions and how these can be tamed and 'managed':

Hazel: Parenting is for life and so is daughtering or and so is sistering. It is for life, it is one of the relationships . . . because it's for life, as well, it's a lot more stressful at times, isn't it, because if a friend gets on your nerves, you can ignore them for a couple of weeks, you know. But if you've got a sister that's got on your nerves and you ignore them for a couple of weeks, there's a little bit of guilt attached to that as well. But my family, and I think most families, don't actually sit it and look . . . I think they sit and look at their physical appearance, am I getting spotty or overweight or . . . but they don't look at their emotional development . . . people don't consider emotional development, they only consider emotion. And you can develop it and you can train it and you can actually work with it and you can actually . . . work with it, you can actually, there are things that will trigger off emotions in your life that you can learn to avoid.

Hazel's wisdom about emotions and harnessing them contrasts with the more disruptive impact of unresolved emotions that we see in Madonna and Roxanne's relationship later on.

Hazel's direct language and comments on relationships are embedded in emotions of sadness and joy:

Hazel: It isn't as fragile, because we are close, because we can have all the ups and downs we like and it is still going to be strong enough to take the lot and it's . . . Basically what I said to Phoebe, don't be frightened of . . . life, of this love, of this family . . . don't be intimidated by it, use it, grow in it . . . and she went . . . 'Yes, I suppose you're right!' [laughs] Well I might be, I don't know! [laughs] Could be totally wrong and we'll all sort of go down the pan together but . . . it just seems more sensible not to be frightened of family love. I mean, Christ it shouldn't be a burden, it should be . . . where you can go for a release and that, and I mean it just gets better and better, doesn't it? I mean the more you work it out, the more you understand it, it's like a computer if you don't know how to work it you're not going to get much use out of it, but if you sit down and read the book and study it you will use it to its full and I think relationships should be like that.

Hazel reflects with humour on the circumstances of her participation in the study. Her reference point is emotions:

Hazel: I'd have said no if I'd still been going through the traumas of it all, because I think you're always . . . life's traumatic full stop. But I think I'd have probably have said, 'Oh yes, it will be a very emotional . . . I'll have to have a box of tissues . . . '

Hazel's astute grasp of the role of emotions in producing knowledge is expressed in this extract which illustrates how power and emotions are entwined:

Hazel: I think that females, and this is general, don't like to take control of their relationships and I think the first time you realise that, is with a sister because your mum definitely had the control when you're young, mum has control. Soon as mum goes to pieces and hands control over to big sister, big sister is now . . . a threat. You're looked at in a better light, it's all . . . . and it's all the things that things imply, isn't it? It's not necessarily what happens to people as a child or with their sisters or without their sisters, it's how they viewed and how they felt about it, it's feelings you're talking about, feelings.

Hazel's description of the negative impact of the *positioned* discourse on their sister tie when growing up highlights the role of emotions as a catalyst for questioning that discourse.

Wising up

Phoebe's role as caring, 'big' older sister developed through her emotional protection of their mother after the death of their stepfather. Her mother in a sense made her into an ally. Hazel and Phoebe are close, best friends at heart, despite the little they say they have in common: they love, respect and are there for each other. Phoebe broke up with her best girlfriend, so perhaps the sisters are best friends in an unusual way – best friends from all their understanding and knowledge of each other.

Phoebe admitted that she took part in the research for Hazel rather than herself, as Hazel rarely asks her for much. She was reluctant to give up her time and found it difficult to revisit the past. At the end of the interview, she, like the other women, jokingly asked me to return on a regular basis. Intrigued by this, I explore its link with the way that women fashion interpretations of their lives. Like the role of emotions, reflexivity in counselling can influence how knowledge is produced.

Psyches talk: reflexivity and therapy

I have hinted at how knowledge can be created before and during the interview, through talk and emotions in Hazel and Phoebe's private lives, and raking these up for the researcher. Unlike other women who had given their sistering little thought or first addressed it only during the interview, Hazel and Phoebe had puzzled over their family and analysed their tie in depth prior to the research. Hazel spoke in a monologue and Phoebe required little prompting. Phoebe's perception of incidents had changed: her present understanding differed from her view of events at the time. Since their girlhood, their knowledge and understanding of each other have evolved and increased.

In addition to Phoebe's reference to counselling at the close of the interview and Hazel's reference to 'emotional development' and 'triggering off emotions' reminiscent of therapeutic language, three other women made similar allusions. Clare said: 'You realise I'm using this as a therapy session don't you [. . .] it's been great, two hours of free therapy!' Two other women were seeing a health professional: for one woman this helped her with employment decisions and finding a language to reflect on sistering. She drew links between her counselling experience and the ease with which she talked to me:

So the reason why I can ramble on and on without you asking the questions is because I've thought about all these things and I've talked about all these things, talked about you know, relationships, family relationships. Well, I suppose I've developed that, the vocabulary of whatever, the vocabulary to talk about it . . . so I can happily talk about it.

The interview was an occasion for reminiscing on parallels between her upbringing in relation to her own children. Her therapeutic experience enabled her 'to break the cycle'. She reflected on her changing subjectivity, particularly emotions and behaviour that she was trying to modify as a mother in order to avoid repeating her own mother's approach with her and her sister:

> I'm thinking and trying . . . although it's very hard actually, also because there are certain things that I have in me about how I react to things er . . . yes, I'm probably very much like my . . . yes . . . when I think of how my angry reactions to my children, I suppose it's then that I maybe . . . things in my mind actually spark off that, that's how my mother . . . that's how things were for us as children because my mother was . . . would have these massive angry outbursts.

Counselling hinted at by Hazel and Phoebe contributed to some women's ability to both reflect and be reflexive about their experience. It also suggests links between therapy, experience, developing a language, and the production of knowledge.

How was knowledge for some women formed from reflexivity in a therapeutic context? Making visible the value of counselling in these sisters' narratives raises the question of women's access to psy discourses[2] (Rose 1996) for interpreting their lives. For Rose, psy enables individuals to access new understandings and ways of acting on themselves: this invention or production of the self is historical as well as ontological. Drawing on Foucault (1985: 6–7), Rose's interest lies in the historical construction of the self 'as experience; that is as something that can and must be thought'. These connections between subjectivity constructed through lived experience and knowledge/language is relevant for sistering. Several women's active construction of their subjectivity through aspects of psy discourses stemmed from their therapeutic experiences.

Rose draws links between psy and 'government' – the Foucauldian notion of governance, or relations of power, which extend to the family and government of the self. These links between subjectivity and power are pertinent in the case of sisters. Psy discourses have provided individuals with techniques for 'shaping and reforming selves' (Rose 1996: 20–1) primarily through language and 'psychological foldings'. The implication of this form of construction of subjectivity lies in its recognition of individuals as 'subjects of freedom'. In other words, 'agentic subjectivity' (Maynard 1995: 274) allows a remaking or 'creation of a reflexively ordered narrative of self' (Giddens 1992: 31) aware of its historical formation and with potential to shape the future. In Chamberlain's work (1997a; b) on formations of subjectivities through narratives of transgenerational migration patterns, this historical self emerges as a global and 'syncretic self'[3] creating the new from the old. Chamberlain recounts how Barbadian women's tales of migration are tightly knit into stories of their female kin. Their narratives of self become tales of the syncretic self or of several lives across many generations, looking back and ahead, where subjectivity takes shape through images, memories and stories of kin and lineage.

Some sisters' therapeutic experiences clearly influence the way they think about and describe their sistering. The words they use draw on ideas from psy discourses and contain images of 'agentic subjectivity' refashioning itself. Rose's 'freedom' and Maynard's 'agentic subjectivity' are instrumental for women experimenting with different positionings.

Conclusion

Hazel and Phoebe's sistering experiences graphically illustrate their move over the decades away from entrenched caring and cared for roles to more flexible positionings. Currently Hazel is Phoebe's 'big sister'. Their narratives depict changing 'dominating positions' (Hey 1997: 84) within their family, from controlling practices to a greater flux of power. Their tales suggest how movement occurs from one discourse to the other in practice and at the level of knowledge through talk and emotions – between them, in counselling and in interviews. The way that they draw on psy discourses (Rose 1996) in their accounts reveals experiences of therapy. Traces of these psy discourses in their thinking also contribute to a vocabulary of emancipation: they reveal the possibility for subjectivities to transform themselves. Sisters move out of the *positioned* discourse facilitating this themselves like Hazel, owing to circumstances like Suzanne and Phoebe, slip out of it temporarily like Beth or remain there like Jeanne. Sisters can also move from the *shifting positions* to the *positioned* discourse, unintentionally, as we shall see in the case of Madonna and Roxanne. These changes occur through a combination of agentic subjectivity – Hazel's 'breaking out' – or circumstances – Phoebe becoming a minimother through life events in her natal family.

Is the *shifting positions* discourse also a friendship discourse? If the definition of friendship includes elements of mothering, 'bitchiness' *and* power as this study and Hey's ethnography (1997) demonstrate, then it certainly is. A broader notion of friendship might encompass role-reversals or shifts in positions of power. This aspect of sistering captures the way that subject positions can change over time and embodies the post-structuralist notion of power as fluctuating rather than stable. This waxing and waning of power between women allows for greater reciprocity than the entrenched positionings of minimothering. In this sense it is a feminist discourse and a positive one. On the negative side, the *shifting positions* discourse is permeable and preserves a space for women to revert back to the *positioned* discourse, as illustrated in Madonna's oscillations in her tie with Roxanne.

6
Lovers and Marriage

As a friendship tie, sistering is characterised by different forms of caring and power relations that fluctuate over time as sisters leave their natal home and enter new phases of their lives. Suzanne's experiences, Jeanne's, and those of Hazel and Phoebe illustrate changes over the decades connected to different ways of interpreting meanings of mothering, being mothered, motherhood and bereavement. The significance of these experiences and life-events lies in the emotional and physical intimacy and distance they create. These women often connected memorable events – such as changing school, starting work, moving and 'coming out' – to key moments of transition in their sistering. Focusing on life-events and turning-points offers another way of describing complex facets of sistering such as changing patterns of dependence and independence. This auto/biographical approach to investigating family histories, which enabled women to call up memories, is outlined in Appendix II.

This chapter focuses on chronological change in sistering marked by the different types of friendship that a single relationship can go through. Leila (age 40) and *Annar's* (age 38) relationship evolved from distance and feelings of resentment in their *companionship* as girls and young women to *best friendship* in their current lives. The trajectory of Leila and *Annar's* tie relies on Leila's story: she planned to tell *Annar* about the study after the interview. The evolution of their bond charts the passage from girlhood in one household to leaving home, growing up and apart, forming and ending sexual relationships, and moving and settling in a new country. This case study highlights the impact of life-events, such as relationship breakdown, marriage, the death of a father and a family rift on changes in sistering.

Prodigal daughter and beauty queen

The positive transformation for Leila (40) and *Annar* (38), of their *distant companionship* to *best friendship*, mirrors the evolution of Suzanne (29) and *Collette's* (25) tie, where *best friendship* followed an initial period of distance, conflict and estrangement. More rivals than friends when they were growing up, distant companions Leila and *Annar* became 'sisterly' in Leila's words, when they reached their thirties, following the death of their father. The family fight with their brothers that occurred some years before this bereavement constituted the other turning-point in their sistering. These two external life-events did not have to do with them directly, in contrast with other moments more internal to their relationship. Events more integral to their tie included their departure from home for boarding school, their divergent educational careers and the vicissitudes of their sexual relationships. The case study focuses on these external and internal experiences as their bond altered from *distant companionship* to *best friendship*, and from the *positioned* to the *shifting positions* discourse.

Growing up

As teenagers, Leila and *Annar* were opposites, fighting about clothes and sharing bedrooms, and their *distant companionship* lasted into their twenties. Enemies rather than buddies as girls, when they went to boarding school they rallied together in an alien environment:

> *Leila*: We were very very different, she was a tomboy and I was very studious and she had a string of boyfriends and I was always, I mean I wanted to do my homework. [. . .] she's very pretty and . . . there was no way that she wouldn't be sought after or fought after for marriage and whatever. And in a way I resented that too. I had to play the part of the ugly sister almost, you know, so that really caused a rift and I didn't know all these years that she had the resentment because she saw me as the intelligent sister and I saw her as the pretty, the beautiful sister so it caused a rift in our relationship for many years.

This period of distance lasted into their twenties before the newfound closeness which emerged in their thirties:

> *Leila*: We were so distant that while I was at university, I was three months, she would never call me once or I would never call her once [. . .] there are a lot of, you know, the complexities, the competition at that age and I was jealous of her and she was jealous of me.

During their teens, growing up in the Middle East and at boarding school in Britain, Leila was located as the older responsible sister. It was Leila's decision to enter boarding school at fifteen and *Annar* followed. Reflecting on this decision Leila says, 'I am a strong person anyway, I know what I want at the end of the day'. Her strong sense of her own subjectivity was present from an early age. Soon after arriving, they were both stunned:

> *Leila*: It was a shock, absolute shock to the system. I couldn't believe it – *Annar* going to bed at 7.30, you know all my protective nature . . . protectiveness towards her, came out 'cos I realised that she'd made a dreadful mistake.

She describes the *positioned* discourse and role that she adopted in her teens:

> *Leila*: we were sent away from [home] to come to England. Then I took on a different role, almost as the eldest sister and protective over her and that kind of role, um, she accepted because she needed for about four or five years. [. . .] It was a role I had to play from a very young age, you know it wasn't just myself I had to look after. I had to look after my sister. And in a boarding school, you know to have an elder sister was a great advantage [laughs]. Cos, you know, I'd have to go and fight her fights for her, you know, if two friends suddenly get hold of her, classmates and . . . make sure that they weren't troubling her. There wasn't anybody for me, do you know what I'm saying, I had that responsibility while I didn't have *that*.

They followed different educational paths that set them against each other. At 10, Leila passed her secondary school entrance exam while *Annar* failed and went to private school, a sort of 'dumping ground'. Leila explains:

> *Leila*: I passed that with flying colours while my sister failed, so already there was a stigma attached to her from a very young age . . . [. . .] because I passed, I was in a state school, I had a very good education.

Education

In Britain, Leila obtained A-levels and went to university. *Annar* completed O-levels and trained as a nurse. As a mother of two she regrets not going to university. After leaving school they became distant: they ended up in different parts of the country during Leila's student years. After her training *Annar* worked and met a man whom she wanted to marry: her parents disapproved and conflict ensued. Yet this episode brought the sisters closer as Leila backed and supported her: 'My protective nature came out and I was really for her,' Leila says. *Annar* later married her 'second suitor'. When her marriage became difficult, Leila offered support. Throughout she respected *Annar*'s privacy and never pried:

> *Leila*: I didn't feel I should force it on her. I mean, I've never, we've had a relationship where neither of us have forced anything on each other. Some sisters, you know, expect it as their right to know.

Both sisters eventually became emotionally involved in each other's sexual relationships with positive outcomes for each of them.

Nevertheless, in their twenties, their different educational paths fostered feelings of resentment. *Annar* felt resentful towards Leila for missing out on university:

> *Leila*: She's told me over the years that, that's been her problem, she suddenly started really resenting me mainly because, um, she didn't get into university and whatever and er . . . and then my father, you know, my parents were very proud of me, while they weren't of her and . . . She always wished that she had done something, so in a way she said she always . . . she was in awe of me.

The resentment that they each felt and kept to themselves created distance, which they bridged only recently. At the same time, Leila has fierce emotions for *Annar*: 'I love her more than any of my siblings . . . er . . . I love her most', she says.

Their relationship was transformed by life- events into *best friendship*. A defining element of their strong bond is what Leila calls 'being there':

> *Leila*: We've both been supportive, it's like . . . I don't know, instinct, or it's like a reflex action when your sister is in . . . in any trouble, you forget all your differences and you go there and you . . . you're 100 per cent there for them . . . well I am for my sister and I'm sure she is . . . well she has been for me. [. . .] With a sister you feel that unconditional love the way you do with a parent . . . I mean I have very very close friends and I could depend on them but I don't know, I think at the end of the

day er . . . with my sister it would be different, I mean if I was in a real crisis it's my sister I would turn to.

Leila's language of 'instinct' and 'reflex action' conveys gut reactions to emotional upheaval. Her understanding of her sister tie is based on 'unconditional love' which in a sense allows her to overlook or embrace 'differences'. 'Being there' is connected to the idea of reciprocity and dependability.

Lovers

A sphere where both sisters have provided support is the sexual, against parental opposition. Like *Annar's* experience of parental disapproval, Leila similarly endured her parents' 'aghast' reaction at a liaison. *Annar's* endorsement of Leila's choice reflects another instance of the sisters' move from the *positioned* to the *shifting positions* discourse. Their support has been reciprocal – dependability and reliance exist on both sides:

> *Leila*: She was very supportive, she's always been very supportive over my relationship[s]. So I suppose that goes both ways. And I think obviously needless, she's had, er, problems in her marriage and I've been supportive . . .

Leila describes *Annar's* support in helping her end a sexual relationship. Moreover, *Annar* agreed to manage part of the break-up for her: 'She cared so much, that she went through the nitty-gritty for me, something that I couldn't handle, she did it for me.'

For Leila, her sister is her best friend, her first port of call in difficult situations, emotional or practical – lending money, for example: 'there's a trust which is both ways.' Leila expands:

> *Leila*: I would only ring her if it was absolutely important and likewise. If she ever rang me I'd know it was absolutely important and I would help. The trust there is 100 per cent. As I said, I mean, I think we're the closest, she's . . . she's the closest human being to me.

Leila is aware of the importance and effect of their different marital statuses and its influence on her feelings for *Annar* and their tie:

> *Leila*: Because I'm older, I first play the protective role over my sister. And then I'm not married and I don't have children so to me, my sister's kids and my sister are very important as family. She's my only

family apart from my brothers, but I'm not close to them. Not in the same way.

Turning-points

What is striking about Leila's narrative is the dual change from *distant companionship* to *best friendship* and from the *positioned* to the *shifting positions* discourse. Similar elements appear as in Suzanne's relationship with *Collette*. The reciprocity between them in their thirties contrasts with the antagonism of their teens and twenties. Leaving behind their positions of 'big' and 'little' sister, Leila and *Annar* moved into *best friendship* where each supports the other. How did this transformation occur?

Leila charts several changes over the years:

> *Leila*: When the competition finally, I mean that, that was in our teens and our early twenties and then er . . . and then we weren't really close and as I said, in my situation I was not close completely and then she had a really bad, um, ten years and her marriage went through a very bad trauma for many years. You know, where she didn't have time to have any relationship with me so we were kind of apart until she worked her marriage out.

Only in their thirties did they became closer through two life-events: a family rift and their father's death. Their rapprochement started during the family rift shortly before their father died. The rift occurred when three of their brothers sided against their father and other brother in the family business, a form of internal takeover bid: 'There is a Judas in our family,' she said.

> *Leila*: We were kind of forced to get together, my sister, me and my father and mother and one brother, and we became very close because then we had to give a lot of support to my dad, so we had to become close, so that probably was the shifting point in our relationship.

This 'shifting point' came with the family rift when both sisters sided with their parents and one brother. This split in family allegiances ended the distance between the sisters that had lasted from Leila's late teens to when she was 24. An important aspect of their reunion during the family rift was the role of talk:

> *Leila*: We were very distant between, I would say . . . 18 to 23 . . . 24 . . . extremely distant . . . and then this rift happened between our family and we were kind of forced to pull together again and then er . . . And

then *Annar* was coming home a lot to help my parents and over this . . . emotional break-up and then after that, I suppose we started getting on again. And then as we matured over [our] thirties we've actually talked about it and said . . . that, look [. . .] we'd never done that before. It does help to talk, doesn't it, to get it out into the open . . .

Their coming together during this family split prepared the way for greater closeness in their thirties in the subsequent upheaval in the wake of their father's death. Leila still wondered about the impact of her father's death on *Annar* a year later, when she was on the verge of a 'nervous breakdown'. Leila speculated on possible links between *Annar's* grief and her marital difficulties: 'Maybe the problem is her own because she's missing her dad so much, you know [. . .] she was going through this terrible loss'.

Some time after their father's death when they were in their mid-thirties, Leila stepped into *Annar's* private life. With her marriage in trouble Leila took charge of *Annar's* well-being: 'Whatever her happiness is, is my happiness' she said, describing her motivation. In this way, she became a more central presence in *Annar's* emotional life:

Leila: I mean, the day that I just went over and took my sister's life in my hands [. . .] I think that kind of jolt[ed] her a bit probably to start . . . getting me back in her life.

Leila dropped everything, drove to *Annar's*, and took her off to seek support. Leila recognises the forcefulness of her tactics, that as older sister it may have been easier for her, in a sense, to relocate herself in the *positioned* discourse in a moment of crisis. Looking back, she wished that *Annar* had been more forthright with *her* during key episodes and spoken her mind. One instance she referred to was a shadowy business deal with a brother, another was a new lover whom *Annar* immediately identified as unsuitable as Leila was on the rebound. Leila seemingly wished that they could have appropriated the *shifting positions* discourse more so that, at crucial junctures, *Annar* could have acted as her 'big' sister.

Current lives

These turning-points – the family rift and their father's death – were significant in contributing to the gradual evolution of their *distant companionship*, except for their years at boarding-school when they drew closer in an alien environment, to *best friendship*. This transformation occurred over a decade, from Leila's mid-twenties towards the end of her time at university, to her mid-thirties. Now at 40, Leila enjoys weekly contact with *Annar*. *Annar* suggested that Leila move to her neighbourhood and Leila said: 'we have become more of a family'. They see each other with *Annar*'s two children and help each other professionally as they both work in the health sector. Their *best friendship*, like Hazel and Phoebe's, exists in spite of differences between them. For example, regarding political divergences, Leila said 'we're like chalk and cheese'. Their *best friendship* is founded on their common experiences, or what Gordon (1994) in her auto/biographical study of female friendship calls 'shared lives', and their new openness – their ability to talk and reflect on their bond and give feedback. Leila said: 'Now I feel I can tell her something, I can tell her something I'm not happy about'.

The sisters have shed earlier emotions of jealousy and resentment and vying over claims for the position in the family of what Leila termed 'the prodigal daughter'. Instead, their changing tie brought them closer through its transitions. Although Leila said that she had never thought about the relationship 'actively', she certainly produced a reflexive narrative, after what she experienced as a thought-provoking and therapeutic discussion. This is how she summarised the relationship:

> *Leila*: I mean, maybe this kind of scenario must happen with a lot of people, where they are very close if there's a small age gap, very close. Then there is this teenage gap where, you know, you . . . the teenage and early twenties when you fall apart and then you come together.

Conclusion

This chapter illustrates how change occurs in sistering at different moments in relationships. Its focus is on triggers for change – specific life-events such as a family rift and bereavement. Inevitably, these turning-points leave their mark on sistering. As one woman succinctly described this series of transitions: 'There is a sort of a path of, sort of, you know, your adolescence days and then you getting married or you decide to live with [a] partner and then you have children and you sort of settle into some sort of cosy, sort of middle aged thing and, you know, and, and it changes . . .'

Change in sistering can happen at two levels, external to the relationship and internally. External change can occur in connection with life-events – leaving home, going to a new school, moving to a different city, acquiring or losing a sexual partner or parent. The different forms of friendship that sistering can take over the decades, from *companionship* to *best friendship* and vice versa correspond to this level. Change can also happen internally, within the relationship, with movement in and out of the *positioned* discourse into or out of the *shifting positions* discourse. This process occurs in Leila and *Annar*'s relationship, which moved from the *positioned* to the *shifting positions* discourse. This was a positive experience for both their tie and their individual subjectivities. Madonna and Roxanne's tie, in the next chapter, displays a contrasting trajectory.

Leila and Annar's tie reveals how relationships change as a result of life-events, in the context of shifting power relations and changing subjectivity. The role of language and whether sisters talk to each other, or not, about their emotions and experiences are significant. Leila and *Annar* each voice their feelings whereas Madonna and Roxanne, as we shall see, attempt to and yet are unsuccessful.

7
Divorce and Bereavement

Madonna (age 31) and Roxanne's (age 39) tie forms part of a complex web of relationships in which women's lives as sisters are enmeshed. Based on their separate narratives, this case study explores the impact of divorce and bereavement on sistering. They moved from *best friendship* and moments of flirtation with the *shifting positions* discourse in their teens and twenties to *distant companionship* and the *positioned* discourse in their thirties. An important feature in both their relationship and in Leila and *Annar's* is the effect of the women's sexual liaisons, which at various times brought them together and distanced them. Transitions in their ties with significant others including mothers, fathers, and lovers alter their subjectivities and their sistering.

Combinations of the different discourses within a single relationship, in the women's current lives and over time, are clearly visible here and throughout the book. In this case study, as in the last, the focus is on turning-points and the transition between *best friendship* and *companionship*. It traces the processes through which sisters imagine other positionings through entering or leaving one discourse rather than another and the pleasures and pains that ensue. These transitions are documented through changing and contradictory positionings and subjectivities.

Tough cookie and prima donna

In Roxanne and Madonna's tie the changes occurred in the opposite direction than in Leila and *Annar*'s bond. Similar transitions connected to bereavement and sexual relationships, in this case the dissolution of a marriage, transformed their teenage *best friendship* to *distant companionship* in womanhood. Whereas in Leila and *Annar*'s bond, their sexual liaisons ultimately brought them closer, the end of Roxanne's marriage had a negative ripple effect on their sistering. The combination of Roxanne's marital 'split', Madonna's experience of living with Roxanne and her 'ex', Madonna's two other sisters' divorces and the death of their father eroded the stability of four nuclear families and marked the end of an era. After sketching out their family background and its shake-up following their father's death, the case study documents their interpretations of their changing relationship over three decades.

Family background

Roxanne (39) and Madonna (31) live in different areas of the country. Roxanne lives with her daughter Lucille (12) and partner Trevor. Madonna, who at one time lived with Roxanne and her ex-husband, is currently single, living in a shared house. They described their background as working-class. Their older sister, Jeanne (45) lives in the same town as Madonna and Leonie (48), lives near Roxanne. A key life-event was their father's death eight years previously. They were closer to him than to their mother, and Madonna enjoyed a special relationship with him. Roxanne remembers:

> *Roxanne*: You know, Madonna had a very different relationship with Dad to the rest of us because she was the youngest and because we'd all paved the way a bit, you know, so you know, Madonna had period pains, Dad would make her a hot water bottle whereas if we had period pains, it was – shut up – your father's around [whispered]. So yeah, the relationships were qualitatively different because Dad had more time, obviously.

After their mother was widowed, she moved out of the family home to live in a nearby neighbourhood.

The loss of their father significantly altered their natal family (Parkin 1997) and shifted the responsibility for looking after their mother onto the daughters. Roxanne and Leonie who live near their mother are the most involved with caring for her. The four sisters' different attitudes towards this brought them closer together and also created tension reflecting, in Roxanne's view, their distinct brands of feminism. Their experiences of higher education (Leonie excepted) and consequent social mobility contributed to their distancing from their mother. Gender, class and education all influenced their individual and sister relationship trajectories. These three elements permeate their different understandings of both their relationships with their mother and with each other.

Girlhood

Roxanne and Madonna were best friends throughout their late teens and twenties. They socialised together and knew each other's friends:

> *Roxanne*: Madonna and I got close from when she was about 18 onwards I suppose, and then, out of all my sisters Madonna and I became the closest. [. . .] With Madonna, Madonna, it was very much like a friendship you know, we'd go to music together, we'd go to the pub together. You know, I'd have her friends and my friends round for meals and we'd all mix together um, so yeah with Madonna it was like a friendship . . .

Madonna corroborates Roxanne's account of their friendship. In addition, she highlights similarities between them that at times created tension:

> *Madonna*: Roxanne and I have got very kind of similar kind of sort of beliefs and values and things, and that's kind of always been a bit of a problem because we have been at kind of, we have been at stages, been very, very close. [. . .] I mean, there was a stage when I actually, I used to live with Roxanne and her, her then husband, so we, we were very close and we still are very close but it's, it's almost been changed just because of the geographical nature of where we live, um.

These changes hinted at by Madonna resulted from two life events: bereavement and divorce.

Bereavement

At 23, Madonna lost her father and five years later when she was 28 (and Roxanne was 36), Roxanne's marriage broke up. Both had long-lasting effects on her relationship with Roxanne. Madonna describes the effects of her bereavement in terms of family structure, emotions and changing patterns of caring between her and her sisters:

> *Madonna*: it's just the whole business of him not being around anymore and, and our relationship not being as, as strong with our mother for any of us, it kind of, things just sort of fell apart a bit for, for a stage, for a time really. Um.

> *MM*: Things fell apart, what between you as sisters or?

Madonna: No, between the family, between the family, you know, kind of not, not, not sort of taking as much care of each other's feelings, I don't think, as we should have been doing, because we were all kind of just in a state of upheaval really.

Madonna's experience of family disruption was compounded by her grief. She recounts how, on the one hand, she found it difficult to witness Roxanne's emotions, while, on the other, these emotions created intimacy between them. Madonna looks back:

Madonna: I was living with Roxanne not, not long after my dad had died and I remember there being, er, being one night where we were both just kind of, just in floods of tears and me not being able to cope with the fact that she was missing him really badly as well, and feeling like she wasn't allowed to kind of miss him in the same way as other people were, for whatever reason, I'm not quite sure about that really, but, but that being quite a kind of turning-point really, the fact that we were able to sort of sit and cry together about the same thing, rather than not, than, rather than it being an experience that you were taking somebody else through, but it being kind of, like a sort of shared experience really.

Madonna, the youngest, grapples with changing dynamics in her tie with Roxanne, resulting from their father's death. She relates her shock at witnessing her older sister's grief. This display of emotion contrasted, she implies, with her expectations at the time of 'taking somebody else through' an event, in this case, an assumption, perhaps, that Roxanne would comfort her rather than pour out her own grief. These expectations were not borne out; instead, grieving, for each of them, became a 'shared experience'. Roxanne commented that their father's death brought her and Madonna very close, a period which coincided with a subtle form of *shifting positions*, an interlude for their relationship where they momentarily moved out of the 'big' and 'little' sister roles, reflected in Madonna's expression 'shared experience'. The interlude remained brief however, disrupted by further events. This phase of their *best friendship* at the time of bereavement also marked the early stages of its ending.

The legacy of bereavement

Reflecting on the aftermath of bereavement, Madonna, eight years on, is still puzzling over its impact. She hints at the role of shifting power relations in the changing family structure:

> *Madonna*: A lot of it is to do with the, the, with the kind of, the sort of change of power I suppose, and things, things have been, there are kind of, like, different sort of stages but what are a very significant stage for me has been since my father died and the kind of, the, the change of the sort of family make-up really.

Madonna captures these changes in the family structure when describing her siblings' movement away from the natal family in order to create worlds and lives of their own. In addition, she draws parallels between this outward mobility and her changing relationships with her sisters:

> *Madonna*: I think that's mainly it, I think what's happened is, it's taken that, that amount of time for us to kind of, sort of go away from the family in our, in our own ways and kind of like, be asserting our own personalities really and our, and our own kind of wants which has been different. I don't know, I'm not sure, I'm not actually sure what, what's, what's made the transition, but relationships have, relationships have changed.

Madonna's hesitant tone reflects the difficulty of verbalising these processes of change and transition, especially pinpointing precise moments or events. One difficulty is disentangling relationship changes from individual changes, or what I call 'changing subjectivity'. Madonna's expressions, 'asserting our own personalities' and 'our own kind of wants', correspond to my understanding of subjectivity, explored in chapter 8. Her musings on the effects of her father's death indicate her awareness of how it marked a break with her past and growing up, modifying her *best friendship* with Roxanne into a form which she could not yet articulate at that moment when it was occurring. These changes and their new *distant companionship* only gradually became clear and explicit to them five years later with the end of Roxanne's marriage.

Divorce

Whereas Madonna's narrative focused far more than Roxanne's on the effects of their bereavement, Roxanne's lingered over the impact of her divorce on her tie with Madonna, an issue that remained complex, painful and unresolved for her. Roxanne captured aspects of their *best friendship* prior to the end of her marriage. She recalls Madonna's empathy after she had moved to start a new job:

> *Roxanne*: Madonna was very supportive through all that because it was very traumatic having moved my partner and my daughter [. . .] away

from his job and her school and everything, so Madonna was really good then, um, and she came to live with us for a bit when she did some [. . .] work [. . .] and so we got closer then, um, and then she lived with us just before me and my husband split up, um, so it ought to put it in, in perspective about why we're not close now.

Roxanne recounts the closeness of that era when Madonna lived with her and her family in contrast with the subsequent distance post-divorce. Her expression 'in perspective' foreshadows problems that ensued with Madonna's anger at the break-up. Roxanne hints at elements that made it difficult for Madonna to accept the 'split':

Roxanne: I think my split with my partner caused all sorts of ripples which I couldn't understand at the time, that you know, I have a bit more of a perspective on now. Um, so none, none of us are very close now because I think, I've just, haven't quite sort of fitted in where I should have done.

For Roxanne the ramifications of her divorce extend beyond the realm of her sister ties. They also impinge on her subjectivity which she alludes to from the vantage-point of others in her words 'fitted in' – how they perceive her in a way that makes her unacceptable. Roxanne's words clearly display the benefit of time for understanding complex turning- points in relationships.

Roxanne examines in detail the intricate web between the legacy of her divorce, her tie with Madonna and her own changing subjectivity. She recalls Madonna's refusal to accept both her divorce and her new partner, Trevor, hinting at anger and possessiveness:

Roxanne: I think Madonna saw me as a bit different and when I split with Stuart I think she wanted me to stay on my own for some reason, you know she wanted me to sort of go it alone and, and she seemed very possessive of my time [. . .]. Madonna wouldn't accept, wouldn't accept us as a couple. She gave me a real hard time about coupledom and, you know, and attacked my feminism and everything, you know, on the grounds of, you know, 'Aren't you an individual on your own, why've you, why've you Trev around all the time?' sort of thing.

Roxanne's hunch about Madonna's expectations of her heterosexual conduct in the wake of her marriage is confirmed by Madonna's words when she says: 'you want to see them being strong really and I suppose with, in whatever relationship, there are always difficulties with men.'

Bogeymen

One interpretation of Roxanne's experience of disapproval in Madonna's eyes is of a younger sister unable to accept her older sister's changing sexuality – from married woman to lover. Madonna admits her difficulty with embracing this new turn in Roxanne's life, with specific mention of the 'new man'. Interestingly, Madonna introduces the notion of power in her analysis, and throughout, she emphasises the way that Roxanne's divorce and new romance have altered their sister tie:

> *Madonna*: I don't know where the kind of power lies with Roxanne really, it's, it's . . . yeah, no, I don't know where that lies really, it's kind of, things have changed because she, she's been in a new relation, well not a new relationship, she's been in a relationship other than, um, than her sort of, her, her long-term partner for like the last, I don't know actually, two and a half years, three years. And things have changed quite considerably there really because of, because of Trev and because I've found it quite hard to sort of warm to Trev that, and I don't know what that's about really.

Madonna finds these transformations hard to encapsulate. In her attempts to verbalise them, she hints at Roxanne's changing subjectivity, changing power relations, and reluctantly points to the interference of sexual relationships in sistering:

> *Madonna*: You know, if I'm honest I don't know why I am finding it so difficult to sort of get on with this person. But, um, but I am and she is very, very kind of, within that relationship and I think she has found the confidence within that relationship to kind of kick a couple of us up the arse really and kind of say, you, you can't treat me like that any more, whatever that treatment is. [. . .] The relationship, the power, I don't know if it's power or what it is really, but the kind of, the importance of that relationship for, for Roxanne has changed quite considerably over the last couple of years and I don't know, and I don't know what that's to do with. And it's one of those things where you kind of think, I can't worry about other people's relationships. I have enough problem kind of like making sure mine are, are working on a sensible sort of positive basis without worrying about how other people are doing it, really.

Roxanne's understanding of Madonna's emotions and the changes in their tie, on the other hand, lies in what she sees as their distinct notions of feminism, experiences of heterosexuality (Roxanne's serial coupledom versus Madonna's more long-standing singledom) and, ultimately following on from this, inconsistencies between principles and praxis. Roxanne says:

> *Roxanne*: I think Madonna would say that, that I haven't behaved in a feminist manner over my relationship with Trev, but I don't understand that, you know, I don't understand that at all. I think that's just, you know because Madonna's on her, yeah, she had a big thing about us touching in front of her, you know, and it was like – you're oppressing me because I'm a single person on my own. But you know I, I will take that argument as long as somebody doesn't offer it hypocritically. But when she was with her bloke, you know they'd be all over each other and it just didn't wash really! [laughs] [. . .] I mean, can you look at the sisters' relationships without looking at men and the way in which men move in and out of women's lives and the way, you know, women's position generally has got to inform how women interact as sisters?

Roxanne touches on the impact of sexual relationships on sistering. Just as Roxanne says 'I don't understand that at all', regarding Madonna's disapproving reaction to her new romance, Madonna similarly says about Roxanne's response to this rift between them, 'I don't know what that's about really'. In their separate accounts the sisters produced a cohesive narrative of knowledge and gaps about their relationship. Madonna says:

> *Madonna*: That's kind of quite hard the fact that I, she, she wants, she wants me to kind of, just take on this new person completely, er, but then at the same time, she's quite happy to say, I don't care what anybody thinks, this new person's in my life and. So that's kind of quite hard because there is a real contradiction in the kind of messages that she's giving out because on one hand she doesn't care and then on the other hand, she's very kind of, obviously very hurt about the fact that, I don't know, I don't know what that's about really.

Madonna's tale of contradictory emotions regarding the impact of Roxanne's new man in their lives and both sisters' incomprehension at recent developments in their relationship signals an impasse between them. One explanation is the absence of dialogue about their emotional responses to recent life events.

Emotions, whispers and silence

Before exploring their other interpretations of the stalemate, I consider their attempts to verbalise their distress to each other. Roxanne tried to talk to Madonna about her feelings with little success:

> *Roxanne*: she's quite a prima donna and so if you challenge her over something she gets all weepy and huffy and, and in the end it wasn't worth it to me, it wasn't worth keep making that challenge because it was in her face, you know, what, what she liked was to be allowed to get away with her humps.

Roxanne initiated contact, which turned into conflict. She found it difficult to spell out the precise nature of her grievances or be open and direct. She speculates on the link between this silence and the distance that ensued between them:

> *Roxanne*: We just ended up having big outbursts which I just thought why, why is this happening and it's happened because I couldn't say what I thought. I realise, you know my, this is my analysis and obviously she would have a totally different one, but I felt that I simply couldn't say what I thought without it causing her grief.

> *MM*: So you didn't, you didn't tell her?

> *Roxanne*: I did now and again, you know, which is I think why she avoids my company but I also thinks she avoids my company because she knows that there's somebody incredibly important to me in my life and I think she's quite jealous.

Here, Roxanne hints at her ultimate and partial interpretation of events when she refers to Madonna's jealousy of her new romance.

Their silence, disclosed by Roxanne whom I spoke to before Madonna, raised doubts in me about Madonna's willingness to talk to me. Roxanne reassured me that she might well participate. With regret she elaborated that 'that's part of the problem, that I've never had the opportunity to talk through the issues with them you know . . . '. She also confessed to feeling nervous at the prospect of my talking to her sisters, especially my not hearing incidents initially from the party concerned:

Roxanne: I feel nervous that you, that you will let them know that you have information, but then that's stupid because they'll know. They'll know that you have all sorts of information. [. . .] I don't think I've told you anything that confidential actually [. . .]

She felt that it would be better for me to hear certain details of her sisters' lives directly from the person concerned, and I concurred. Roxanne's assumption about my interview technique was correct: 'I presume that's how you'd work anyway. You'd start as if from scratch.'

Jealousy

As a result of their silences Madonna and Roxanne each resorted to their own interpretations of their dead-end. Jealousy, or the 'green-eyed monster' in Mildred's words, loomed large as an explanation: sexual jealousy, and also sister jealousy regarding possessiveness of Madonna as the family 'baby'. For Roxanne, jealousy over sexual relationships certainly shed light on tensions in her tie with Madonna in the context of Madonna's lack of 'traditional success with men'. Roxanne also mentioned age: her new partner's age placed him as a near contemporary to Madonna in contrast with Roxanne's ex-husband who was older than herself. She guessed that Madonna found this age issue threatening. Roxanne describes her frustrations at trying to resolve these sister tensions over her new lover and her disbelief at the plausibility of the jealousy interpretation:

Roxanne: Friends on the outside sort of said that to me and I thought what, you know, what does that mean? I've never ever let Trev get in the way of us meeting up, or, you know, me having time available, but in fact I went out of my way because she showed how irritated she was. I'd like, you know, put Trev off for an evening or say, you know, come down and we'll be on our own and then I got to thinking why should I do that, you know, this person is part of my life and she's either got to accept that or we can't have the sort of relationship that I want. But then other people, friends also said, maybe it's also a jealousy about you and men because she had, she had a, she had a real sort of go about Trev. [. . .] So people put it to me that maybe she was really pissed off that not only had you got this nice bloke who you believe in but, but there was this other nice bloke who's nearly 12 years younger than you and she, she was maybe jealous of that. I didn't want to accept that though because I actually believe that she's brighter than that, you know.

Madonna also referred to jealousy as a cause of her difficulties with Roxanne, in this case over her greater intimacy with Jeanne. Madonna refers to mixed family allegiances and the vying between her three older sisters for the ability to privilege their tie with her as the 'little' sister and, by extension, their 'baby'. In this setting of rivalry for the affection and 'ownership' of their 'baby' sister, Madonna finds herself in an awkward position: whereas she gets on with all of them, they have conflictual relationships with each other. Madonna speculates that Roxanne might be jealous of her *close companionship* with Jeanne:

> *Madonna*: There's always been a bit of kind of like, um, oh I suppose you'll be going to Jeanne's for Christmas again, or you, that kind of thing, or I expect you talk to Jeanne about things like that or

Madonna's example of Roxanne's anger at Madonna for maintaining her loyalty to Jeanne illustrates this jealousy. Madonna recounted Roxanne's anger at her refusal to act as a go-between between Roxanne and Jeanne, who have little contact:

> *Madonna*: We have different relationships and you must kind of sort it out between the two of you which they never do [. . .]. Roxanne finds it much harder to deal with because it's like, I'm closing down on her and because she, you know, because she, by that, by that sort of stage in the conversation she's kind of fairly hyped up, it's like, well what do you fucking mean, why won't you tell me, you know and it's that sort of, um, it's like I'm hiding something and it's like I'm in allegiance with somebody else. I mean, there's a real kind of feeling of like sort of mixed allegiances and kind of, which is really hard to deal with, very hard to deal with because I feel like I'm not being loyal to, to either of them. [. . .] They'd rather deal with it through a third party rather than . . .

When Madonna says 'it's like I'm closing down on her', there is a hint of the shifting power relations between her and Roxanne which I turn to next.

Growing pains

Madonna herself is aware of how she is situated in the *positioned* discourse as the family 'baby', an enviable location that brings certain benefits. She is the only one to receive Christmas presents from her sisters since they decided only to buy gifts for each other's children. On the other hand, she reflects on the shocks that she as the youngest, faced as, one after another, her sisters divorced. Her reaction to Roxanne's 'split', in the context of her experience of the break-up of her two other sisters' marriages, sheds light on the negative aspects of her positioning as the 'baby' sister. Roxanne's 'split' aroused similar emotions that she had already experienced with the earlier divorces. Madonna's vivid awareness of this pattern and its emotional impact is striking. Recalling Leonie's divorce, when she was 15, she positions herself in relation to Leonie and her ex-husband as 'both of their babies':

> *Madonna*: I hated her [elder sister Leonie] for the fact that he'd gone away, you know, because I was, I was both of their babies you know. And it was and I kind of, the minute, the minute I'd reached where I realised how, what a disgusting like child I'd been, being so horrid to my sister because she'd been dumped by her husband, you know it was just, I kind of, I kind of vowed never to do it again really. Um, so I, I think I have, I've always tried to be very loyal to both Roxanne and Jeanne in the sort of, the break up of their marriages, but at the same time it has been quite hard, it was very hard with me with Roxanne and Stuart because I did, I did like Stuart an awful lot. Um, it wasn't quite so hard with [laughs] with Jeanne and Thomas because I didn't actually like her husband very much, so that was kind of, that was OK. Um, but . . . yeah, but there were, there were definitely divided loyalties in terms of feeling very much like into, you know, for the sake of sisterhood, I should have been there for Roxanne but sort of, sort of somewhere emotionally feeling a bit kind of upset really.

Significantly, Madonna refers to herself as the 'baby' or 'child' in relation to Leonie and her former husband. With a gap of 17 years between them Madonna and Leonie unsurprisingly regard each other as 'mother' and 'child'. Madonna recognises her renewed anger at each family fragmentation. At the same time, she was determined to learn from the first divorce and to support her sisters, subsequently. In practice, however, this proved problematic owing to the demands of her own subjectivity in the midst of these break-ups. Her insights into her own emotions highlight her conflicting response, torn between, on the one hand, her sisterly loyalty and, on the other, her rage and sadness at the dissolution of couples upon whom she depended.

Madonna's weariness of these emotions third time round became manifest when Roxanne divorced. She touches on the web of relationships that connect sisters and their lovers and the impossibility of not becoming ensnared in these changing emotions and ties:

> *Madonna*: Then Roxanne then splitting up with Stuart, it was like, oh I'm not doing this again! I'm not going through all this shit again of like dealing with somebody else's relationship break-up and that I think, that's what it was, it was feeling like I was dealing with other people's relationships and, and, but that's what happens with sisters, because you do get drawn into their relationships, because they're kind of so important really, because they, they kind of mould the people that they become and certainly influence the people that they are, you know.

She eloquently articulates her resentment, her wish to remain distant from the emotions and the difficulty of keeping aloof from the significant others in her sisters' lives.

Furthermore, Madonna recognises the inconsistency of her lack of understanding of her sisters in contrast to their unstinting support of her own heterosexual trials and tribulations. They, she says, have stood by her:

> *Madonna*: Followed me through the most outrageous relationships and been just incredibly supportive until I've seen the, sort of seen the light myself really. So, I haven't done very well by them have I? [laughs] And that's all right because I'm the kid sister!
>
> *MM*: [laughs]
>
> *Madonna*: So, yeah, quite, yeah.
>
> *MM*: So it sounds like there are times when it's quite nice to be the kid sister?
>
> *Madonna*: Oh, yeah, definitely.
>
> *MM*: To revert to that.
>
> *Madonna*: Definitely. I try not to do it. I really do try not to do it, um but um . . . um.
>
> *Madonna and MM*: [laugh]

Madonna's reflexivity on the ups and downs of being the 'kid sister' reveal its contradictions and her difficulties with abandoning this long established role. Her enjoyment and pain at her 'kid sister' position in the realm of heterosexuality is reminiscent of her ambivalent feelings when she was temporarily positioned as Roxanne's 'big sister' after their father died.

Bye bye baby

Madonna's ambivalence about adopting the 'big sister' position at specific transition moments linked to bereavement and marital break-up illustrates the challenges of shedding the 'kid sister' skin. Indeed, as she says herself, this position enabled her, in a sense, to let herself off the hook at certain moments when she felt put upon by her older sisters when they reverted to something she abhorred, such as telling her how to organise her life. Madonna muses pertinently on her new-found awareness of her own power and its likely connection with the difficulties that she has encountered in her changing relationship with Roxanne:

> *Madonna*: I've never had any power [laughs] up until now, um, I, I think, up until the last kind of year, literally the last year or so. I've always been not, actually that's not quite so true of my relationship with Roxanne, um, although because I am the youngest, I've always tended to see that being the problem, that I've been treated as the youngest where in actual fact, that's not always been the case. And I, and, and kind of, now I've sort of peaked 30 and you know, I'm sort of, you know, I'm in my thirty-somethings and it's and it is obviously very difficult for them to see me as the baby anymore. Um, but things have, the, the power has kind of shifted. I'm now kind of very, quite obviously seen as a woman by the rest of them and, and have a power which to be honest, until sort of two years, 18 months ago, I actually didn't realise I had. And that, and I think that's been the kind of like, I think that's, thinking about the sort of difficulties and the transition in the relationships, I think that's been a lot to do with it. I was very unaware of the power that I had um because I was, I did find it very easy to slip into thinking, they're just treating me like a child again, you know it's like, they've been there, they've done it and they're telling me what to do again, you know, when will they stop doing it.

Madonna's detailed account presents a fascinating exploration of her analysis of the shifting power relations between her and her sisters, especially Roxanne.

Madonna grapples with the implications of leaving behind the 'kid sister' position almost for good and the emotional hurdles involved. Her words encapsulate the difficulty in practice of moving out of one discourse and into another. The emotional demands of the *shifting positions* discourse where roles fluctuate are one consequence of abandoning the *positioned* discourse. Madonna vividly describes this process:

> *Madonna*: It freaks me out, I mean I can't cope with any of them when they're upset but, um . . . that's a bit of a contradiction really, isn't it? I've just said that it's easier to cope with but, but I do find it very difficult. But I'm, I, but I have realised as I've sort of, the last couple of years, that I have to deal with that if I want to be taken seriously as a grown up, as a grown up sister. I have to cope with the fact that they will come to me in tears occasionally and that I can't look to them and just to being the sort of caring older sisters really.

Madonna continues:

> *Madonna*: I find it, I find it really quite hard when the roles are reversed and they are, they are being very vulnerable because it does make me feel incredibly grown up, you know incredibly old. The fact that they are there doing that with me and I think, shit, you know, they must be, they must be relying on me. That's never been, that's never been so much the case with Roxanne and I, and yet I still have a, I still haven't, I still haven't acknowledged it until really recently. You know there have been times when Roxanne and I have just been in the most awful slanging matches and, and she's been saying things to me, but I, and I've been thinking, but I'm the kid, you know, but I'm the kid sister. Why are you saying this to me, I, I shouldn't be expected to do that, I'm the young one. But then, but then being very aware of the fact that there never has been that kind of power thing between the two of us anyway but that's me kind of hiding behind the kind of kid sister apparel really.

Madonna's narrative reflects the challenges of attaining greater parity in sistering. The way that she toys with holding on to and letting go of her position as 'kid sister' in her relationship with Roxanne suggests its lure and seductiveness and the costs of bidding it farewell.

Hello baby doll

The other side of the role-reversal proves as complex for Roxanne as for Madonna, but in a different way. As Madonna became aware of her new power, she struggled in order to come to terms with her ambivalence towards the potential emotional requests her sisters might make of her as new 'big sister'. For Roxanne, however, an unforeseen consequence of Madonna's ambivalence about shedding her 'little sister' skin and moving out of the *positioned* discourse, was to find herself positioned by Madonna as 'little sister'. Roxanne elaborates on this new negative phenomenon:

> *Roxanne*: She's treated me like I'm a little sister actually, that's how people observe it, that's how Jeanne observes it. She was once round on one of the rare occasions that we're, we're all together and she said to Madonna, God you talk to her like she's your little sister! And she does. And for a long time I accepted it because my relationship with her was so important to me and it was, you know, she was like a friend, she, out of all my sisters she was the one that I could say, she's like me, you know, I feel that I can relate to this person, we have similar politics, we have, you know she's a feminist um, she's arty, I'm arty, you know there were loads of things that were very similar.

> *MM*: Mmmm.

> *Roxanne*: So I didn't want to lose that. So I would put up with her treating me like a little sister and I would put up with her sulks and, but then, I know it sounds corny, but then Trev became too important to me, you know I, I thought at last I've found a relationship where I feel like I can be me and I could see the way my sisters weren't allowing me to be me so I thought, stuff this, and started confronting Madonna and I did say to her, you know why, why is it not OK, and she actually said, well because I have different expectations of you.

> *MM*: That you'd be some kind of tough cookie?

> *Roxanne*: I don't know really, she could never really explain it. Just, she'd just say, there's no point in you quoting Jeanne to me and what I allowed Jeanne to do without getting in a huff with her because you're not Jeanne, you're not like her! I expect different things of you. But I didn't know what, you know, I didn't know what I wasn't living up to.

Their lack of dialogue leaves them in a stalemate. When Roxanne considers the new turn that her tie with Madonna has taken, she realises how difficult exiting the *positioned* discourse and moving into the *shifting positions* discourse are. Noting the shifting power relations between them, she reflects that perhaps her relationship with Madonna was more manageable when they each took on conventional age-related 'big' and 'kid' sister roles. Their narratives reveal the hurdles in the transformation of their relationship. Unlike Leila and *Annar*'s tie, Roxanne and Madonna's has changed in a negative way for them.

Roxanne: Like my relationship with Madonna was easier.

MM: When there was a slight imbalance?

Roxanne: Yeah, yeah . . . Because equality is difficult isn't it?

MM: Yes!

Roxanne and MM: [laugh]

MM: That's [what] I was thinking about.

Roxanne: Most people find it difficult.

MM: It, it, it, it's um.

Roxanne: Most, I think, most relationships are, are premised on some sort of inequality. That inequality may fluctuate but I think quite often where relationships appear to be going well, you know somebody has the upper hand or somebody is in a position of mentor or guide or whatever [. . .]

Roxanne identifies the changing power relations between them, the difficulty of attaining a balance or equality, and their silences:

Roxanne: It's difficult to negotiate when you've had something very different.

MM: Um.

Roxanne: In any relationship, isn't it, it's not just sisters, it's like anything at all where you've had something different, to then, for one person to become more powerful is just too often, too difficult for it to work.

MM: But why, why do you, well you've talked about why it hasn't happened with your sisters, but are you, are you, are you disappointed, does it bug you?

Roxanne: Yeah, I can't say. It doesn't, I do feel, it's not so much disappointment as lack of justice. You know, I've always had a very very strong sense of justice ever since I was a kid when I got blamed for things that I hadn't done, you know and I do, I do feel strongly that people have a right of reply, um and it's and it's more that . . . that I wish, that I wish that it, it was possible to talk through the issues with them but it isn't. It just isn't [. . .]. And with Madonna it's just, it would be too painful for her, she doesn't want us to be equals, she wants to be able to talk badly to me which she's done all her adult life and I've taken it. And I'm disappointed, yeah with Madonna I am, because we are, as I said, out of them all, we are the most similar, we have the most in common. You know, I like, I like lots of things about her um, but not enough to tolerate her spoilt behaviour because it's like saying, it's like saying beat me over the head, you know, and I'm worth more. I have a much stronger sense of myself I think than I ever have before and I'm just not prepared to put up with as much crap as I have been in the past. Life's too short.

MM: Yeah.

Roxanne: But I do, but I do, you know back to what you said, I do, I do miss, it seems odd, I think it's more about me thinking I should need something from a family but I don't, you know I don't seem to miss them that much really.

Roxanne's sadness, disappointment and resignation to the stalemate are palpable. Both sisters are unhappy with the status quo and yet neither is able to resolve the complex issues involved. Instead, the impact of the transitions linked to bereavement and marital break-up has transformed their relationship from *best friendship* to *distant companionship*.

In addition, their tie has become stuck in its path out of the *positioned* discourse, when Madonna was always the 'kid sister' with its benefits and disadvantages. In spite of their experiments with shifting positions, this process has stalled in a negative way. For a positive outcome they would each need to be more accepting of the other's changing subjectivity. Roxanne would have to respect the privacy of Madonna's independent bond with Jeanne and her refusal to mediate between Roxanne and

Jeanne. Madonna would have to respect Roxanne's sexual autonomy and her new partner. For Madonna to shift emotionally into Roxanne's 'big sister' in moments of crisis, she would also have to embrace the new responsibility that comes with this caring role.

Distant lives, still voices[1]

Madonna and Roxanne's sistering tales of their current lives corroborate each other. They agree on the new distance between them, the silences and diminished intimacy and contact. Madonna looks back at her changing relationship with Roxanne:

> *Madonna*: I don't, well maybe no, didn't used to be Roxanne's baby, but I used, I definitely used to be Roxanne's friend, you know. We kind of used to sort of hang out together, do you know what I mean and go clothes shopping and things, when I, especially when I was living with her. And um and that's moved on I suppose just in terms of being in different places, her being in a different relationship than when I was living with her. Um, I think that, that's been, I mean that is, that is to do with men. That is to do with men and the fact that I haven't completely denounced her ex-husband completely and taken on this new partner.

And she continues:

> *Madonna*: We kind of, we kind of throw it at each other Jeanne and Roxanne and I really. Jeanne, not so much, but Roxanne and I certainly do in terms of well, I can't, no, I can't explain it, I really can't explain it. We don't talk healthily about, well; things aren't going well at the moment. I mean, Roxanne, I, I get the feeling at the moment that Roxanne, well it's not a feeling, I know, Roxanne will not talk to me about anything bad that happens between Trev and her because she doesn't want me to think that there is, there could possibly be anything bad in that relationship. So it's, it's um, you're kind of at a bit of a dead end street really in terms of that and I think that's how men affect us really, the fact that they kind of close down certain areas for, for conversation, that our friendship doesn't override the, the traumas of a, of our personal relationships. It kind of, it acts as a, as a kind of barrier really because we're too frightened to admit that we're doing things wrong. [. . .] I think it's, it's not always been the case about things but, but I think there is, I mean we, [sighs] are we competitive? I don't know but I, I, it's almost that it's almost that fear of not wanting to be seen to be doing things wrong.

Madonna attributes their changing relationship to the impact of men in their lives, especially in Roxanne's life, and to the reduced talk flowing between them. Roxanne, however, notes the way that change has been gradual as evinced in new contact patterns:

> *Roxanne*: I think a lot about the issues and why it is how it is at the moment. I've thought, thought it through endlessly really recently because it's so noticeably different, not noticeably different, it's just, it's been quite gradual actually but I know now that it's reached a point where we are not regularly keeping in touch whereas before I always knew that Madonna would ring every now and then . . . whereas I'm sure that now, it's very much, you know, I'll ring her and then she'll respond and I think well I can rise above that, you know. I will do that just because partly because I want to have the higher moral ground I suppose [laughs]!

Below the bubble

Roxanne and Madonna no longer get 'below the bubble' in their dealings with one another. The 'inter-connect personal' element described by Roxanne which she used to enjoy, including moments of telepathy, has vanished. Instead, they find it difficult to talk about recent changes in their tie. Madonna, the former 'baby sister', resisted becoming a go-between for Roxanne and Jeanne, who have little contact. There is also jealousy as Madonna is now closer to Jeanne than Roxanne. In addition, Roxanne's new partner and their distinct attitudes towards their mother have also caused conflict.

After Roxanne separated from her husband, she and Madonna grew distant. She felt treated as a 'little' sister, so in a sense their roles reversed. Madonna felt angry about the break-up and, according to Roxanne, possibly jealous of her new partner, who is almost the same age as Madonna (and Madonna is single). Roxanne says, 'None of us are very close now because I haven't fitted in where I should have.' Roxanne's words, that as a child 'I'd been seen as wayward', conjures up an image of the family rebel. One interpretation is that she has rebelled against both Jeanne and Madonna's positioning of her as 'little' sister. After confronting Madonna about being treated like a 'little' sister big outbursts ensued: 'I couldn't say what I thought without it causing her grief.' Roxanne's understanding of all this is: 'my sisters weren't allowing me to be me'. Two life events changed their sistering: their father's death and Roxanne's divorce. Roxanne sees herself as the most 'feminist' of all her sisters and also as not being 'prepared to compromise'.

From Roxanne's perspective, several factors contributed to her estrangement from Madonna and her other sisters, including disagreements about how to 'be' with their mother. When Roxanne says, 'I don't need to do these things to keep people happy', in the context of feeling let down by her elder sister Leonie, she is also referring to Madonna – Madonna's lack of support in Roxanne's new sexual relationship and attitude towards her as a 'little' sister. Roxanne elaborates:

> *Roxanne*: So there's all these factors, you know that have converged at this particular time, for me, when I'm the happiest that I've ever been in my life, so perhaps I need them less as well, you know. But I think it's also as I said, it's to do with getting older and not needing that sort of approval [. . .]

Roxanne's changing subjectivity plays a significant role in her tie with Madonna. One interpretation is that she has safeguarded her subjectivity at the cost of distancing herself. This is perhaps a negative instance of shifting positions where Roxanne (39) has moved out of her new positioning as 'little' sister by Madonna (31) through separation. Although this was a positive move for Roxanne's changing subjectivity, she felt its negative impact on her tie with Madonna. In other cases, this flexibility is positive, with each sister in turn adopting the 'big' or 'little' positioning for example Hazel (34) and Phoebe (35), and Suzanne and *Collette*. Roxanne's attempts to move out of the *positioned* discourse have had a negative effect on her sister ties since her sisters have resisted Roxanne's move away from the 'little' sister position. Despite this price of distance, conflict and anguish, Roxanne also hints at another facet of this process when she says 'perhaps I need them less'.

Roxanne was less successful than other sisters were, whose changing subjectivity and moves out of 'big' or 'little sister' positionings were positive for both their sistering and each woman's subjectivity. Phoebe managed to end her positioning as 'big' sister and swap roles with Hazel. This change in behaviour is implicitly connected to their individual changing sense of self, which in Phoebe and Roxanne's cases, becomes less 'other' or duty-oriented and more self-directed. In Phoebe's case, Hazel accepted this change; in Roxanne's, her attempts to modify both her subjectivity and the dynamics of her tie with Madonna led to conflict and resistance. This was partly owing to Madonna's hesitation and caution about fully embracing the 'big sister' position, especially regarding the management of emotions.

Conclusion

After a brief experiment to shift positions, Roxanne and Madonna's tie stalled in a negative way. Their sistering trajectory charts a painful uncaring role reversal, which they both feel uncomfortable with leading to a stalemate. In the aftermath of their father's death they remain unhappily locked into 'big' and 'little' sister positionings. Other life-events, Roxanne's divorce and new romance, led Madonna to position herself as Roxanne's 'big sister'. Madonna's new 'big' sister position constitutes perhaps a reaction to the dissolution of yet another family unit, in addition to her natal family, which she had relied on in earlier decades in order to construct herself as 'kid sister'. Madonna's apparent rebellion against so much family fragmentation, through her move from 'kid' to 'big' sister, is marked by feelings of extreme ambivalence. A central factor in these changing ties is the level of awareness about emotions and different perspectives on moments of transition in relationships. Reflexivity as understanding, as a means of transcending power relations, and of acknowledging differences can be key in bridging divides. One explanation for Roxanne and Madonna's inability to extricate themselves from the *positioned* and into the *shifting positions* discourse, which one of them hints at, is their inability to face and incorporate their differences positively into their sistering.

8
Changing Subjectivity

Another factor in bringing about what Smiley (1991: 308) calls a 'changed sisterly condition', which Suzanne, Jeanne, Hazel and Phoebe, Roxanne and Madonna refer to, is the role of their own changing subjectivity. Their eloquence about how women attempt to refashion their sister identities beyond fixed notions of mothering and being mothered illustrates this process in detail. This chapter looks further at the influence of subjectivity – a reflexive, multiple, rational and emotional changing self – on sistering. It is partly through talk, silence and emotions that subjectivity is constructed and experienced materially. The chapter focuses on the self's movement or lack of movement within constricting or supportive forms of sistering. The emphasis here is on how feminine subjectivities develop over time in the context of caring practices, life-events and their unpredictable impact on power relations – in effect, how girls and women make themselves 'subjects within subordination' (Hey 1997: 141).

The chapter explores how these changing subjectivities can transform, or not, the very relationships in which they evolve as they emerge from either within or outside sistering. Typically, in *best friendship*, changing subjectivity is generated from within the tie; whereas in *distant companionship*, it develops outside it. In both instances, changing subjectivity can either influence the sister tie or not. Two case studies of *best friendship* trace how changing subjectivity emerges through a crisis and loss. For Chloe (20) and Annabel (20), the loss of Annabel's girlfriend led to changes in both her subjectivity and her bond with Chloe. For Rae (30) and Bukhi (25), the loss of Bukhi's boyfriend and Rae's motherhood changed the dynamics between them. In contrast, two *distant companionships* reveal how changing subjectivity develops outside sistering. For Clare (50), her disability and awareness of difference distanced her from *Stella* (52), and Clare's subjectivity evolved through other friendships. For

Rowena (37), jealousy and emotional distance from *Grace* (34) also affected her subjectivity, which similarly evolved outside this tie.

Chloe and Annabel

Living and studying in different cities, Chloe and Annabel, both aged 20, spend less time together than when they lived at home as teenagers, yet this has not significantly altered their tie. They speak on the phone and meet during holidays. Although they are currently single, they recently spent a social summer together with their boyfriends. The dominant emotions in their narrative – anger, jealousy and appreciation – can be traced chronologically to conflict in their early years:

Chloe: We used to fight like cat and dog! [laughs]

And to rivalry over boyfriends in their teens:

Annabel: Mmm, yeah, I think I was jealous. I was jealous that Isaac got on with Chloe as well, but that was at the stage where we were, we were only just starting to be friends, and, weren't we?

They also reflect on a moment in their mid-teens which marked a break with their early years of fighting, competition and 'personality clashes' when Annabel, at that time 'very naughty, like I did stupid things' who took Chloe for granted, 'calmed down' and they began to talk. Chloe explains:

Chloe: I think there, there got to a stage where Annabel realised what she was like or doing and, um, she just sort of settled down and um, I think, um, a few, um, instances, um, brought us closer together and we were able to understand each other and talk about things, which we'd never sort of, really, really done.

Their appreciation during the interview for each other was explicit. Annabel said, 'we appreciated each other'. It was also embedded in the style of their interaction and talk – confiding, for example – and in their laughter throughout. Appreciation was the dominant emotion in their dynamic and dialogue. How was their subjectivity constructed through these emotions? And what role did these play in the evolution of their relationship?

Their joint narrative was structured through episodes detailing key emotional events: their account of their sistering was primarily constructed through *emotions*. Moreover, the style of their narrative was an intimate one of *confiding* between them as a twosome, and between them and me. Significant emotional moments in their tie coincided with a turning-point in their 'sense of self' or subjectivity, their relationship, or both – subjectivity and relationship. An example of loss and sadness in their mid-teens illustrates the connections between talk about emotions, an intimate or private style of talk, and changing subjectivities and relationships.

The turning-point in their teens was prompted by crises with their girlfriends. Danielle, Annabel's best friend, became mentally ill, signalling the end of their best friendship; and one of the sisters' mutual friends, Emily, lost her mother. Annabel describes her sadness when she was 15 to 16 at Danielle's illness and the ending of their friendship:

Annabel: She went very, er, I mean she was naagh, she, you know cut herself up, um, made herself sick and and just basically, was just causing mayhem in the, and disrupting the school routine, let alone, you know, mine, and, you know, she was just disrupting everything and it was just this attention-seeking thing which I couldn't handle because I had to take on . . .

MM: Yeah.

Annabel: Her, you know, I had to help her and you know [. . .] the teacher used to say to me, you know, 'Oh go, go and see how Danielle is Annabel', you know, 'off, off you trot, see how she is' and then, it just used to, it was just so much of a strain and it was, I mean, I couldn't bear just watching her you know, my best friend. I mean it was really upsetting.

This event, however, brought about changes in the twins' relationship:

Annabel: It was very upsetting for me because it was like losing a, I mean fortunately, I, you know, I've, well Chloe's my best friend now, I mean. Fortunately, you know, but Danielle was the only best friend that I've ever had, as in a friend-friend [. . .] My best friend Danielle and, and I don't know whether you noticed that, that I was

Chloe: I don't know, I mean maybe it was the first time that you noticed, not noticed me, but didn't take for granted, that I was there and I don't know, I think

Annabel: I think, I mean

Chloe: I can't remember the exact time or anything but we just, I think you appreciated me being there for someone you know, to talk to.

Annabel: Yeah, yeah and also I mean like when Emily's mother died of cancer. Yeah and I suppose I, I was very, I never really talked about much, many things and I suppose that

Chloe: I think it was a time where we both grew up.

Annabel: It happened, those two instances happened at very similar times and then we just suddenly realised, oh right, we, we've got some understanding here and um

Chloe: Yeah and we realised that, you know, I guess we did, we just started talking, I can't

Annabel: We appreciated each other.

This moment where talk about emotions coincided with distressing events for each of them regarding their girlfriends also changed the power relations between them. From a position where Annabel was dominant, they moved to a situation in which they describe themselves as more equal:

Chloe: Things, people, it's nice to have someone your age, er, around.

Annabel: I just realised that, I mean, we, we could actually talk about about, how we were feeling and

Chloe: Yeah, and Annabel was no longer sort of, trying to, looking down upon me or anything.

Annabel: Trying to be impressed, trying to be the

Chloe: And, you know regarded me as an equal I suppose that's, that's what it was.

Annabel: That was the start.

Chloe: And I didn't, I thought oh, that's really good, you know, that she can do that now and, um, and I suppose it got better and better, I mean we tolerated each other better and, you know, you just, I don't know, suppose as you grow up, you do, you just appreciate

Annabel: Yeah, I mean I had to grow up, I mean I had to, not, I mean, I thought, I was growing up really fast, you know, at the age of 13 or 14 and I think I did, but I actually grew up or matured properly at the age of 15 or 16 because I really had to be sensible and mature about, you know, what was happening to Danielle and I had to be, I had to grow up. I really had to calm down, you know, and things took a more serious tone at that stage and, and I think that's when we started talking and I accepted Chloe or rather, you accepted me more. It happened at the same time.

Chloe: Mmm. Well, no, yeah, well it's a two-way thing isn't it?

Annabel: Mmm.

Chloe: Definitely.

Annabel: Because before we just didn't really accept each other, did we? Because I think I was the dominant one and

Chloe: Yeah.

Annabel: You couldn't stand that.

Several themes emerge here: acknowledging and accepting difference, moving out of the *positioned* into the *shifting positions* discourse, and changing subjectivity – through references to tolerance/acceptance, domination/equality and maturing/growing up. What stands out in their joint story is the important change that occurred when Chloe and Annabel started discussing how they felt about distressing events surrounding their friendships with Danielle and Emily. This change happened in both their relationship *and*, in Annabel's case, her subjectivity or sense of self. This is an example of changing subjectivity generated by external events leading to positive changes in the sister bond.

Rae and Bukhi

Another case of critical external events provoking crisis and change in sistering related to strong emotional reactions is Rae (30) and Bukhi's (25) bond. Events in their *best friendship* reveal patterns similar to those found in Chloe and Annabel's tie. Their separate narratives were similarly structured around emotions and understanding them. Their contact and the strength of their tie is greater now that they are older and live in the same city rather than in the family home. When they were growing up, the age gap led Rae to keep her distance from her two younger sisters, Bukhi and *Mira* (22). Now however, they are very involved in each other's lives through work and childcare. They have contact at least two to three times a fortnight – on the phone, at work, at home when Bukhi babysits for Rae's daughter Sasha (1), and during shopping trips or meals out.

Several features of their tie stand out: Rae supported Bukhi's move to the city where she was already living, put her up on arrival and encouraged her to enter higher education as a mature student. Bukhi was Rae's birthing partner, and here she summarises the trajectory of their sistering:

> *Bukhi*: I think as soon as she moved to [the city] that was just a really big change in how we got on. Because she'd always, she's only five years older than me but it just seemed a lot, a bigger gap than me and my sister [*Mira*]. I think it's because my brother [San, 29] was like . . . I used to think well, there was those two and then there was us two and she left home quite young so . . . I don't think I knew her as well before she left home and I think once she left home, because I wanted to leave home as well, that was like, we were able to start getting to know each other really well. And then I think the major thing was when she had Sasha and she asked me if I wanted to go to the birth and I was like . . . really pleased that she'd asked me and that was . . . that was the best thing that I've ever . . . that was just amazing going to the . . . amazing seeing the birth and Rae! And I felt really really close to her, got really involved beforehand and afterwards. It's like I was saying before, now I feel like . . . I can give her back, she did a lot for me when I was first in [the city], now I feel I can sort of help her with Sasha and look after Sasha and just . . . it's more like, I can talk to her and give her advice sometimes now. Whereas before it was always Rae usually and I was always like . . . oh, I don't know what I'm doing, whereas it seems to have changed a bit now and we're sort of more . . . . .more like on a level . . .

Bukhi's snapshot of their changing relationship traces its evolution into a phase of mutuality where their actions and involvement in each other's lives became, over time, reciprocal.

Their narratives centre on 'emotional ups and downs'. For Rae, these concern her anger and sadness at Bukhi's distress regarding a break-up, coupled with her love for her:

> *Rae*: I had a lot of respect for her and I was really happy. As well as just, you know, her being my sister and I, I do love her a lot.

Bukhi feels upset about both her break-up and how she 'took out' her anger on Rae:

> *Bukhi*: I think we'll always be, I think we will always be really close now, I don't think I'll go back to, I think before it was like, phases but I think that was like, because I was sort of growing up – couldn't imagine not getting on with her for a long period of time now. I don't think so; no. [. . .] I think that time was a bad time for me anyway. And I know that I took it out on her a bit.

This heightened emotion regarding what Hey (1997) terms 'boyfriend management' is a central feature of their narratives where emotions, the intimate style of talking and change are embedded. Rae recounts this difficult time in her twenties when Bukhi decided to leave her boyfriend and they handled the ending together:

> *Rae*: Well, she told me everything, well more or less everything when she was upset. It was an immediate, you know, she, she could go to the pub or wherever and have a drink with people and and get by, whereas if I went with her and we were on our own, she'd say, or if, or if she came and spoke to me, she'd say, oh I'm upset about this and this happened and that happened and she'd tell me everything. So I would kind of go through her emotional ups and downs with her.

In her distress over the break-up Rae's feelings of 'upset' turned into anger and she 'exploded':

> *Rae*: She came up with this whole spiel of, I haven't got anything to, er, anybody to love, well nobody loves me, more or less. And I know that she was upset and we've all been there and, and said those things or felt

those things and I just felt so angry that she was in this position. I did-n't blame her entirely but I felt that she was the only person that could get herself out of it but I couldn't, I just couldn't logically say, well, do this or do that. So I just exploded myself because I never do, I always kind of say, oh well, I just, I was upset that she, that she was sort of at the end of her

MM: Tether?

Rae: Yeah.

A further effect of the 'boyfriend management' episode on them illus-trates how intertwined emotions and the process of change is. Rae's out-rage and exasperation at both Bukhi's reaction to the break-up – 'grief' – and at her own distress at Bukhi's experience is intricately expressed below. A number of themes appear: first, Rae's astonishment at the change in Bukhi – 'she was slightly losing it a bit'; second, Rae's intensely emotional response to this change – Rae starts to cry and shake. Third, there is Bukhi's shock at her sister's emotions expressed physically and the change this prompts in her: in Rae's words, 'she immediately snapped out of her grief'.

Rae: I just felt I, I couldn't give anything and the only thing that I could give, there was just a really sort of black on white view of, look Bukhi, how can you say that? I mean, and I started crying and I said, look how can you say? How can you be this far? How can some, another man do this to you, get you into this state? Look at you, I can't cope, I can't bear to see you like this, you need help, you need to go and speak to some-body, you're going to, you need, you, I just thought she was going to do something ridiculous. I knew that she wouldn't because I, I've got this kind of confidence in her anyway that she's not, you know, sort of suicidal or anything like that, but I just felt emotionally she was um . . . she was losing it a bit and not, not the sort of full person that I've always known her to be and she was becoming one of these people who, she says, oh I'm depressed because of this. Well I think, well go abroad, you know, go on holiday, I'll give you the money to go on holi-day, I, I'll lend you, I'll borrow the money. Go away with this person and, and you, you need to do something. Anyway so I, I, and I just started crying and I started shaking. Then, then she immediately snapped out of her grief and sort of said, 'Oh my God Rae, I've never seen you like this'. And she was starting to say to me, calm down, calm

down. I said, 'I can't calm down, I can't see you like, I can't cope with
you like this'. And I was really upset and then . . .

This example illustrates how emotions and change are tightly enmeshed
at the micro-level in relationship interactions. Changes in subjectivity
and relationships also operate at the macro-level over the course of time
in a tie. Rae sums up this phase of emotional upheaval: 'But, um, it was just
a really difficult time, but it did bring us closer together.' This contradictory moment in their tie coincided with a period of change in both their
own sense of self or subjectivity and in their sistering, by bringing them
'closer together'. How do these narratives of change emerge?

Narratives of change (Sandmaier 1995; Mathias 1994) or 'reflexive personal narratives' (Giddens 1992) are significant for understanding subjectivities and relationships. Women's subjectivity and sistering are
constructed by and through change to do with emotions, a specific style
of emotional disclosing, talk and contact. Another element structuring
Rae and Bukhi's narratives is power relations: we have seen in previous
chapters how the *positioned* and *shifting positions* discourses may contradict and yet co-exist within *best friendship*. How do these shifts appear in
narratives of changing subjectivity?

Tensions between multiple and contradictory 'subject positions'
(Bloom and Munro 1995: 99) surface in Chloe and Annabel, and Rae and
Bukhi's bonds. We saw how the *positioned* discourse reproduces elements
of mothering–daughtering. As eldest sibling and daughter, family members including Bukhi and herself positioned Rae as the 'responsible' one
in charge. As a ten-year-old she prepared 'tea' for her three siblings as both
parents worked. Rae describes this process of positioning herself as 'big'
sister in relation to the 'boyfriend management' episode:

Rae: Maybe I was upset at the fact that I couldn't help her and I wanted
to. I've always felt semi-responsible for her because I kind of helped her
move to [the city]. I mean, I don't feel like that any more. I had felt at
the time semi-responsible and I just, I couldn't bear her to be so upset.
And I, I hated this man for, for treating her like he did.

During Rae's pregnancy and especially after Sasha's birth, the sisters
swapped roles when Bukhi became an older sister. After asking Bukhi to be
her birthing partner they attended antenatal classes together:

Rae: And she gave me, she gave me a lot of confidence and she was
almost like my older sister I felt, plus she, she, she, she's had more

experience in some ways because she's had more boyfriends than me and I've always felt that she's more, not lots more boyfriends, that's silly. She's had more friendships with people, um, and she's quite wise I think and she really helped, she really helps out. And I could talk to her about lots of things but if I'm, I really trust Bukhi, and if I'm worried about something I, I tell her.

Bukhi's version corroborates Rae's: .

> *Bukhi*: I've been able to help her out a lot now, so I feel . . . I think I feel better about it . . . we get on a lot better because I feel that I can help her out now whereas before she was always sort of helping me out and it was always me that was sort of messing up or . . .

This role reversal reflects how positions or roles within the relationship are not fixed: sisters can oscillate between 'helping' and receiving help.

These shifts between different subject positions occurred in the context of *best friendship*, changing subjectivity and changing relationships for Rae and Bukhi. Awareness of changing subjectivity, talk, being the 'big' sister, their changing bond, and emotions are laced through Rae's narrative:

> *Rae*: I know now that whatever I say, it's up to her and she's her own person and she'll, I'll never know everything about her. It was like, it was getting to that thing where she was telling me everything and I was going through the ups and downs with her but having the frustration of not being able to do anything myself. [. . .] With Bukhi I couldn't just say to her, because she couldn't just finish with him, and um she couldn't, it wasn't, it was too easy for me to say that. I had to go, I had to let her make the decision, especially being an older sister. Um . . . but it just brought us closer together because especially that time when I got upset, then she got upset because I was so upset and then it was, it was, it was one of the first times that I felt that she, she really cared about how I felt in this, because I did feel involved with her and I didn't expect her to keep it to herself. I mean, you know, she had to tell me or somebody and I was the one, which I'm, I'm glad of because I do want to share the good times and the bad times with her. Um, she just loved him, that's all. She couldn't help it. She, you can't act rationally if you love somebody and I didn't want her to love him, so that was all.

As Bukhi gradually accepted the break-up, became an aunt and grew up, she felt closer to Rae:

Bukhi: I'd split up with my boyfriend, everything was a complete mess really. And then I started not getting on with Rae as well. And it just seemed like, Oh God, it's never ever going to get sorted out. But . . . it did . . . I think it was just time, I just got over not going out with this guy and stopped taking it out on Rae, I think. And then she had Sasha and that brought us together, all that feeling from before . . .

A crucial aspect of this process was Bukhi's sense of her changing subjectivity over the years:

Bukhi: I always used to feel a bit like that, overshadowed by Rae . . . and probably act differently when Rae was there whereas now I think, as I've got older, I've got more of a sense of who I am and that I can behave how I want to behave – whether Rae is there or not, I'll still be the same sort of person and maybe it's, she's doing the same thing. [. . .] As I've become older, I've become more aware of myself anyway and what I want to do and a bit more happy within myself. I think that's one of the main things [. . .] . . . I just think that I've grown up more and it's been great that she's been here. To sort of help me out while I've been doing that.

At the same time, she recognises how her own changing self was inextricably tied up with her changing relationship with Rae:

Bukhi: It sort of swings around, but I do think, yeah, there's definite phases but I think that's because people change, don't they, and you go through your own phases yourself.

Chloe and Annabel's and Rae and Bukhi's *best friendships* illustrate how agentic change occurs in relation to events external to sistering: in the first case, loss of a girlfriend, and in the second, Bukhi's loss of her boyfriend and Rae's motherhood. Internal events, in contrast, might include forms of betrayal. In both case studies, the women's subjectivities changed within their sister ties and partly as a result of these. Furthermore, their subjectivities then influenced their sistering dynamics with shifts in both instances from dominant and dominated subject positions to greater reciprocity. Significantly, these changing relationships are marked by both positive and negative change, which the sisters recognise and discuss.

Clare and *Stella*

In contrast, Clare (50) and *Stella's* (52), and Rowena (37) and *Grace's* (34) *distant companionships* reveal ties where little change occurs within sistering or in individual subjectivity in that context. Nevertheless, their subjectivities do change outside their sistering. There is only one perspective on these ties as I spoke only to Clare and Rowena and not to their sisters. Their narratives reflect gaps and silences in their sistering linked to physical disability and geographical distance. Their ties hardly alter over the years except for increased distance, which they neither acknowledge nor discuss.

Clare, single, and her older sister *Stella*, married with four children, live in different parts of the country and have little contact. They were 'never close'. As teenagers, they did not do things together. And although Clare envied *Stella* her 'older sister status' and wanted her to take on this role, Stella did not act the part:

> *Clare*: I wanted her to be an elder sister, and I think . . . I don't know I think she pushed me away a bit, I wanted to dress like her and be like her and my mother says I wanted to go to the same school as she did and we certainly went to the same schools all the way up until I was 12, but she was never a big sister to me. And I suppose, I had to just go out and find my own friends.

Although they get on 'quite well now' – 'we do get on superficially' – the distance between them is palpable:

> *Clare*: Yes, she said to me, oh fairly recently, 'Oh well, you always get what you want . . . in the end, don't you?' which is actually [not] necessarily true at all.

Infrequent contact and little physical intimacy mark their distant tie. They see each other approximately four times a year, mainly when Clare visits her mother who lives near *Stella*. At a recent family gathering, Clare was struck by their physical distance:

> *Clare*: She can't bear touching, she doesn't . . . I never kiss her . . . actually I did kiss her at her twenty-fifth wedding anniversary for the first time ever, I think.

Clare is partially disabled and as a child found it difficult to carry out some routine activities, but her disability was never mentioned among her par-

ents or two siblings: 'it was just expected that I would get on with it, and
so I did.'

> *Clare*: I've never discussed it with my sister, ever! [laughs] Other than
> she used to help me with my hair. I mean, for instance, I remember it
> was difficult as a teenager and I would sometimes, very, very rarely, ask
> for help with something and the response would be, why? Why can't
> you do it yourself? I know, it's quite incredible, and possibly that has,
> possibly that is, I don't know, it is quite complicated. My sister is very
> different from me.

Clare's disability remained invisible in the family even when, at the age of
11, she decided to wear a prosthesis. Even in her adulthood, it remains
silenced:

> *Clare*: Nobody ever asked me what it was, that caused me to then say, I
> would like to have a prosthesis and I did find it very difficult. I found it
> very difficult to wear it and I found the whole thing as a teenager very
> difficult.

Educational achievements created further distance, as happened to Leila
and *Annar*. *Stella* failed her school exams while Clare sailed through with
little work. Clare described herself as more outgoing than reserved *Stella*.
Both sisters trained as English teachers: Clare stopped half-way through
when her father died. It was Clare, age 19, who broke the news to *Stella*:

> *Clare*: . . . we weren't able to [be] close which I always felt was rather sad
> and I sort of felt that she resented it was me that was giving her this
> news.

Clare returned home to support her mother, and *Stella* went on to qualify.
At the end of her training *Stella* returned home and 'took over' from Clare
to be with their mother.
  They both felt neglected by their mother, a hard-working solicitor, and
resentful of the little time she spent with them. Whereas *Stella* nursed this
resentment, Clare just got on with things, obliged in a way by her disability to do so. Paradoxically, her physical difference became a strength and
she describes her changing subjectivity explicitly:

> *Clare*: It's been easier for me because I've built on successes, if you know
> what I mean. Because I've had to deal with things and succeeded in

dealing with them, that gives you a springboard all the way up your life.

Growing up, the girls were positioned as carers in the household. Clare's father, from when she was ten on, became an invalid and 'grandfatherly figure' and so the sisters in this 'matriarchal family' took over. In their teens, both were positioned as minimothers: 'My mother never cooked, you see. My sister and I did the cooking from when we were twelve.' Lunch was the main meal of the day prepared by a paid worker: during weekends and holidays the daughters took it in turns to cook. This gendered division of labour fuelled their resentment towards their brother, who was waited on by their mother.

Both sisters were sent to boarding school partly owing to their mother's strong work ethic and long hours, and partly to remove the problem of domestic labour requested from both daughters. Unhappy at school, Clare returned home and competed for maternal attention. *Stella's* return from boarding school for the holidays exacerbated Clare's quest for maternal intimacy. By 'getting things nice' to compensate for her guilt for sending *Stella* away, their mother only fuelled Clare and her brother's resentment against *Stella*.

In their twenties, the sisters' paths diverged further as each struggled to leave the nest and detach herself from their mother. Clare's incisive reflections on the links between mother–daughter and sister relationships in terms of emotions and power relations echo Suzanne, Hazel and Phoebe's comments. Recalling their mother's 'beastly' reaction when *Stella* met her future husband soon after their father's death, Clare speculates on the key role mothers play in sister ties where they can divide or unite daughters:

Clare: I think that must make a huge difference to all women, I suspect this is what ferments sister relationships, not for men . . . so they either work or they don't and it will work depending on the mother. [. . .] I think there are two things, if the sisters are thrown together so that, and . . . the personalities are such that they have only each other, then against some, whatever it is . . . some . . . some problem, whether it's the mother or family or isn't . . . so they unite, then I think you get a very strong bond. I think you probably also get a very strong . . . the healthiest strongest bond where there isn't, where the mother has a good relationship with both children and the jealousy doesn't, it must be very difficult . . . I mean, obviously, hugely difficult to bring up children. But to do it in such a way that jealousy doesn't arise.

Clare touches on mothers who can 'play off' sisters against each other:

> *Clare*: The reverse is if, that if the mother then divides them, if she actually divides them, and of course my mother actually would do this quite deliberately, it would be part of her . . . how much do you love me? I mean, it was never said, but she . . . for instance, she had a beastly little dog and she always had this dreadful Pomeranian and he was really snappy and not just snappy, I mean he would really bite. And she would say, go on, try and take him away from me [laughs] . . . knowing that you would go, and I think she played us off against each other. Yes, it's a power thing as well.

Mothers can divide and set daughters against each other or let them flourish leading to solidarity:

> *Clare*: If the relationship is good [. . .] between the mother and [daughters] and the mother is happy and content in herself as a person er . . . and [. . .] she can deal with her own problems without putting it onto the children then she can perhaps manage a relationship.

Domestic circumstances – an employed absent mother – and Clare's isolation in the family owing to her disability led her to develop kin and friendship ties outside the home. She became close to a now deceased aunt who looked after her as a newborn when her mother started a new job. She made friends more easily than her siblings, sometimes even 'acquiring' their friends, which created resentment. Her girlfriends date from several eras in her life. There are those she has known for decades scattered around the country and whom she seldom sees. There are her two closest friends whom she has known for 5–6 years, one of whom she rings up several times a week; and others who have also experienced a disability in their family.

She bonded with two cousins on different sides of the family, Joan (45) and Agatha (65), becoming close to the latter when they both shared the care of Agatha's dying older sister, Enid (70). Many of Clare's complex emotions regarding *Stella* surfaced when *Stella* became involved in caring for Enid, an 'interesting scenario'. Clare maintained the most regular contact with Agatha and Enid. Clare and Agatha both cared for Enid while she was dying. However when Enid died, *Stella* not Clare was at Enid's side, causing Clare to feel resentful. This bereavement resonated with Clare's father's death when the sisters' roles were reversed. Clare, the closest relative to Enid geographically, rushed to her when she discovered that she was terminally ill:

Clare: I dropped everything and I went down and what happened was that for about six weeks Agatha and I more or less between us packaged it out, so that I would go down on Thursday . . . Friday and stay through to Monday and then Agatha went down on Monday to Thursday and so either Agatha or I were there.

Clare was almost affronted when *Stella* became involved:

Clare: We didn't really need her, you know, and she was obviously, sort of . . . didn't . . . she didn't have a role to play, whereas we'd sort of established this role.

A further interpretation of Clare's resentment of *Stella's* arrival on the scene can be traced to Clare and Agatha, as younger sisters, positioning themselves as carers for Enid, mothering her during her final days. They did not relish *Stella*, as older sister, taking on that role. This reading is interesting in the light of Clare's girlhood wish for *Stella* to behave *more* like an elder sister. When *Stella* assumed some responsibility for caring for their cousin, Clare felt almost jealous:

Clare: Somehow or other Agatha and I, and we both felt this, sort of resented *Stella*'s presence and we weren't quite sure . . . I know, it's very odd. Very odd, I don't know why we did . . . er . . . and I felt all the resentment I did as a teenager. And then, er . . . I missed the death in the end, I mean it sounds as though I was looking forward to it, which I wasn't, but you know what it's like, and yet it was a funny situation because the whole thing was that there was so much laughter there, it was a very uplifting experience actually, and er . . . But anyway I'd gone back to have a bath because we'd been there, up all night and I'd just gone back for a quick bath and feed, and er . . . was going back and she died while I was away, and Agatha said to me, she said, it was actually *Stella* who was standing by her and not me because . . . [. . .] And I know it was that *Stella* just didn't know . . . what . . . She wanted to play a part and I felt really bad that we felt that we didn't want her. Awful, but it's what we felt. And I really was very resentful that it was *Stella* who came told me that Enid had died. In fact, I was quite cross. I think she just thought I was upset. I don't think she realised I was cross.

This episode is also about exclusivity. Enid's death brought Clare and Agatha closer: 'Agatha is older than I am, but we are, but Agatha and I are, we . . . we have the genetic thing and we read the same books and we laugh at the same things'.

At intervals, Clare mused on the delicate and discreet process of breaking away that she experienced in order to embrace her subjectivity – one largely constructed through difference. Her narrative is punctuated by moments of reflection: pondering on how her disability shaped her, she stresses her independence and an unwillingness to consider herself different. Yet in other ways, she clearly positions herself as 'different' from other family members. So, her self-description as the 'black sheep of the family' enables her to distance herself positively by rejecting the dominant family work ethic. Proudly, she asserts her 'laziness':

> *Clare*: I think, I probably found quite early on that I could get away with a very bare minimum and then do things in a rush at the end and just about scrape and that's the story of my life!

> *Clare*: I've had [a] very unstructured life so I've always expected things to turn up and sometimes they have and sometimes they haven't and I will . . . go with whatever is going really.

She conveys succinctly her awareness of her own subjectivity:

> *Clare*: I was the favourite in a way apart from . . . because I have a . . . I do have an outgoing personality and I will always make friends now whether or not this is because, you know, it wasn't there in the family. I mean, one can sort of make those things that, you know, you didn't, there wasn't enough mothering there and so you go and find people to, surrogate people to be friends with.

In a sense, Clare's subjectivity has hardly changed since her girlhood when she made her own friends outside her family circle. The sisters' paths have evolved differently, with Clare remaining single, working and establishing her own social networks, and Stella, marrying and raising a family.

As adults, Clare and *Stella* 'are moving much into a very mellow, rather nice phase', yet Clare is aware of not wanting to bond too much with her 'niblings' – nephews and nieces – now in their twenties (Parkin 1997). Contemplating a possible rapprochement with *Stella*, she realises, somewhat like Jeanne, that this could be engineered if she felt more enthusiastic:

Clare: She would like to be more intimate I think, but she doesn't know how, and I suppose this is my fault, I do, and she doesn't, and I could. I'm the one who could actually make the moves.

Much of Clare's narrative is structured around the body, her arm – its physical and verbal absence in her own life, in the family and in her relationship with *Stella* – and around difference. Themes of disability and difference, their silencing in the family, by her parents – out of parental guilt, Clare suspects – by her sister, and also by herself, pervade her tie with *Stella* and her construction of her own subjectivity.

As she contemplates both past and present, Clare discerns her own insensitivity towards *Stella*, the lack of direct communication between them stemming from their girlhoods, and *Stella*'s own misunderstanding of Clare – all of which shape their *distant companionship*:

Clare: I think I was pretty rotten to her really! [laughs] I think I was insensitive. She didn't understand and I think I . . . I suppose I didn't either but . . . I..could . . . I should have shown more sensitivity to her at various times I think . . . [. . .] We are much . . . closer than we were but we'll never be very close because we don't share the same interests, you know. And the same tastes.

In effect, Clare's subjectivity, while formed inside the family, developed and changed outside it – and outside the sister tie. Unlike the previous examples of *best friendship*, Clare and *Stella*'s *distant companionship* hardly evolved over time.

Rowena and *Grace*

Rowena (37) and *Grace*'s (34) *distant companionship*, like Clare and *Stella*'s, is also marked by separateness and silence. Any change in Rowena's subjectivity occurred outside her tie with *Grace* who lives in Alaska. In their girlhoods, they too fought physically, had separate friends and argued over boyfriends. When one of Rowena's old flames wanted to go out with *Grace*, it was less a case of jealousy, than 'cringing' because both found him 'awful'. In another instance, Rowena remembers one of *Grace*'s boyfriends whom *Grace* always thought Rowena was trying to steal.

Rowena's feelings of ambivalence about *Grace* stem from their school days: *Grace* was conscientious with homework and exams, whereas Rowena worked in bursts of adrenaline and felt anxious about exams. Rowena remembers their competitiveness; attending the same single-sex grammar school, comparing exam results and returning home separately with their own friends. She freely admits her long-standing jealousy of *Grace*. However, as they both work in male-dominated environments, they discuss the stress involved. Rowena, a management consultant, is proud of *Grace*'s achievements as a geologist:

> *Rowena*: At the same time as being jealous of her, I've been very, very proud of her as well, very proud of her. That she went into very much a man's world . . . [. . .] I felt immensely proud of her . . . that there she was travelling, proud, at the same time jealous, because I felt I couldn't have done it myself, to have travelled alone. And then she ended up in Alaska and she's never come back since.

Rowena was not positioned as an older sister and did not experience herself as a minimother, reminiscent of Clare's description of *Stella* not being an older sister to her. Rowena was not the older sister who looked after *Grace*: they did not have a 'leading relationship'; *Grace* 'looked after herself'. As these counterexamples indicate, older sisters do not automatically become minimothers.

Rowena paused in her narrative to consider patterns of silence and exchange among different family members. She acknowledged her option to disclose or withhold personal, sensitive emotional information to *Grace*. She became more aware of these options during the interview as she mulled over her silence to *Grace* and other kin about a recent operation:

> *Rowena*: I haven't told my sister er . . . I mean until I said that now, it hadn't occurred to me a) that I hadn't told her and b) that I might tell her, I mean I haven't actually told my mother either. The only person I've told in my family is my older brother, er . . . but then, that's actually because I hadn't seen my mother . . . and in fact, I've almost avoided ringing her, just because . . . for one period, I ∧∧ very much feared telling her. Anyway, I shall see her this weekend and I shall probably tell her this weekend. Yes . . .

A recent significant change that had occurred in Rowena's life in connection with motherhood was her decision to give up working. With support from mainly non-kin, her changing subjectivity emerged outside the context of her sister tie:

> *Rowena*: I'm in a bit of a limbo, at the moment I've got no desire to go back to work. I thought at one point, I could never give up work, er . . .

but that's all the identity the work gives you, was too important to me, but things have changed.

She contrasts herself to *Grace* in terms of decision-making, describing *Grace* as more 'grounded' and self-sufficient, able to make decisions alone, whereas Rowena experiences herself as more indecisive and needing to bounce ideas off others:

> *Rowena*: Something about that thing of self-sufficiency as being . . . standing on your own two feet and not depending on . . . others.

Another important facet of Rowena's subjectivity is her identity as a parent: she comments on how she and her friends have become parents at a similar time while *Grace* remains child-free. Hence, she discusses parenting issues more with her friends and mother than with her sister. Aware of the geographical distance, she speculates that if *Grace* has children, the cousins will have little contact.

However, one crack that Rowena discerns in the exterior that *Grace* presents to the world is her sensitivity about body size. When Rowena overheard someone call her 'fat Gracie', she realised that *Grace* might be jealous of Rowena's slighter build:

> *Rowena*: There was a big thing about, 'I'm happy the way I am you know'. She gives off this exterior of being very happy the way she is and of being very self-sufficient. And I've always presumed she is, but sometimes, occasionally maybe there's a crack, and this fatness thing is maybe a bit of a crack, I don't know.

These comments reflect Rowena's gradual understanding of *Grace*'s subjectivity, more fragile than it appears, in contrast with the 'self-sufficiency' that she exudes.

Recalling the past, Rowena's narrative combines reminiscences and recent reflections on family relationships. She notes how aspects of the present can 'spark off' memories, especially the replication of familiar patterns. Her awareness of parallels between past and present in relation to her parenting makes her avoid comparing her children in order not to foster competitiveness. Motherhood and sibling rivalry books have prompted her to revisit early conflict in her sistering. As a parent, she wants 'to break the cycle', just as Suzanne, in Chapter 4, mentioned regarding her two daughters.

Rowena's contradictory feelings towards *Grace* encompass not minding the lack of closeness, yet feeling sad about this absence as *Grace* is 'somebody I go back to year dot with'. While aspiring to greater intimacy and contact, she acknowledges that over the years their bond has been stretched and not always positive.

These *distant companionships* reveal silences and gaps related to jealousy and geographical distance in Rowena and *Grace*'s case, and physical disability and difference in Clare and *Stella*'s tie. In both, there is either little change, change in the form of increased distance, which the sisters do not discuss, or change, in their individual subjectivities outside their tie.

Emotions, talk and silence

The emotions of sistering – anger, jealousy, sadness, possessiveness, appreciation and joy – reverberate throughout these narratives. Talk, silence and emotions all mould these changing ties. Emotions encompass the range of feelings that sisters experience about each other, their sistering, and their relationships with other kin and friends. The significance of emotions, in addition to contact, and talk – in sisters' discussions in their lives *and* in the research narratives – lies in their role in constructing different forms of sistering, and knowledge about these. As Coates (1996: 263) says about friendship: 'Talking with friends is constitutive of friendship; through talking, we do "being friends"'. Sister talk encompasses a range of topics from emotions and the body – sexuality and health – to 'everyday talk' and work, in a variety of styles: bickering, teasing, having a giggle, gossiping, confiding, asking and giving advice, and listening. There was also 'catching up', playful and serious talk (Coates 1996: 285).

Talk, and its absence, characterise each of these case studies. Rae and Bukhi's talks during Bukhi's break-up with her boyfriend led to greater understanding between them. Bukhi stressed her desire to be listened to rather than being told what to do, and her contradictory wish for both honesty and not wanting to feel upset by what she hears. She describes this form of listening as support:

> *Bukhi*: At other times it just sort of goes backwards and forwards and I'll have some sort of . . . I mean I split up with my boyfriend the year before last and I was in a real mess. I didn't know what I was doing and Rae was really good then, because she didn't . . . it seemed like, instead of her telling me what to do . . . Whereas before I felt like she'd tell me what to do, she was just listening to what I was saying and say well . . . you know, you could do this. But she wasn't really *telling* me what to do

and then I'd sort of say what I wanted to do and she'd say, yes fine. And basically I felt that everything I was saying I wanted to do, she was saying, that's fine, I'll just support you and that was all I needed.

Bukhi also wanted Rae to be more direct and open, to tell her when she was getting on her nerves:

Bukhi: I was just annoyed with her I was just fed up with ... I think I felt that she wasn't being honest with me all the time and I was saying, you don't er ... you don't seem to tell me when I'm getting on your nerves whereas I can tell you and ... I said ... I just basically said to her, you get on my nerves because you're so nice all the time and I just don't believe somebody can be like that, I just don't believe that that's normal. And of course, she got really upset and then ... and that was exactly what I didn't want to do, so we just ended up half-shouting at each other and she was just really, really upset and I just felt so guilty and I don't think I quite managed to say what I wanted to say. – Do *you* understand what I'm saying now? [little laugh] I think all I was trying to say was that ... I just wish you'd tell me if I got on your nerves or if you didn't want me to do something or ... whereas I didn't feel that she was doing. Whereas I suppose you don't, I don't think you do it with anyone *do* you, [to] be completely honest but I felt that because it was my sister, that you could sort of say ... you know ... you're being a complete idiot. And I suppose it's hard to say that to someone without upsetting them. But then, I suppose ... now, it's a bit better because we do talk about things like that but it's all really good. [...] I think I went through a stage where I felt that she wasn't being honest with me about what she thought I was doing, what I was doing or what she really thought. And I suppose she couldn't win because I suppose if she had been honest I probably would have just ... gone spare or something.

And in Chloe and Annabel's *best friendship*, a new kind of talk about emotions which played a vital part in bringing them closer together developed between them in their teens. Simultaneously, their bond evolved and moved out of the *positioned* into the *shifting positions* discourse. And talk between Leila and *Annar* led to their rapprochement as thirty-somethings after years of distance.

In *distant companionship*, silence is the more pervasive feature illustrated by Rowena and *Grace*, and Clare and *Stella*'s ties. Central aspects of their sistering remain unspoken – Rowena's jealousy and sadness at the geographical distance, Clare's disability and its construction of difference over the decades. Occasionally, these silences surface in the actual interview. The taboo topic of boyfriends was broached between Eve (18), Celia (16) and Amy (13). This embarrassing moment revealed Celia's resentment towards Eve, as the eldest, for never raising the issue, thereby making it impossible for Celia to mention it or for them to compare notes:

Celia: I do tell Eve a lot about myself, don't I Eve? I mean I will come in and jump and say

Eve: Mm, but I never get it all.

MM: You know that?

Eve: I know quite well that she's going to stop to ask something, I'll ask a leading question maybe and then she'll shut up.

Celia: Yeah, yeah, yeah, yeah, um yeah.

Eve: It's very closed.

Celia: It's not all my fault, you don't tell me everything either, do you?

Eve: No. [laughs]

Celia: I've never known about any man in your life!

After touching on their intense privacy surrounding hetero/sexuality, they puzzled over its meaning as the interview drew to a close:

Celia: No, I shall get out and say, 'God! I wish you'd told me that before', I, really

Eve: Yeah.

Celia: And so you should have. Oh God! It's really really good for our relationships.

Eve: Yeah.

Celia: Just to say, 'Ah, I didn't realise you felt like that!'

Eve: So tell us about, you know.

Celia: Tell me.

Acknowledging the taboo was restricted to the interview. Eve and Celia recognise their silence explicitly, but this exchange is merely an interlude, not necessarily marking a new stage in their relationship.

Silence need not have such a potentially disruptive effect. Alice (36) referring to her bonds with her four sisters explains positive silences:

> *Alice*: [. . .] so it's just chit-chat really, nothing um, and sometimes we don't talk at all really, because there's nothing to say! [laughs] But there is nothing uncomfortable about that silence. It's just, you know, that, that's how it is.

Emotions, talk and silence underlie the caring and power 'practices' (Morgan 1996: 188) through which sistering take shapes materially. Different experiences of these practices lead to distinct forms of friendship, companionship and feminine subjectivity. The intersections between changing subjectivity and these practices illustrate how subjectivity is experienced materially as well as discursively through the *positioned* and *shifting positions* discourses.

Conclusion

This chapter has established links between power relations, through the *positioned* and *shifting positions* discourses, changing subjectivity, and the role of emotions, talk and silence in sistering. Change in sistering occurs through women's experiences of power relations, their reflections and emotions about these and ability to name them. It is through power, emotions and language – the naming or 'verbal bodies of acknowledged knowledge' (Smith, cited in Stanley and Wise 1990: 34) – that women acquire knowledge about their experiences, act upon it (movement) or not (immobility). Their emotional response to their insights and perceptions vary. Some women feel unhappy and sadder than others do about their knowledge and understanding. Chloe and Annabel became best friends after Annabel ceased acting as the dominant sister and their tie moved out of the *positioned* discourse. This change occurred after she and her girlfriend Danielle grew distant. Can sisters be located in the *positioned* discourse and be best friends? Probably not, as illustrated by the strain Annabel experienced when positioned as Danielle's minder during her best friend's breakdown. These moves in and out of the two discourses occur partly through the emotions that sistering gives rise to and women's interpretations of their significance, and partly through verbalising or silencing their meanings.

The chapter examined the extent to which subjectivity changes within or outside sistering. Comparisons between four case studies reveal distinct patterns, which emerge in the links between different types of tie, *best friendship* and *companionship*; feminine subjectivities; and material practices of caring and power made up of emotions, talk and silence. Rae and Bukhi's, and Chloe and Annabel's *best friendships* illustrate agentic change, in this instance connected, respectively, with motherhood and the loss of a boyfriend, and the loss of a girlfriend. In both cases, positive and negative changes happened which the sisters discussed. In Clare and Stella's, and Rowena and *Grace's distant companionships*, changing subjectivity occurred against a background of on-going features – jealousy, geographical separation and physical disability. It developed outside their sistering, in other contexts and relationships. The distant companions, although they clearly reflect on their sistering in their narratives, unlike the sister best friends, are not reflexive about it with each other. They are also less happy in their sistering relationships.

Conclusion

Sistering occurs within the social and cultural context of femininity and its prescriptions, notably caring. Like mothering and daughtering, sistering is characterised by caring, power relationships and elements of friendship. This book shows how inextricably connected power and caring become in intimate relationships – as sources of control and regulation as well as of nurturing and autonomy. These case studies offer a collective testimony about an invisible aspect of femininity in women's everyday lives – their experience of being a sister and of sistering. One of this book's aims is to create new knowledge about a marginalised aspect of female culture, based on women's own words and emotions. Another is to identify the different forms that sistering can take and explore their meanings among a small, fairly homogeneous group of women. What has emerged is the absence of rules or explicit expectations in this tie and the need for these to be defined and renegotiated as they evolve over time. As a result, I have generated a specific vocabulary for naming and interpreting women's sistering experiences. My intention is that readers will add their own terms to this vocabulary and that this process will lead to further thinking about the family – as a key site where gendered identities develop. Finally, I intend this book to contribute to change in how we live our lives: new understandings can inspire sisters to rewrite family scripts.

Part of my project is to argue that sistering is as fundamental as mothering and daughtering in the construction of feminine subjectivity. The different subject positions that are available for girls and women to take up, such as best friend, close or distant companion, minimother or cared-for sister through practices of caring and power relations, are closely connected to what it means to be feminine in our culture.[1] These subject positions permeate each other and can coexist within a relationship as sisters move from one position to another at a single moment in time òr over decades. In this way the book documents the complexity of what it means to be a sister, and the difficulty of modifying meanings and patterns of sistering which women and significant others around them assume to be fixed. How can and do sisters rewrite their family scripts?

One way in which sistering alters as women grow older stems from circumstances beyond their control external to their tie. When young women like Roxanne and Madonna evolve from best friends in their teens to distant companions as adults, or vice versa, as in the case of Leila and *Annar*, this type of change is connected to circumstances external to the relationships. Turning-points and life-events influenced the oscillating patterns of dependence and independence between them. Bereavement and divorce in their families altered the shape of their sistering. Other sisters, such as Chloe and Annabel, Rae and Bukhi, and Suzanne mentioned different key moments leading to transitions, such as changing school, acquiring and losing girlfriends and boyfriends, leaving home, starting work and becoming a mother. The main factors accounting for the process of relationships changing over time were age and life-stage.

In contrast to these unexpected changes, another way that sistering alters is through internal shifts triggered by factors additional to age and life-stage: fluctuating power relations and subjectivity. Subjectivity, explored empirically, is embedded in emotions, talk and silence, as well as in the women's reflexive knowledge about their own and their sister's trajectories. This material and discursive self is potentially independent and self-determining while simultaneously embedded in kinship ties. The case studies document how subjectivities can bring about change, distance or connection, by mapping their formation and transformation through shifting power relations. These internal changes occur when sisters move in or out of minimothering and the cared for position and swap roles, with varied outcomes in different cases. Hazel and Phoebe, and Suzanne and *Collette* were far happier with their role-reversal than Madonna and Roxanne. This study illuminates how subjectivities are made up of 'a conjunction of diverse social practices produced and positioned socially, without an underlying essence' (Lather 1988: 577).

Women spoke eloquently of their reactions and feelings about their changing subjectivities and sister ties. Some felt happy with or accepting of their sistering while grappling with their own subjectivity: Bukhi recovering from the break-up with her boyfriend, Alice ambivalent about her singledom, or Jeanne anxious to resist being both 'mothered' and 'mothering'. Jeanne was struggling with her subjectivity and yet accepting of her complex and difficult ties with her sisters. Madonna and

Roxanne, and Clare, on the contrary, felt happy with their subjectivity and uncertain about some of their sister ties. Some women felt perplexed about their subjectivity and their sister tie: Beth had mixed feelings about her minimothering and wanted to feel closer to Louise. Others felt confident about both their subjectivity and their sistering – Hazel and Phoebe, Rae, Leila, Leonie, Suzanne, and Louise. Subjectivity, significantly, evolves within and outside sistering. Sister best friends are more likely to develop their subjectivity within sistering, whereas for distant companions their subjectivity is more likely to flourish through friendship or other kin ties.

The book extends research on family life and, as Morgan (1996) suggests, offers a more complex appreciation of the interrelationships between different levels of power in the context of domestic ties. This attempt to theorise intimate relations of control and subordination leads to an understanding of the processes of change and variation, as well as of stability and continuity in family relationships. Furthermore, this study contributes to a sociology of family relations that 'still requires accounts that [. . .] allow for the possibility of change through human agency' (Morgan 1996: 8). It is women's emotions and subjectivity as rational actors, which guide their agency – actions to bring about change. The book also adds to our understanding of a same-sex tie. The focus on caring, power relations and formations of subjectivity make it relevant for exploring other socially invisible bonds and support networks among lesbians, gays and even brothers in their private lives.

This book charts continuity and change in sistering. The variety and fluidity of sister ties in women's lives elucidates a hidden dimension of changing family forms and postmodern families. While not the only possible reading of the women's narratives, it is one of several potential interpretations in keeping with the postmodern project which challenges and rejects 'the lust for authoritative accounts' (Lather 1988: 577) in the deconstruction of the 'totalising discourse' (ibid.) and the power relations inherent therein. The case studies reflect a specific group's experiences – women who have active sister relationships – and may have limited relevance for other types of involvement between sisters. Nevertheless, the importance of new family forms and transformations in intimate ties, including sistering, indicate a greater affirmation of non-sexual ties. This is the result of demographic, economic and social changes including the demise of marriage and traditional gender roles (Thorne 1992; Stacey 1992).

One issue that arises in the context of these social and gender transformations concerns the nature of biological kin ties: are they more dependable than fragile sexual relationships or friendship? The association of biology with images of stability or permanence is especially visible in sistering. To what extent is there anything unique or essential to sistering? The myth about sisters, and kin ties more generally, that 'blood is thicker than water' carries the idea that biological bonds invoke stronger loyalty than other non-kin ties – that kin will 'come through' in times of hardship. Yet narratives of sistering reveal a more complex picture than what the myth indicates. While several women experience the myth as reality, others question it and see little direct link between the biological dimension of sistering and its quality and role in their lives. Nevertheless, the myth about sisters' bonding has been attractive and significant for the discourses and practices of female friendship, political lesbianism and feminist activism reflected in debates about 'sisterhood'. In fiction and popular culture, ideas of sorority and fraternity have influenced representations of same-sex friendship ties as well as those between lesbians and gay men (Cartmell *et al.* 1998).

Challenging the myth about sisterly bonding opens up a space for rethinking sistering as a socially constructed tie. This exploration of the contradictory absence and visibility of the sister myth and sister ties in politics and fiction is set against the ongoing debate about how biological ties are socially constructed. Challenging the notion of the family as a biological entity, feminists such as VanEvery (1995) question beliefs that living arrangements are immutable or biological. Instead, they argue that families are socially and historically constructed. I want to suggest that sistering is socially constructed just as feminists emphasise that the social organisation of intimacy, sexuality, reproduction, friendship, mothering, fathering, the sexual division of labour and gender are. Kin bonds, 'fictive kin' and a 'love ethic' form part of a new culture of intimacy, created rather than given.[2] In the case of biological sisters' private lives, as we have seen however, this new ethic of negotiation often exists more as a possibility, its potential overshadowed by complex emotions, and entrenched discourses and practices of caring and power relationships. Interestingly, several interventions in health promotion, social and welfare work apply this notion of sistering as socially constructed in an attempt to recreate aspects of the tie in specific social contexts.[3]

This re-creation of a familial tie in social settings raises crucial issues about its construction as both biological and social. I investigated sistering as a socially constructed bond in order to understand its formation and evolution. Sistering, similarly to mothering, constitutes a form of 'social reproduction' which includes 'the activities and attitudes, behaviours and emotions, responsibilities and relationships directly involved in the maintenance of life on a daily basis and intergenerationally' (Laslett and Brenner 1989). These activities, including care, are organised in and outside households and networks of kin: all this labour is structured by gender. However, the biological connection can be significant, for example, in relation to hereditary diseases. Full discussion of the biological *and* social construction of the tie – an issue fiercely debated in the context of work on the sociology of the emotions, the body, health and illness (Bendelow and Williams 1998) – lies beyond the scope of this book.

Feminist politics is another realm where the notion of sistering as socially constructed is influential. Several of the women refer to the impact of feminism in their thinking and attitudes not just to their sisters but also to other female ties – with girlfriends and mothers. Some aspire to 'sisterly' bonds with women generally. What are the links between private sistering, a bond whose qualities are both invoked and yet decried as oppressive, and 'sisterhood', its public form in the sphere of feminist politics? It may be possible to bridge gaps and divides of difference and power inequalities in both private sistering experiences and the public sphere of feminist politics through similar processes. Bonds can potentially be created across differences in feminist politics, similarly as for relationships based on biological ties – by acknowledging these differences, voicing and working with them.

Turning from 'sisters in private' to 'political sisters',[4] we find that terms connected to sistering and friendship provide distinct metaphors of political solidarity. Trawling through this terminology reveals a fascination with the power of associations around *sister* to connote women united in spite of their differences. The Spanish *hermana* for sister conveys the sympathy and practical support offered by siblings and close friends; while *compañera* or comrade suggests egalitarian companionship in political struggle and partnership; and *sister* also has a political resonance (Lugones and Rosezelle 1995). *Sister* used in a religious context denotes a constructed familial and political tie based on race not blood in the history of resistance to slavery in the African American community. In the white Anglo context, it refers to an egalitarian kinship tie of bonding, trust, affection and reciprocity – possibly an attempt to recreate the support networks of some black kinship groups. These distinctions indicate the varied political meanings of *sister*.

Yet friendship potentially offers a more realistic political metaphor of women's solidarity than sisterhood. 'Pluralist friendship' suggests the possibility of women bonding across differences and committed to 'perceptual changes' in the knowledge of the other (Lugones and Rosezelle

1995: 141). This utopian vision, of neither an institutional, legal nor unconditional bond, can encompass plural realities and selves who are differently positioned, yet are difficult to sustain in practice. A more attainable goal is that of 'compañerismo', or 'comradeliness' which captures more successfully the importance of acknowledging difference in the political realm than do images of sisters, sistering or sisterhood. Perhaps this goal is also relevant for women's private lives with their sisters. Possibly, this investigation of sistering more than the simple celebration of sisterhood will allow a reinvigorated return to values and ideas that have motivated the political activism and cultural work of women.

Overcoming differences through 'verbal bodies of acknowledged knowledge' (Stanley and Wise 1990: 34) provides a key element in both women's personal lived experience as sisters and in the public arena of political sisterhood. Other feminists also abandon the notion of a female 'nirvana' (Hey 1997: 126). Although Hey recognises that girlfriendship provides some form of escape from invisibility in the male domain of schooling, she 'ultimately refuses the notion of a 'better' because 'feminine' culture by attending to the real material difficulties and differences which girls' relations articulate' (Hey 1997: 36). 'The difficulty for girls,' Hey says, 'is that of seeking out empowering places within regimes alternately committed to denying subordination or celebrating it' (Hey 1997: 132).

The postmodern and auto/biographical accounts of subjectivity in this book suggest that tensions within sistering can illuminate our understanding of the interaction between subject and society, in this case between an autonomous self and one embedded in family networks. This auto/biographical perspective reveals internal changes within sistering as well as the interaction between these ties and changing subjectivities. I analysed this process through notions of power relations and discourses rather than structures, and subjectivity and positionings rather than agency alone. Here subjectivity is embedded in change and positionality rather than resistance.

This book documents the possibility for shifting feminine subjectivities to emerge inside and outside sistering, both a confining and a supportive space. With its focus on agentic subjectivity and power dynamics in the context of changing sister relationships, the book shows how women grapple with contradictory sistering subject positions: 'they invest in some, reject others, create their own meanings for the choices they make, and position themselves in hierarchies' (Usher 1996: 140). This exploration of sistering maps a neglected experience, a hidden culture and its pre-eminence as a source of feminine subjectivity.

Appendix I: The Sisters

A brief description of the participants is provided in this appendix. Names and some geographical and biographical details have been changed in order to protect the identity of the women. Names in italics refer to participants' sisters who did not take part in the research. Details of how I found these 37 girls and women are provided in Appendix II. The participants fall into four age groups (except for the youngest, aged 6 and the eldest, aged 50): sisters in their teens, twenties, thirties and forties.

Teenage sisters

Hilda and Adrienne

I interviewed Hilda (age 9) and Adrienne (age 12) together. They live with their mother who is single, a mature student and works part-time. Hilda goes to a small girls' primary school; Adrienne, until recently, attended a local state school and is about to go to an independent secondary school. The important people and relationships they refer to are: Hilda's best friend Gwen, her ex-best friend Juliette and her special friends. One of Adrienne's ex-best friends is Sultan, her other friends are Hilary and Lamia. Their 'mutual people' include two different sets of cousins. Their relationship is one of *close companionship* with elements of *best friendship*. They are white English and middle-class.

Judith and Nicole

I interviewed Judith (age 16) and Nicole (age 10) together. They live with their parents, who both work full-time. The sisters attend different schools and have distinct social networks. They enjoy different leisure activities and do few of them together. Nicole is more lively than her older sister. Judith has a Saturday job and is studying for GCSEs. They argue frequently and talk openly about the differences between them. They do not have a confiding relationship partly, in their eyes, owing to the age gap. Their relationship is one of *distant companionship*. They are white English and working-class.

Eve, Celia, Amy and Isabel

I spoke to Eve (age 18), Celia (age 16) and Amy (age 13) together in a small group discussion. I interviewed their younger sister Isabel (age 6) separately. They live with their parents, apart from Eve, who has recently left home to work in a nearby city. Eve is about to study for a degree and her younger sisters are at school. Their parents both work in local government. The sisters pursue sporting and musical activities. Important people in their network include grandparents, cousins, neighbours and school friends. The ties between them are of *close companionship*. They are white English and middle-class.

Zoë, Sofia and *Gita*

Zoë (age 17), and Sofia (age 16) are the eldest daughters in an Asian family of three sisters, their younger sister *Gita* is 9. I interviewed them together. Zoë had a tendency to dominate and talk more than Sofia. They live in an Asian neighbourhood of their city with their parents and *Gita*. Their mother used to work as a nurse; their father is an artist. Zoë is at college doing a business course and Sofia is studying for A-levels. The important people in their lives include their parents and their friends. They are close to their cousin-brother Ranjeet (age 21) and cousin-sister Manjeet (age 17) who live in a different city. Zoë and Sofia's relationship is one of *best friendship*. They are British Asian and working-class.

Sisters in their twenties

Chloe and Annabel; *Vicki* and *Gemma*

I spoke to Chloe and Annabel (age 20), the only twins in the study, together. Chloe is training to be a midwife and Annabel is studying for a degree. Now that they live in different towns they see each other less than when they were schoolgirls. They are both single. The important people in their lives include their two older sisters *Vicki* (age 29) and *Gemma* (age 28), who live in other towns, Annabel's ex-best friend Danielle (who is a year older), Chloe's best friend Medina and a mutual friend of theirs, Emily, whose mother died when they were at school. Annabel knows several friends in different circles. The men in their lives include Louis, Annabel's most recent ex-boyfriend, and Paul and Robert, Chloe's most recent ex-boyfriends. Their relationship is one of *best friendship*. They are white English and middle-class.

Revi, Vandana and *Shari*

I interviewed Revi (age 21) and Vandana (age 25) together. They are the eldest in an Asian family of five siblings. Their younger sister *Shari* (age 17), two brothers and parents live in the Middle East. Revi and Vandana are both married to Asian men, who have lived in the UK for over a decade and work full-time. The sisters, both mothers with a toddler each, have been living in the UK for three and two years respectively. They live in adjacent neighbourhoods in the same city. Revi is a home-maker and lives with her husband and child. Vandana is studying part-time at a local college and lives with her husband and in-laws in an extended family. The important people in their lives are their children, husbands, their sister *Shari* and a few girlfriends. They are *best friends*. They are Asian Pakistani and working-class.

Beth and Louise

I spoke to Beth (age 27) first and Louise (age 22) several months later. The sisters live in different towns in England. Louise has just completed her degree and Beth is training to be a dentist. Their parents are Scottish though the family home is in the north of England. Their brother Colin (age 24) is temporarily living with Beth and her partner. Louise lives with her boyfriend. Their relationship is one of *distant companionship*. The sisters are white Scottish, of working-class origin and now middle-class.

Mildred, Frieda, *Jane*, *May* and *Sarah*

I interviewed Mildred (age 26) and Frieda (age 24) together in the house they share with two men. They are the eldest in a closely knit family. Their sisters *Jane* (age 21), *May* (age 19) and *Sarah* (age 18) all live in different cities. They all meet up regularly at family reunions with their parents. Mildred, an arts administrator, is single and Frieda, training to be a nurse, has a boyfriend, Philip. Mildred and Frieda describe their relationship as one of *best friendship*. They are white English and middle-class.

Suzanne and *Collette*

I interviewed Suzanne (age 29) alone. She lives with her partner Frank and two daughters, Juliet (age 5) and Helen (age $2\frac{1}{2}$). She is a full-time mother and Frank works full-time as a builder. Her sister *Collette* (age 25) lives in the same neighbourhood and they have almost daily contact. *Collette* used to work in a community centre and now works with her mother in a nearby café. *Collette* is a single mother and has a son Tristan (age 10), and a boyfriend. Suzanne plans to embark on a training course for women to become a gardener. The important people in Suzanne's social network are *Collette* and their mother. Her father died when she was a teenager. After a turbulent relationship with *Collette* when they were teenagers, they are now *best friends*. She is white English and working-class.

Rae, Bukhi and *Mira*

I first interviewed Rae (age 30) and later her sister Bukhi (age 25) although their preference was to talk to me together. Rae is the eldest in a family of four siblings. Rae and Bukhi live in different areas of the same city after having moved away from their home town where their parents and siblings still live. They are less close to their brother San (age 29), married with two children, and their sister *Mira* (age 22) who still lives with their parents. *Mira* has just completed a degree, works part-time and has a boyfriend Ricky. Bukhi feels sad that she and *Mira* are less close than they used to be when Bukhi still lived at home. Rae is married and has a daughter, Sasha (age 1). She is a decorator and sculptress. Bukhi is single, studying for a degree, works part-time and lives with her best friend Nina and Nina's husband. When Bukhi moved to the city, she lived with Rae and her family temporarily before finding a place of her own. Their relationship is one of *best friendship*. They are of mixed British Asian parentage and middle-class.

Sisters in their thirties

Hazel and Phoebe

I interviewed Hazel (age 34) first and Phoebe (age 35) several months later. They live in different nearby towns. Phoebe trained as a health visitor and works as a playgroup leader. She is married, with two children (age 6 and 8) and pregnant. Hazel trained as a beautician, and is currently a mature student. She is divorced and lives with her new partner and three children from her marriage (age 6, 11, 14). She described herself as a housewife/part-time student. Phoebe is the eldest of four siblings: their half-brother Oliver (age 30) lives near Phoebe with their mother; their younger half-sister *Denise* died at 19. Phoebe and Hazel's father left the family when they were toddlers and their stepfather died when they were children. Their mother raised the family single-handed. The sisters see each other with their children and at family gatherings, rarely as a twosome. They speak on the phone fortnightly, not out of duty, just to see how the other is. They visit each other by train as neither has easy access to a car. Phoebe has more frequent contact with their mother than Hazel. Their relationship is one of *best friendship* with elements of *close companionship*. They are white English and working-class.

Rowena and *Grace*

I spoke to Rowena (age 37) alone. Her sister *Grace* (age 34) works in Alaska where she has lived for the last decade. The sisters have three brothers (age 40, 30 and 28). Rowena lives with her husband (age 50) and her three children (age 8, 5, 3). Rowena's parents live in a nearby town and she sees them regularly. Rowena is a management consultant and *Grace*, a geologist who lives with her *de facto*. Rowena described herself as 'a temporary full-time mother'. They are not a close family. The sisters see each other infrequently and do not maintain close contact. When they were growing up Rowena's relationship with *Grace* was one of competitiveness and is now one of *distant companionship*. Rowena is close to her cousin Aysha and several female friends. She is white English and middle-class.

Lauren, *Muriel*, *Shirley* and *Marie*

Lauren (age 37) is the eldest in a family of five siblings. She has a brother Paul (age 31) and three sisters: Muriel (age 36), Shirley (age 34) and Marie (age 30). I spoke to Lauren only. She is a solicitor, a single mother and lives with her son Ryan (age 3) in England far from her siblings who all live in Wales, where she grew up. She is the only one among her siblings not to be married. They each have two children. Her brother Paul is a waiter, *Danielle* is unemployed and setting up her own business, *Shirley* is an infant school teacher, *Marie* works in a textile factory. Lauren and Ryan have regular contact with Ryan's father and with Lauren's family. Ryan spends his holidays with Lauren's parents and siblings, in spite of the distance between their respective homes. The other important people in Lauren's life are her women friends. Lauren's sibling relationships are *close companionships*. She is white Welsh, comes from a working-class family and is now middle-class.

Eliza, Alice, *Diane*, Rosemary and *Joy*

I spoke to Eliza (age 38), Alice (age 36) and Rosemary (age 30) separately. They approached their two other sisters, *Diane* (age 31) and *Joy* (age 28), who decided not to take part in the study. The five sisters all live in the same city. They all get on and see each other regularly. Eliza and Alice are both accountants and Rosemary is a physiotherapist. *Diane* and *Joy* both have professional jobs. All the sisters live with partners except for Alice who is single; *Joy*, the youngest, is about to get married. Eliza is the only mother: she and her partner Pete have two sons, Chris (age 5) and Andrew (age 1). Their social networks are very entwined: Alice works with Eliza's partner Pete; and Pete and Rosemary's partner D.J. together. Their relationships are ones of *close companionship*. They are Black British and middle-class.

Sisters in their thirties and forties

Leonie, Jeanne, Roxanne and Madonna

Leonie (age 48), Jeanne (age 45), Roxanne (age 39) and Madonna (age 31) are four sisters in a family of seven siblings. Their brothers figure marginally in their narratives: one lives in England, one abroad and the whereabouts of the third are vague. I interviewed Roxanne first and she then approached her sisters about taking part. Roxanne and Leonie live in two adjacent towns and their mother lives in the same urban area. Their father died almost a decade ago. Jeanne and Madonna live in the same town in a different part of England. Leonie, the eldest, is a seamstress, divorced with two sons, and her eldest has just left home. Roxanne is a college lecturer and Jeanne is a family doctor. They are both divorced: Roxanne lives with her daughter Lucille (age 12) and new partner Trevor; Jeanne lives with her son Dylan (age 13) and new partner Thomas. Madonna, the youngest, is training to be a singer, single and lives in a shared house. The relationships between them vary between *distant* and *close companionship*. They are white English, originally from a working-class family and now middle-class.

Anne, Flora, *Hailey* and *Diana*

I spoke to Anne (age 38) first and Flora (age 40) a few months later. They live in different towns in the same part of England. Anne is single, Flora is married and lives with Rupert and their two daughters (Clara age 13) and (Josephine age 8). Anne is a writer and Flora a theatre director. They are the eldest in a family of four daughters. Their sister *Hailey* (age 33) is single and lives in the north of Ireland where the family come from. *Diana* (age 30) is married and works in Europe. Anne and Flora are not very intimate yet they see each other the most, owing to geography, usually with Flora's children, as well as at family gatherings. Their relationship is one of *close companionship*. They are white Irish and middle-class.

Sisters in their forties

Leila and *Annar*

I interviewed Leila (age 40) alone and not *Annar* (age 38). They live in different neighbourhoods of the same town. Leila is single, *Annar* lives with her husband and three children (age 10, 7 and 2). Leila trained to be an optician and *Annar*, a nurse. They are the youngest in a family of six siblings: they have four older brothers. They were raised and educated in the Middle East and Britain. Their father died a few years ago and their mother is still alive. After a distant and competitive relationship from their teens to their thirties, Leila and *Annar* now have a 'sisterly' relationship of *best friendship* even though they do not have a lot in common. Leila is Asian Indian and middle-class.

Carmen and *Rita*

Carmen (age 47) is the eldest in a family of six siblings. When she finished school, she left Puerto Rico and came to the UK. She is single, works as a secretary and personal assistant and lives with her two sons (age 14 and 8). Her sister *Rita* (age 33) is 14 years younger, works as a secretary and lives in Madrid with her husband and two daughters. Carmen left home at 18 when *Rita* was 4 and they picked up their relationship when *Rita* moved to Europe in her early twenties. Three of her four brothers (Clark, Montgomery, Gene) live abroad; the fourth (Lawrence) lives in the same city as Carmen. His late wife – her sister-in-law Ellen, who died four years ago (age 42) – became her best friend. The other significant people in her network include her neighbour Moira and her cousin Teresa (age 48), with whom Carmen is closer than with her sister. Carmen and *Rita*'s tie is one of *distant companionship*. She is Black of mixed Caribbean parentage and middle-class.

Sisters in their fifties

Clare and *Stella*

I interviewed Clare (age 50) on her own, *Stella* (age 52) did not take part in the study. Clare is the middle child in a Scottish family of three siblings. She lives with her dog Ruby, works as an urban, freelance journalist and has a new boyfriend. *Stella*, a social worker, is married and lives with her husband and two children in a rural area in a different English region. Their brother (age 46) is married with three children and lives near *Stella*. The sisters rarely see each other, except at family events, and their tie is one of *distant companionship*. Clare's disability is neither acknowledged nor discussed in the family. Their widowed mother lives in the same county as *Stella*. The important people in Clare's network are her cousins Joan (age 45), Agatha (age 65) and Agatha's sister, Enid, who recently died (age 70), and her women friends. Clare is white Scottish and middle-class.

Appendix II: Method and Methodology

This appendix describes the way that I found the sample and its socio-demographic characteristics. It also outlines the different techniques that I used as part of the auto/biographical method, which enabled the women and I to talk about sistering. I was influenced by several principles of feminist methodology and I begin with these.

Feminist methodology

The study was carried out from a feminist theoretical perspective: feminist theory allows women's gendered subjectivity and sistering to be placed at the centre of women's lives.[1] I combined feminist standpoint theory, feminist post-structuralism and auto/biographical work in sociology in an 'eclectic project' (Maynard 1995) even if they do not easily coexist. Standpoint theory influenced the methodology of the study; auto/biography, the method of collecting and analysing the data; and both standpoint theory and post-structuralism, my epistemological and ontological positions.[2]

Grounded in Marxist concepts of class, ideology and economy, Dorothy Smith's (1988) materialist feminist standpoint theory posits a 'materialist conception of knowledge underlying the idea of a standpoint' (Bubeck 2000: 187). The idea of a standpoint, black or lesbian for example, is that women's experiences offer a different and even better perspective of the world. These form a basis for what Smith (1974: 11) calls 'situated' knowledges, which are socially and historically located. On the basis of these standpoints, Smith (1988) advocates a sociology for women which refutes knowledge as expertise in favour of knowledge derived from women's experiences. She visualises a form of knowledge that remains accessible to those who have contributed to its production. This new sociology 'would have the capability of continually opening up a different experience of the world, as women who have not yet spoken now speak' (Smith 1988: 222–3).

In this context, documenting women's lives from their own perspective then requires particular attention to method and methodology. Participatory methods during fieldwork and data analysis are considered valuable tools for creating knowledge from women's own standpoints while at the same time ensuring that respondents are treated with respect during the research (Reinharz 1992). Smith (1988) highlights the way that this conception of research facilitates the involvement of participants in the active construction and interpretation of the social processes and relations that constitute their lives. Reflexivity constitutes a central tenet of a feminist methodology whereby the researcher documents the production of knowledge and locates herself in this process for 'the subjectivity of the researcher herself is part of research production' (Harrison and Lyon 1993: 105).[3] I collected and analysed women's experiences according to five elements of feminist standpoint methodology: I paid attention to reflexivity, power relationships, participants' subjectivity, my subjectivity, and emotions. I have written elsewhere in more detail about my attempts to put these principles into practice (see Mauthner 2000; 1998).

Recruiting participants

The main characteristics defining the sample of women studied were their active sister status and their age. I wanted to speak to women who had some form of contact with at least one sister, even if infrequent. I limited the age of the participants to teenage and adult sisters. This project was designed to fill a gap in previous research, which focused on sister relationships in infancy, and among elderly women. As I wanted to chart changes and continuities in sister ties across women's lives I focused on four decades. All the women I spoke to, apart from three (Isabel age 6, Hilda age 9 and Clare age 50), were in their teens, twenties, thirties and forties.

Access routes

Finding women keen to talk about sistering presented challenges experienced by others researching families and friendship. I accessed the women through four routes. First, I contacted 18 women through snowballing from my own networks. Researchers investigating lone motherhood, mother and daughter-in-law ties, and divorce have also used snowballing (Duncan and Edwards 1998; Cotterill 1992; Vaughan 1987). I decided not to interview women whom I knew at first hand: my contacts put me in touch with other women at one step removed from me. Second, I interviewed two women from a project I was employed on at the time, who I knew had sisters and who I had already interviewed.[4] Third, I found four women in the health centre where I was recruiting for the same project. Fourth, I found 13 women by snowballing from participants to their sisters and in two cases, their friends. I adopted a flexible approach to the interviewing process like Cotterill (1994): I started out interviewing women individually and in pairs before interviewing related sisters, separately.

Limitations of the sample

This access route yielded a small purposive sample appropriate for an exploratory study. However, certain sister relationships are excluded, and others under-represented. Women who have no contact with their sisters are absent. Many of the 32 women I approached and who refused to participate probably declined for this reason. The reasons they gave included not having a sister, having a sister who lived abroad, lack of time or interest. The principal limitation of the sample is its homogeneity: it is predominantly white, urban, middle-class, heterosexual and biological. Certain types of relationships and women are under-represented: inactive sister ties, women with difficult or conflictual relationships, step relationships, black, working-class and non-heterosexual women. Although these exclusions were not intentional, accessing the sample through snowballing from my own networks inevitably contributed to its homogeneity. As a result, while class and ethnicity could have yielded rich insights into cultural differences (these are merely hinted at in some case studies – Zoë and Sofia, and Lauren and her sisters), the numbers of black, mixed-race and working-class women were too small to allow for this. The prime focus of the research was to chart sistering experiences through descriptions of some specific processes. Other forms and meanings of sistering among other women remain to be explored.

The women in the sample

The 37 women aged between 6 and 50 came from diverse geographical, socio-economic and ethnic backgrounds. They all lived in England. Twenty-six women were white; five, Asian; three, black Caribbean and three, black from mixed ethnic backgrounds. Twenty-seven were middle-class and ten working-class. In determining their class, I took several factors into account – education, housing and occupation – and assigned them to a class accordingly. I gave more importance to education and housing to younger sisters, and more importance to education and occupation to older employed women and mothers. Twenty women were single and 17 had a partner. All the women were heterosexual apart from one who was lesbian. Sixteen were mothers and 21, childfree (see Table AII.1). Their occupations and employment situations were varied (see Table AII. 2). They came from 19 family sets including nine all girl families and ten families of mixed siblings.

An auto/biographical method

The auto/biographical approach to studying lives was ideally suited to documenting a hidden aspect of female culture and mapping changes in sistering over time. Theories of auto/biography in sociology provided a method[6] with which to interview sisters and analyse their narratives of sistering. The term auto/biography refers to a recent move by sociologists to view auto/biography and biography as intermeshed rather than as separate activities. Stanley (1993; 1992; 1987) sees each as entertwined and inseparable and, for her, the research process includes elements of both the researcher and participants' biographies.[7] As a sister myself I brought aspects of my sistering experiences to the research, which I acknowledged with the women during the interviews. I experimented with distancing myself from them and disclosing to them until I felt comfortable mid way between these two positions (see Mauthner 1998).

Three other features of auto/biography influenced my interviewing technique: its focus on connections between the past and present, between the individual and the social, and between turning-points and changes across the life-course.[8] Linking past and present enabled me to place identity, emotions and memory and the link between individual experience and familial processes at the centre of personal accounts (see Griffiths 1995b; Evans 1993). This method allowed me to examine

Table AII.1: Summary of the sample

Class	Ethnicity	Marital Status	Sexual Identity	Mothering Status
27 middle-class	26 white	20 single	36 heterosexual	21 child-free
10 working-class	11 black/ Asian[5]	17 partnered	1 lesbian	16 mothers

Table AII.2:   Characteristics of the sample

Women	Adrienne	Alice	Amy	Annabel	Anne	Beth	Bukhi	Carmen	Celia
Age	12	36	13	20	38	27	25	47	16
Ethnicity	White	Black	White	White	White	White	Asian	Black	White
Nationality	English	British	English	English	Irish	Scottish	British	P. Rican	English
Class	Middle-class	Middle-class	Middle-class	Middle-class	Middle-class	Middle-class	Middle-class	Working-class	Middle-class
Education	Secondary school	BSc	Secondary school	A-levels	BA	BSc PhD part-time	A-levels	Higher National Diploma	Studying for GCSEs
Occupation	School pupil	Accountant	School pupil	Studying BA degree	Writer	Trainee dentist	Studying BA degree Part-time work	Mother Secretary and PA	School pupil

Women	Chloe	Eliza	Eve	Flora	Frieda	Hazel	Hilda	Isabel
Age	20	38	18	40	24	34	9	6
Ethnicity	White	Black	White	White	White	White	White	White
Nationality	English	British	English	Irish	English	English	English	English
Class	Middle-class	Middle-class	Middle-class	Middle-class	Middle-class	Working-class	Middle-class	Middle-class
Education	A-levels	BA	A-levels	MA	Nursing qualification	Trained as beautician	Primary school	Primary school
Occupation	Trainee midwife	Mother Accountant	Gap year travel and work prior to BA	Mother Theatre director	Trainee nurse	Mother Studying for GCSEs part-time	School pupil	School pupil

Women	Jeanne	Judith	Lauren	Leila	Leonie	Louise	Madonna	Mildred	Nicole
Age	45	16	37	40	48	22	31	26	10
Ethnicity	White	White	White	Asian	White	White	White	White	White
Nationality	English	English	Welsh	Indian	English	Scottish	English	English	English
Class	Middle-class	Working-class	Middle-class	Middle-class	Middle-class	Middle-class	Middle-class	Middle-class	Working-class
Education	BSc	Studying for GCSEs	BA	BSc	Left school at 15	BA	BA	BA	Primary school
Occupation	Mother Family doctor	School pupil Part-time work	Mother Solicitor	Optician	Mother Seamstress	Gap year travel/work post-BA	Training to be a singer	Arts administrator	School pupil

Women	Phoebe	Rae	Revi	Rosemary	Rowena	Roxanne	Sofia	Suzanne	Vandana	Zoë
Age	35	30	21	30	37	39	16	29	25	17
Ethnicity	White	Asian	Asian	Black	White	White	Asian	White	Asian	Asian
Nationality	English	British	Pakistani	British	English	English	British	English	Pakistani	British
Class	Working-class	Middle-class	Working-class	Middle-class	Middle-class	Middle-class	Working-class	Working-class	Working-class	Working-class
Education	Trained as health visitor	MA	Secondary School	Physiotherapy Diploma	BSc	MA	GCSEs	Left school at 16	Secondary School	GCSEs
Occupation	Mother Playgroup leader	Mother Decorator/sculptress	Mother Learning English as a second language	Physio-therapist	Management consultant	Mother FE College Lecturer	Studying for A-levels	Mother	Mother Part-time FE student	Studying at FE College

changes in individual women's lives and their sister relationships in the broader social context of transformations of intimacy informed by discourses and practices of caring and power relations. Lastly, auto/biography alerted me to connections, triggered by life-events, between changes in individual women's lives and change in their sistering experiences, and vice versa.

Auto/biographical work in sociology offered a method for collecting and interpreting the narratives. This method provides a conceptual link between the individual and the social, subjectivity and discourse: it incorporates and weaves together changes in individual subjectivity and in sistering. In this sense, auto/biography forms a lynchpin between the four discourses. As Morgan says, the strength of this approach enables us to understand the social through changing subjectivities:

> The growing interest in auto/biography shifts the attention away from the categories used to describe collectivities, structures or social institutions and towards a processual understanding of a social actor following a variety of careers or trajectories. [. . .] we have a fluid sense of a movement through and across a variety of statuses and identities. (Morgan 1996: 187–8)

While piloting this method I carried out two focus groups: one with a group of mature women students and another with three related teenage sisters. The first discussion generated many of the themes of the interview guide: exclusivity, 'duty' and 'caring', reciprocity, 'unconditional' emotion, selective memory and the difficulty of remembering past events, the taboo of sexuality, age differences, sadness and joy. The women talked about whether 'blood is thicker than water' which raises questions about how much sistering is a 'natural' biological or socially constructed phenomenon. I observed sister dynamics in the second group and how the girls encouraged each other to remember and jointly describe aspects of sistering (Kitzinger 1994). Groups were less suited to sisters in their thirties and forties. When I suggested this to one participant, she warned me of the danger of a group interview verging on 'family therapy' and she opted to talk to me alone. Her comment reflects the nature of the interview as a managed episode of social interaction (Holland and Ramazanoglu 1994). While the teenage discussion and subsequent pair interviews were useful for observing sister interactions and encouraging joint recollection, when the women spoke to me alone, they could reflect on their experiences in more depth and with more privacy.

The interviews

When I first contacted the women, I sent them an information sheet describing the research and an availability sheet for them to complete and return to me. At the start of the interview I reiterated the aims of the research. Finding participants was a lengthy process and required careful negotiation between sisters, my first contact and myself. I contacted participants' sisters only if both parties consented. Throughout I adopted a flexible approach: some women offered to contact their sisters on my behalf to request their participation, others preferred me to. I interviewed those women, whose sister(s) did not take part, either because she lived abroad, refused to participate or was not invited to by participants, *individually*. I spoke to other sisters together in *paired interviews* when they were willing and got on. In other cases I interviewed each member from a set of sisters *separately*. I gave all the women the option to talk to me with their sister(s). The combination of *individual*, *pair* and *separate* interviews reflects the different consent patterns according to age: older sisters were less willing to talk in pairs than teenagers or sisters in their twenties (see Table AII.3).

I interviewed most of the women in their own or their sister's home and some in my office during 1994. The interview included several auto/biographical activities. I filled out a demographic questionnaire, before handing them an Ecomap for mapping kin and friendship networks and a Flowchart of life-events and turning-points to complete (Department of Health 1988). The Ecomap allowed the women, especially the teenagers, to focus on sistering in a visual way. The Flowchart helped them recall key events and develop an overview of their relationship over time. Both techniques encouraged them to reflect on a taken for granted tie.

The Ecomap involved drawing connecting lines between the respondent placed in a circle in the centre of the page and other key members in their social network. They drew different types of lines to indicate various ties – strong, weak or stressful. The Flowchart, a review of life events in the general sense of the term (Riessman 1989), required women to reflect on changes to do with the birth of a sister, changing school, girlfriends and boyfriends, leaving home and changing patterns of closeness–distance and dependence–independence. For the interview, I devised topics rather than questions covering life events and relationship transitions including: contact patterns, school years, the age gap, significant events in the women's lives and changes in relationships with sisters and significant others. These topics allowed us to explore the tensions and pleasures of sistering rather than cover the exact same ground through chronological or linear questions and answers. The interviews had a loose structure and so the order in which we discussed these topics varied. The interviews, lasting approximately one and half-hours, were taped and transcribed, and I wrote fieldnotes and a research diary.

The 29 interviews included four with teenagers; seven with sisters in their twenties; eleven with sisters in their thirties; and six with sisters in their forties and fifties (see Table AII.3). I also spoke to Isabel, a six-year-old girl. As we talked she drew the qualities she liked about her older sisters: Celia's hair and flute-playing, her and Amy in the bath, swimming, book-binding at an after-school club with

Table AII.3: Sample by age and type of interview

Age	Individual Interviews	Paired Interviews	Separate Interviews	N Interviews	N Women
Pre-teens	0	0	1	1	1
Teens	0	4[9]	0	4	9
Twenties	1	3	4	8	11
Thirties	2	0	10	12	12
Forties	2	0	1	3	3
Fifties	1	0	0	1	1
Total	6	7	16	29	37

Eve, her mother reading her a story and her father taking her to school on his bike (see Mauthner 1997; Williams *et al.* 1989).

Ethical issues

Privacy was sometimes hard to secure (Brannen *et al.* 1994): I interviewed several women with toddlers and, in one case, a husband present. Ensuring confidentiality was another difficulty: when I interviewed two sisters separately, I guaranteed each confidentiality and anonymity. I did not disclose or use any information received from one woman when I interviewed her sister/s. Some felt concerned that some information might get back to other family members involved during access (fathers or husbands). I reassured them that I covered the same themes with everyone and that I would not use what one woman had said to inform the questions that I asked her sister. While most said, mainly at the start or end of the interview, that 'nothing they said would they mind the others knowing', this was contradicted by details revealed, usually concerning sexual relationships. I asked participants why and how they felt about taking part: reasons included helping me out, doing their sister a favour, fascination, a desire – in pair interviews – to find out what their sister thought, their belief in the sister tie and memories of 'closeness' between a mother and her sister. I have written in more detail about the challenges and sensitive aspects of confidentiality and ethics in these auto/biographical interviews elsewhere (see Mauthner 2000; 1998).

I adopted several measures central to a feminist methodology for carrying out ethical research (Stanley and Wise 1990). I explained the research clearly, negotiated access and consent, approached the interview as a social interaction rather than 'therapy', respected their privacy if they did not want to elaborate on certain themes and protected their confidentiality from one interview to the next with related sisters. I asked for feedback at the end of the interview, wrote and thanked them for participating and sent them a research summary.

Analysing the data

I analysed the data in three simultaneous stages based on Strauss's (1987) reformulation of grounded theory as an inductive and deductive process.[10] My material included interview transcripts, Ecomaps and Flowcharts, fieldnotes, my research diary and interview summaries. I completed a coding grid in the form of a table for each interview and wrote these up as case studies. First, I explored the narratives using concepts that guided the study – for example, friendship and contact patterns. Simultaneously I identified themes emerging from the narratives – conflict, distance, pleasures, and emotions – and looked for patterns and made comparisons across cases. I then developed coding categories from the theoretical concepts of power relations, talk, and subjectivity in interaction with the narratives. So the coding scheme incorporated theoretical concepts and themes from the data. The categories emerging as dominant were those most confirmed by the data: for example, power relations.

I also analysed the interviews through case studies whose methods are largely those 'of disciplining personal and particularised experience' (Stake 1994: 245). I examined patterns within and across cases and selected for in-depth analysis those, which best illustrated concepts or the four discourses. This focus on the specific rather than the general ties in with the auto/biographical method which drew my attention to transitions, turning-points and life events. Grounded theory, case studies and auto/biography all share a constructivist epistemology.

Producing knowledge

My decision to write about knowledge production in this appendix rather than in the main text is to ensure that the book is as accessible to as wide a range of readers as possible, especially women curious about the complexities of sistering, like those who shared their experiences with me. I want to briefly acknowledge inevitable tensions in my theoretical framework. These stem from the two contradictory epistemologies that I draw on – feminist standpoint theory and feminist post-structuralism. The auto/biographical method however brings together, through language, the two discordant epistemologies: experience, the material and the emotional on the one hand; subjectivity, discourse and narrative on the other.

Epistemology concerns the context and process of the production of knowledge, the relationship between knower and would be knower and the question of what is knowable.[11] It corresponds to a philosophical grounding for deciding what kinds of knowledge are possible and ensuring that they are both adequate and legitimate (Maynard 1994). Feminist sociologists of all persuasions share a concern with investigating hidden experiences even though there is no single feminist theory or feminist epistemology. Indeed, the different 'complex and evolving' feminist theories are difficult to classify (Maynard 1995: 261). Yet there is agreement about the need for *feminist theory* 'at its best when it reflects the lived experience of women, when it bridges the gap between mind and body, reason and emotion, thinking and feeling' (Tong 1992: 237).

Despite the consensus that there is no single feminist epistemology owing to the pluralism of feminist theories and the 'anti-hegemony' of any one feminist discourse (Stanley and Wise 1990: 47), commonalities do exist. All feminist epistemologies challenge modern, traditional or positivist epistemology which posits reality as a rational, completely knowable, transparent, accurate 'mirror of the mind' (Nash 1994: 67). In contrast with traditional sociological knowledge posited on a series of dualisms – reason/emotion, mind/body, subject/object, objective truth/ideology (Maynard 1994), feminist epistemologies are concerned with gendered experience and challenge the notion that facts are objective or value-free. They all have a moral/political stance; values and power are organising concepts which precede epistemology and analysis starts at that point; they address the disempowerment of women underpinned by other epistemologies; and they stress the importance of self or subjectivity (Griffiths 1995a).

My epistemological stance draws on several standpoint theory principles (Smith 1988): the 'everyday world as problematic', women's views as particular and privileged, and acknowledging the presence of the researcher's subjectivity and reflexivity (Smith 1988). These principles validate the investigation of an invisible female tie and thereby assume that experiences including emotions and memories of relationships are knowable (Kuhn 1995). I was influenced by Stanley and Wise's (1990) interpretation of Smith's (1988) outline of a sociology for women which refutes knowledge as expertise in favour of knowledge derived from women's experiences. Smith visualises a closer link between experience and knowledge, where this knowledge remains accessible to those who have contributed to its production. Smith writes (1988: 222–3): 'It [the new sociology] proposes discourse organised differently, where knowledge does not become a body of knowledge, where issues are not crystallised, where the conventions and relevances of discourse do not assume an independent authority over against its speakers and readers.'

Crucially, Smith's broad understanding of 'text' or knowledge produced from experience, unlike that of other thinkers, implicitly includes both the written and the spoken. In his work on hermeneutics, Ricoeur, for example, distinguishes between discourse, language and text: text is equated with writing rather than 'living speech' (1981: 198). The importance of Smith's incorporation of both the written and the spoken in the notion of text is epistemological: fusing the two connects the production and the producers of oral and written narratives, in this case the women and myself. Stanley and Wise (1990: 34) capture this epistemological point as 'verbal bodies of acknowledged knowledge' which derives from the above passage of Smith's. This expression succinctly and implicitly brings together the verbal or textual (language), the spoken or oral (talk) and abstract aspects of knowledge production (discourse). In the context of sistering, it refers to both talk between sisters in contrast with silence, and the potential exchange of knowledge between them about their positionings in the four discourses.

Knowledge, in the context of standpoint theory, stems from lived experience and a tangible social and material reality. Liz Stanley and Sue Wise's *fractured foundationalism* argues for the idea of 'overlapping . . . material realities' (Stanley and Wise 1990: 41).[12] Foundationalism is the 'insistence that "the truth" rather than a number of truths, exists independently of the knower' (Stanley and Wise 1990: 41). Drawing on Durkeim's philosophy based on the existence of a material reality 'out there' they espouse a revised version of foundationalism as 'fractured'. This means that a truth independent of the knower exists, as well as these 'overlapping . . . material realities'. The epistemological implication of recognising an independent truth, and these 'material realities' is that knowledge can be produced out of women's material experiences, including their emotions (Ramazanoglu and Holland 2000, 1999; Holland and Ramazanoglu 1994).

In the project of deconstruction and post-structuralism on the other hand, knowledge or reality, as Nash (1994: 66) writes is 'produced discursively, *within* a system of rules that govern what can count as a real object or process, or a "true" or "false" statement. Within such systems reason and experience are themselves no more than discursive constructions legitimating certain statements and denying others authority; they are seen as having no privileged access to an extra-discursive world.' Knowledge is equated with narrative or texts created through language; experience is always contextualised, and subjectivity is constructed and embedded in practices of social control. Knowledge is produced by deconstructing 'the discursive practices through which the social world is portrayed' (Maynard 1995: 269). Knowledge is thus produced from narratives.

Another vital element of Foucault's work and deconstruction for feminist theory is the connection between knowledge and the desire for control or power in modern societies (Nash 1994: 68). The equation between knowledge and power is central to feminist epistemologies, politics and, by extension, the interpretation of sistering narratives. One tenet of feminist epistemologies and politics is that knowledge leads to empowerment: here the context is the social construction of subjectivity in the family and the extent to which women as sisters can or do rewrite their familial scripts. As Nash (1994: 69) explains: 'knowledge positions subjects within certain discourses by enabling certain possibilities and excluding or repressing others'. My interest is in the link between knowledge, specific positive or negative discourses that operate around sistering *and* the possibilities for resisting or embracing these. Indeed, Alcoff (1988) sees discourses as enabling and as offering the possibilities for resistance, as well as constituting the currency through which power and control are mobilised. Maynard (1995: 269) adds: 'The subject is presented as being divided against itself and as the product of conflicts and contradictions between its various parts and its positioning in various discourses.'

In feminist post-structuralism there is a tension regarding the space for the 'materiality of human existence' (Maynard 1994: 22), which becomes replaced by text or discourse. As Foucault says, 'the very act of speaking about experience is to culturally and discursively constitute it' (Foucault 1981; 1986; cited in Maynard 1994: 23). This turn towards culture – words, language, text, representation, and discourses – away from the material – economics, the sexual division of labour and labour market – Maynard (1995) argues, marks one of the most significant developments in feminist theory in the 1990s. She writes: 'it is possible for feminism to hold on to some of the most helpful insights which are offered by Lacanian and post-structural perspectives, while at the same time retaining a commitment to some of its earlier tenets which have recently been challenged' (Maynard 1995: 274). The earlier tenets that she refers to concern the material and the importance of experience.

Women's sistering highlights the significance of both the material reality of experience and emotion and the fact that these exist and are constituted through narrative and language. Language, the production of knowledge, the material, and power relations are all inextricably linked. 'Language is the medium through which we can express knowledge of material conditions and power relations,' Ramazanoglu and Holland (1997: 5) explain.

This distinction between 'talk', the practice of speaking about emotions and the body; 'language' or the word as text or utterance that plays a key role in connecting experience, narrative of experience and knowledge; and 'discourse' or the structures of power and thought; is significant for three reasons. First, this distinction highlights the link between experience and language in the production of knowledge. Second, it illuminates the centrality of talk, and silence, in the emotional and material production of subjectivity. Third, the social invisibility of sisters that is reflected in a linguistic absence to describe their ties was mirrored in the research process (see Mauthner 1998). It is partly through talk, silence and emotions, that subjectivity is constructed and experienced materially. I use 'discourse', 'language' and 'talk' in distinct ways: by 'discourse', I mean structures of power and thought. 'Language' refers to the medium of the word as text or utterance: language plays a key role in connecting experience, narrative of experience and knowledge. By 'talk' I mean the practice of speaking. The influence of feminist post-structuralism has been at the levels of both ontology, hence my examination of the centrality of narrative and discourse in constituting 'reality' through language, and epistemology, where the main concept for understanding the creation of knowledge from speaking subjects' narratives, is subjectivity.

This tension between the lived, the material, and its representation through language is not easily resolved. However notwithstanding the epistemological tensions, there are many benefits from combining elements from both feminist standpoint theory and feminist post-structuralism with the auto/biographical method for documenting women's lives as sisters.

Notes

Introduction

1 The terms tie, bond and relationship are used interchangeably and do not imply an essentialist approach to sistering. The book covers ambivalence and distance between sisters as much as closeness.

2 My understanding of caring stems from Hochschild's (1983) notion of emotional labour. The book does not examine sistering in relation to class and race, which for Skeggs (1997) are intrinsic to femininity, nor other models of femininity based on heterosexual appearance and glamour, full-time domesticity and mother-intensive child-rearing (see Hey 1997; Stacey 1992).

3 See Almack (2002); Weeks *et al.* (1999a, b, c, d); Dunne (1996); Weeks (1995); Giddens (1992); Weston (1991); and, for an opposite view, Jamieson (1999).

4 See government-funded empirical initiatives such as the HEA Family Health Research Programme (Hogg *et al.* 1996), the ESRC Population and Household Change Programme (McRae 1999), and the ESRC Children 5–16 Programme (Hallett and Prout 2003). Moreover, the creation of the National Institute for Parenting and the Family perpetuates the focus on parent–child relationships, at the expense of other non-nuclear kinship ties.

5 Powell and Steelman (1990) and Hudson (1992) use this term. Hudson defines 'sibships' as fraternities, or sororities I would add, in the context of Jane Austen's fiction. She highlights their literary and social innovation in their embodiment of ideal communities based on values of loyalty and reciprocity. She says (1992: 2): 'Based on mutual respect, individual worth, and shared beliefs and concerns, they herald a new dimension in the English novel to the extent that they are relatively egalitarian societies.'

6 Thorne (1992) identifies five themes central to feminist rethinking of the family. First, feminists have sought to challenge assumptions that any specific family arrangement is natural, biological or 'functional' across time and space. Second, rather than starting with 'the family' as a unit of analysis, feminists have focused on underlying structures of domestic life and intimate relationships – gender, age and generation, sexuality, class and race. Third, feminist analysis has led to a much more complex view of family life; for example their examination of the family as a site of power struggles (Delphy and Leonard 1992). Fourth, they have raised questions about family boundaries. By challenging traditional dichotomies between private and public, family and society, they have recentred social theory and brought hidden topics into view. Lastly, the public/private dichotomy is linked to ambivalence embedded in feminism between values of individualism and equality, and values of nurturance and community.

7 A total of 40 families were interviewed in 1993–94 for *The Natural History of the Family Project*, a qualitative study commissioned for the Health Education Authority's *Family Health Research Programme* (see Holland *et al.* 1996).

8 My Foucauldian understanding of discourse, described in chapter 3, includes enacted practices.

9 See Schutz's (1972; Schutz and Luckman 1973) theory of inter-subjectivity suggesting that subjectivity is formed in relation to the Other. My study draws on the work of Hollway (1984), Lauretis (1986) and Alcoff (1988) on the subject, agency and positionality. See also Mason's (1999) argument for a relational understanding of subjectivity in sociology.

10 There is a move in sociology towards acknowledging the role of emotions in a more embedded understanding of social agency and interaction (see Hochschild 1983; Williams and Bendelow 1998).

11 The names of women such as *Annar* who could not or declined to take part in the study and yet still appear in their sisters' narratives are italicised in order to reflect their involuntary presence and absent narratives.

Chapter 1

1 Giddens (1992: 155; 158) uses this term as a synonym for negotiation in the context of the 'pure relationship . . . entered into for its own sake, for what can be derived by each person from a sustained association with another'. For a critique, see Jamieson (1999).

2 See Dunne (1996); Edwards *et al.* (1999); Weeks *et al.* (1999 a, b, c, d); Mason (1996); Finch and Mason (1993); Cornell (1991); Hoffman-Riem (1990).

3 See Fabera and Mazlish (1987); Reit (1985).

4 See Cartmell *et al.* (1998); Private Lives (1996); Grant (1994); Mackay (1993); Cahill (1989); McNaron (1985). And interest in siblings as metaphors of same-sex ties in fiction flourishes in queer studies (see Flannery 1997; Sedgwick 1997).

5 See Fox-Genovese (1991); Morgan (1984).

6 Most of this work concerns siblings including: delinquency (Rowe *et al.* 1992); learning (Marjoribanks 1991; Lynn *et al.* 1989; Rubenfeld and Gilroy 1991; Powell and Steelman 1990; Hauser and Wong 1989; Goodman 1987); and sexual identity (Blanchard and Sheridan 1992a; b). For work on early years rivalry, birth order and sibling bonding, see Murphy (1992); Dunn (1984); Bank and Kahn (1982); Dunn and Kendrick (1982); Lamb and Sutton-Smith (1982); McFarland (1938). For work on jealousy and coping with the new birth, see Allred and Poduska (1988); Schachter and Stone (1987); Jalongo and Renck (1985); and on parenting and divorce, see Brody *et al.* (1992); Ihinger-Tallman (1986); Taylor (1982). For studies on genetics and on terminal illness, see Downing (2001); Fulker *et al.* (1999); Green *et al.* (1997); Lessor (1993); Salvi *et al.* (1992); Wilson (1992); Wallinga *et al.* (1987); Koch-Hattem (1986).

7 See Doucet (1995); Cotterill (1994); Ribbens (1994); Sharpe (1994); Mason (1987); Brannen and Collard (1982).

8 See Mason (1996; 1989); Edwards (1993); Finch and Mason (1993); Vaughan (1987).

9 Hey (1997); O'Connor (1991); Oliker (1989); Lasser (1988); Raymond (1986); Nestor (1985); Faderman (1981); Smith-Rosenberg (1975).

10 One exception is Griffin's study (1992) of three friendship groups of girls aged 12–16 of different races where the distinguishing features were: 'having a laugh', 'talking' and physical closeness.

11 See Gage (1989); Fallon (1988); Hey (1986); Cockburn (1983); Serfontein (1979); Barker (1977); O'Broin (1976); Baring Brothers & Co. Ltd. (1970).
12 For an interdisciplinary approach to birth order see Sulloway (1996).
13 See Bernart *et al.* (1992); Vandereycken and Vrecken (1992); Casper (1990); Waters *et al.* (1990); Lewis (1987); Artley (1993); Laviola (1992); Muram *et al.* (1991); Oliver (1988); Dipietro (1987); Dyke (1987); Fortenberry (1986); Bates *et al.* (1983).
14 See Brody *et al.* (1989); Matthews *et al.* (1989); Matthews (1987).
15 These contradictory findings could be owing to the small sample sizes in both studies.
16 See Southall Black Sisters (1990); Brah and Minhas (1985); Bryan *et al.* (1985); Khan (1979).
17 See VanEvery (1999); Bernardes (1993); Segal (1983); Barrett (1980).
18 See Brah and Shaw (1992); Southall Black Sisters (1990).
19 See Mirza (1992); Ghuman (1991); Brah (1979).
20 For studies of siblings and disability, see Gladstone and Montgomery (1990); Begun (1989); Brown *et al.* (1989); Lapalus-Netter (1989); Murphy and Della-Corte (1989); Senapati and Hayes (1988); Stoneman *et al.* (1988). Other work examines: the impact of a disabled child on other siblings (Gallagher and Powell 1989); autism (McHale *et al.* 1986); and Down's Syndrome (Cuskelly and Dadds 1992; Gath and Gumley 1987).
21 See Coates and Silburn (1970); Young and Willmott (1962); Mogey (1956); Willmott and Young (1960); and for a contemporary example, O'Brien and Jones (1996).
22 See also Bell and Coleman (1999); Medick and Sabean (1984); Leyton (1974).
23 See Hey (1997); Apter (1990); Oliker (1989); O'Connor (1990; 1987).
24 See Lawler (2000); Nice (1992); Fischer (1986); Cohler and Grunebaum (1981).
25 The term 'sibling solidarity' also appears in Gold's study (1987) of siblings in later life.
26 See also Allan (1977b) for class variations in friendship patterns.
27 See Side's (1999) review of different feminist attempts to theorise friendship.
28 See Jerrome's study (1984) of the 'Tremendous Ten', a friendship group of 11 middle-aged, middle-class women brought together by their class and age.
29 See O'Connor (1992) for research on women's friendship at other stages of the life-cycle including adolescence and old age and during singledom, divorce and widowhood.
30 Dunn (1993) mentions power relations, negotiation and reciprocity between young siblings; and McNamee (1997) examines gendered conflicts over leisure and domestic space among teenage siblings.
31 Fishel's data consists of 150 questionnaires and a sub-sample of 50 interviews with women aged 18–82.
32 Mathias interviewed 75 women aged 15–87.
33 Sandmaier interviewed 80 brothers and sisters aged 26–79.
34 For links between sibling aggression, masculinity and adult violence see Bennett (1990); Mangold and Koski (1990); Felson and Russo (1988); Brody *et al.* (1987b); Gully *et al.* (1981); Straus *et al.* (1980).
35 See also Ross and Milgram (1982).

Chapter 2

1 See O'Connor (1992); Morgan (1990); Finch (1989); Oliker (1989); McCall (1988); Montgomery (1988); Gullestad (1984); Jerrome (1984).

2 Coates (1988b) recorded a group of white middle-class friends in their late thirties and early forties over nine months who met once a fortnight at each others' houses in the evening to talk. This notion of 'cooperative talk', she notes, needs to be tested against parameters of class, ethnicity and age.

3 See Aughingen (1990); Hays (1988); Reis and Shaver (1988); Reisman (1981); Fischer *et al.* (1977).

4 See Aukett *et al.* (1988); Helgeson *et al.* (1987); Derlega *et al.* (1986); Aries and Johnson (1983); Wright (1982); Bell (1981); Rands and Levinger (1979); Powers and Bultena (1976); Weiss and Lowenthal (1975); Cozby (1973); Booth (1972); Komarovsky (1967).

5 See Brannen *et al.* (1994) and Monck (1991). Monck interviewed and gave questionnaires to 142 girls aged 15–20 who scored high or low on measures of eating disorders. She found that at 19 girls were slightly more likely to name their boyfriend than their girlfriend or mother as intimate confidant. Yet sisters do act as confidantes regarding menstruation, sexual and reproductive health: see East and Felice (1992); Thompson *et al.* (1991); Prendergast (1989); Ortiz and Nuttall (1987).

6 These figures correspond to specific dyads which the women described in detail and do not cover the full range of dyads in their lives or in the data.

7 All the women's names have been replaced with pseudonyms. Geographical, occupational and some demographic details have been omitted or modified in order to protect their anonymity.

8 The following transcribing conventions are adopted throughout the book: [...] indicates excised text; ^^ signals an inaudible word; ... corresponds to a pause; and [laughs] denotes descriptive comments that I have added. The speech of women such as Revi, Vandana and Carmen, for whom English is not their first language, has been left intact.

9 Jeanne, whose name appears twice in this table, has been included in the 13 *close companionships* while her sisters, Madonna and Leonie, whose names appear here only once, have not. They have been counted in the ten *distant companionships* (see Table 2.3), where their names appear twice.

10 Lauren, as other women did, mentioned her brother Paul (31) with whom she had less contact, in passing. Several women described the role, both positive and negative, of brothers in their lives, and the effect of sister-brother ties in shaping sister bonds.

11 In this table, Roxanne, Madonna and Leonie, whose names appear twice, have been included in the total number of 10 *distant companionships* while their sister Jeanne, whose name appears once, has not. She was counted as part of the 13 *close companionships* (see Table 2.2).

12 I am using 'responsibilities' as Finch and Mason (1993: 166) do instead of notions of duty and obligation.

Chapter 3

1 See Henwood (1995); Nice (1992); Apter (1990); Fisher (1986); Chernin (1984); Rich (1984); Cohler and Grunebaum (1981).

2 Hey (1997) and Miller (1990) explore the Gramscian (1971) construction of hegemony in the private world in relation to heterosexuality and homosociality.

3 See Holland *et al.* (1991a); Phoenix *et al.* (1991); Thomson and Scott (1991).

4 Early feminist postmodernists influenced by the philosophy of Jacques Lacan and Jacques Derrida include the French deconstructionist thinkers Luce Irigaray, Hélene Cixous and Julia Kristeva: their particular interest was in re-interpreting Freudian psychoanalysis (Tong 1992).

5 Frazer borrows the term discourse register from socio-linguistics where the 'legal register' or the 'classroom register' have long been studied (1988a: 192). She contrasts the 'tabloid press' register versus the 'feminist' register as well as the different 'dialects' used depending on the context. She identified three registers (1988a: 194): (i) the tabloid journalism register; (ii) the 'feminist' or 'critical' style of talk; and (iii) two forms which oppose the critical register – individualism and conservatism/traditionalism.

6 Although Frazer highlights the weakness of this approach, its behaviourism and by-passing of the 'cognitive' (1988a:199), its strength for my study lies in her depiction of active forms of feminine subjectivities, in a specific site – school.

7 See also Holland *et al.* (1998) who provide a complex account of the role of both experience and reflection (or intellectual knowledge) in young women's struggle with and resistance to gendered power relations in the process of hetero/sexual empowerment.

8 Hey (1997) and Lees (1993; 1986) illustrate teenage girls' 'policing' of each other through language.

9 See Brown and Gilligan (1992); Gilligan *et al.* (1990).

10 I use 'discourse', 'language' and 'talk' in distinct ways: by discourse, I mean structures of power and thought. 'Language' refers to the medium of the word as text or utterance: language plays a key role in the study in connecting experience, narrative of experience and knowledge. By 'talk' I mean the practice of speaking between sisters.

11 See Duck (1991; 1990).

12 Mens-Verhulst (1993a; 1993b) uses a similar notion of active subjectivity in the context of women shaping their 'mothering' and 'daughtering' relationships.

13 Walkerdine (1986; 1985) examines the different subject positions available to girls and women in relation to discourses of regulation in schooling and the family. And Finch and Mason (1993) use the term 'structural position' in relation to family relationships, which includes material and moral commitments.

14 For an account of sub-cultures as forms of resistance to class and femininity, see McRobbie and Nava (1984); McRobbie (1977). For other work on resistance see Mann (1996); Rossiter (1994); Jerrome (1984); Brown and Gilligan (1992); Gilligan *et al.* (1988).

15 See Holland *et al.* (1992; 1991b); Steedman (1986).

16 For an empirical illustration of this idea see Anyon (1983).

17 My notion of changing subjectivity, existing between oscillating interdependent social selves echoes the work of earlier sociologists on inter-subjectivity and

sociability – Alfred Schutz, George Herbert Mead and Georg Simmel (see Frisby and Featherstone 1997; Joas 1991; Miller 1982; Reck 1981; Schutz and Luckmann 1973; Schutz 1972, 1966).

Chapter 5

1 See Smith (1988), cited in Stanley and Wise (1990: 34).
2 Rose (1996: 4) refers to the 'psychosciences' including psychology, psychiatry and related disciplines that have emerged since the last half of the nineteenth century as 'psy'. His project is to use psy to propose a genealogy of subjectivity.
3 Syncretism refers to the attempt to sink differences and effect union between different sects or philosophical schools (Fowler and Fowler 1964).

Chapter 7

1 This is adapted from the title of Terence Davies' film, *Distant Voices, Still Lives* (1988), a fictionalised and autobiographical account of his childhood growing up in a working-class family in Liverpool.

Conclusion

1 While I am making an assumption about the female and gendered aspect of sistering among women, as others do regarding mothering and daugthering (Lawler 2000), I am not making a case for essentialism. My attention to caring and power relations does not mean that although these structure femininity, it is restricted to these. While Delphy (2000) calls for us to let go of the illusion of femininity 'in *any* shape', I argue that sistering, similarly to mothering and daughtering, remains nevertheless for now an important aspect of how femininity is socially constructed.
2 African-American conceptions of 'family', for example, which according to Collins (1992) connect households and larger communities and link generations, revolve around female kin such as other mothers and blood mothers. See Chamberlain (1999); Jamieson (1998); Weeks (1995); Weston (1991).
3 Elements of sistering, sibship and 'buddying' are used in US peer work including Big/Little Sisters/Brothers and Resource Sisters/Compañeras projects for improving behaviour and promoting nurturing among children, teenagers, pregnant women and gay men (Lugo 1996; Frecknall and Luks 1992; Whitehead and Nokes 1990; Seidl 1982). See also Illman (1993) for a Thai community soap opera about sisters and safer sex.
4 Gordon (1994) uses this expression in her compelling historical portrait of a group of girlfriends in pre-Second Wave Feminism 1950s white South Africa.

Appendix II

1 See Maynard (1994); Maynard and Purvis (1994); Olesen (1994); Mies (1983); Ramazanoglu (1989a; 1989b).

2 Epistemology refers to a theory of knowledge about the social world in contrast with ontology which corresponds to a theory of reality or 'being'. Influenced by Nash (1994) I address the epistemological tensions that surface in trying to reconcile these two theories elsewhere (see Mauthner 2001).
3 See also Hughes (1998); May (1998); Harding (1987).
4 See Holland *et al*. (1996).
5 Five Asian women, three black Caribbean women and three women of mixed parentage.
6 This is a way of distinguishing between method, methodology, epistemology and ontology in the research process.
7 Other researchers work with different definitions. Whereas Crapanzano (1984) distinguishes between 'life histories', a response to a request from an outsider, and 'autobiographies', accounts originating with the narrator, Blair *et al*. (1995) distinguish between life-history, which is delivered orally, and auto/biography or the story of one's own life or a written account of someone else's.
8 See Stanley and Morgan (1993); Vaughan (1987); Burgoyne and Clark (1984); Weiss and Lowenthal (1975).
9 This figure includes three paired interviews and one group discussion with three sisters.
10 In grounded theory, the emphasis is on the process of generating theory through emerging categories from data in contrast with the older social science tradition of verifying theory (Glaser and Strauss 1967). Although Glaser and Strauss (1967) first conceived of grounded theory as an inductive method, I used Strauss's (1987) reformulation. Two decades after devising grounded theory Strauss (1987) refined the coding to include *in vivo codes* which stem from the language of participants and *sociologically constructed codes* 'based on a combination of the researcher's scholarly knowledge and knowledge of the substantive field under study' (Strauss 1987: 33). *Sociologically constructed codes* can add more sociological meaning to interpretation than *in vivo codes* and clearly acknowledge the influence of knowledge external to the data. So while primarily an inductive approach (moving from data to theory), grounded theory also includes coming to the data with concepts, an *a priori* perspective or even elements of 'formal theory'. Formal theory corresponds to a conceptual area of enquiry, for example feminine subjectivity, whereas substantive theory is developed for an empirical area such as the sociology of friendship/kinship. There is also 'grand theory' which is 'generated from logical assumptions and speculations about the 'oughts' of social life' (Glaser and Strauss 1967: 34).
11 See Maynard (1995); Guba and Lincoln (1994); Nash (1994); Alcoff and Potter (1993).
12 Stanley and Wise (1990: 41) borrow this idea from Gross (1987). See also Stanley and Wise (1993: 194).

Bibliography

Adkins, A. and Leonard, D. (1993) Family work and the educational careers of working class girls in England. Paper presented at *Education in Europe: an Intercultural Task* Conference, organised by the Network for Educational Science (based in Amsterdam), Budapest, 17 September.

Alcoff, L. (1988) Cultural feminism versus post-structuralism: the identity crisis in feminist theory, *Signs* 13, 3: 405–36.

Alcoff, L. and Potter, E. (1993) Introduction: when feminisms intersect epistemology. In Alcoff, L. and Potter, E. (eds) *Feminist Epistemologies*, Routledge, London.

Allan, G. (1990) British studies in the sociology of friendship: a view of the past decade. Paper given at the *5th International Conference on Personal Relationships*, Oxford, July.

Allan, G. (1989) *Friendship: Developing a Sociological Perspective*, Harvester-Wheatsheaf, Hemel Hempstead.

Allan, G. (1979) *A Sociology of Friendship and Kinship*, Allen and Unwin, London.

Allan, G. (1977a) Sibling solidarity, *Journal of Marriage and the Family* 39: 177–84.

Allan, G. (1977b) Class variation in friendship patterns, *British Journal of Sociology* 28: 389–93.

Allred, G. H. and Poduska, B. E. (1988) Birth order and happiness: a preliminary study, *Individual Psychology Journal of Adlerian Theory, Research and Practice* 44, 3: 346–54.

Almack, K. (2002) Women parenting together: mothering and family life in same sex-relationships. Unpublished PhD dissertation, University of Nottingham.

Anyon, J. (1983) Intersections of gender and class: accommodation and resistance by working-class and affluent females to contradictory sex-role ideologies. In Walker, S. and Barton, L. (eds) *Gender, Class and Education*, Falmer Press, Lewes.

Apter, T. (1990) *Altered Loves: Mothers and Daughters during Adolescence*, Harvester-Wheatsheaf, Hemel Hempstead.

Argyle, M. and Henderson, M. (1985) *The Anatomy of Relationships*, Heinemann, London.

Aries, E. J. and Johnson, F. L. (1983) Close friendship in adulthood: conversational content between same-sex friends, *Sex Roles* 9: 1183–96.

Artley, A. (1993) A family execution, *The Independent*, 18 July.

Aughingen, E. A. (1990) Friendship and sibling dyads in everyday life: a study with the double diary method. Paper presented at the *Fifth International Conference on Personal Relationships*, Oxford, July.

Aukett, R., Ritchie, J. and Mill, K. (1988) Gender differences in friendship patterns, *Sex Roles* 19, 1/2: 57–66.

Avioli, P. S. (1986) Sibling relationships: an unrealised potential support for the elderly. Paper presented at the *New Jersey Psychological Association*, Saddlebrook, New Jersey, 26 April.

Ayres, J. (1983) Strategies to maintain relationships: their identification and perceived usage, *Communication Quarterly* 31: 62–7.

Bank, S. P. and Kahn, M. D. (1982) *The Sibling Bond*, Basic Books, New York.

Baring Brothers & Co. Ltd (1970) *Merchant Banking Today*, Baring Brothers and Co. Ltd, London.

Barker, T. C. (1977) *The Glassmakers: Pilkington – the Rise of an International Company 1826–1976*, Weidenfeld and Nicolson, London.

Barrett, M. (1980) *Women's Oppression Today: Problems in Marxist Feminist Analysis*, Verso, London.

Bates, Ü. Ü., Denmark, F. L., Held, V., Helly, D. O., Lees, S. H., Pomeroy, S. B., Smith, E. D. and Rosenberg, Z. S. (1983) Daughters and sisters. In Bates, Ü. Ü., Denmark, F. L., Held, V., Helly, D. O., Lees, S. H., Pomeroy, S. B., Smith, E. D. and Rosenberg, Z. S. (Hunter College Women's Studies Collective) (eds) *Women's Realities, Women's Choices: An Introduction to Women's Studies*, Oxford University Press, New York and Oxford.

Bedford, V. H. (1989) A comparison of thematic apperceptions of sibling affiliation, conflict, and separation at two periods of adulthood, *International Journal of Aging and Human Development* 28, 1: 53–66.

Begun, A. L. (1989) Sibling relationships involving developmentally disabled people, *American Journal on Mental Retardation* 93, 5: 566–74.

Bell, R. R. (1981) *Worlds of Friendship*, Sage, London.

Bell, S. and Coleman, S. (eds) (1999) *The Anthropology of Friendship*, Berg, Oxford and New York.

Bendelow, G. and Williams, S. (eds) (1998) *Emotions in Social Life: Critical Themes and Contemporary Issues*, Routledge, London.

Bennett, J. C. (1990) Nonintervention into siblings' fighting as a catalyst for learned helplessness, *Psychological Reports* 66: 139–45.

Bernardes, J. (1993) Responsibilities in studying postmodern families, *Journal of Family Issues* 14, 1: 35–49.

Bernart, R. de, Ferrara, M. and Pecchioli, S. (1992) L'importanza di essere fratelli, *Terapia Familiare* 38: 21–30.

Blair, M., Dawtrey, L. and Holland, J. (1995) *E826 Gender Issues in Education: Equality and Difference – Study Guide*, MA in Education, The Open University, Milton Keynes.

Blanchard, R. and Sheridan, P. M. (1992a) Proportion of unmarried siblings of homosexual and nonhomosexual gender-dysphoric patients, *Canadian Journal of Psychiatry* 37, 3: 163–7.

Blanchard, R. and Sheridan, P. M. (1992b) Sibling size, sibling sex ration, birth order, and parental age in homosexual and nonhomosexual gender dysphorics, *Journal of Nervous and Mental Disease* 180, 1: 40–7.

Bloom, L. R. and Munro, P. (1995) Conflicts of selves: nonunitary subjectivity in women administrators' life history narratives. In Hatch, J. A. and Wisnieswski, R. (eds) *Life History and Narrative*, Falmer Press, London.

Booth, A. (1972) Sex and social participation, *American Sociological Review* 37: 183–92.

Borland, D. C. (1987) The sibling relationship as a housing alternative to institutionalisation in later life, Special Issue: Family and Economic Issues – Diversity in the Lifestyles of Older People, *Lifestyles* 8, 3–4: 55(185)–69(199).

Brah, A. (1979) Inter-Generational and Inter-Ethnic Perceptions Amongst Asian and White Adolescents and their Parents. Unpublished PhD thesis, University of Bristol.

Brah, A. and Shaw, S. (1992) Working Choices: South Asian Young Muslim Women and the Labour Market. A Report for the Department of Employment, Research Paper No. 91.

Brah, A. and Minhas, R. (1985) Structural racism or cultural difference: schooling for Asian girls. In Weiner, G. (ed.) *Just a Bunch of Girls*, Open University Press, Milton Keynes.

Brannen, J. and Collard, C. (1982) *Marriages in Trouble: The Process of Seeking Help*, Tavistock, London.

Brannen, J., Dodd, K., Oakley, A. and Storey, P. (1994) *Young People, Health and Family Life*, Open University Press, Buckingham.

Brody, E. M., Hoffman, C. and Kleban, M. H. (1989) Caregiving daughters and their local siblings: perceptions, strains and interactions, *Gerontologist* 29, 3–4: 529–38.

Brody, G. H., Stoneman, Z. and McCoy, J. K. (1992) Associations of maternal and paternal direct and differential behaviour with sibling relationships: contemporaneous and longitudinal analyses, *Child Development* 63, 1: 82–92.

Brody, G. H., Stoneman, Z. and Burke, M. (1987a) Family system and individual child correlates of sibling behaviour, *American Journal of Orthopsychiatry* 57, 4: 561–9.

Brody, G. H., Stoneman, Z. and Burke, M. (1987b) Child temperaments, maternal differential behaviour and sibling relationships, *Developmental Psychology* 23, 3: 354–62.

Brown, H. and Cowman, K. (1999) Exploring suffrage friendships. In Symes, R. A., Kaloski, A. and Brown, H. (eds) *Celebrating Women's Friendship: Past, Present and Future*, Raw Nerve Books, York.

Brown, L., Long, E., Udvari-Solner, A., Davis, L. *et al.* (1989) The home school: why students with severe intellectual disabilities must attend the schools of their brothers, sisters, friends and neighbours, *Journal of the Association for Persons with Severe Handicaps* 14, 1: 1–7.

Brown, L. M. and Gilligan, C. (1993) Meeting at the Crossroads: Women's Psychology and Girls' Development, *Feminism and Psychology* 3: 11–35.

Brown, L. M. and Gilligan, C. (1992) *Meeting at the Crossroads: Women's Psychology and Girls' Development*, Harvard University Press, Cambridge, Mass.

Bryan, B., Dadzie, S. and Scafe, S. (1985) *The Heart of the Race: Black Women's Lives in Britain*, Virago, London.

Bryant, B. K. (1989) The child's perspective of sibling care-taking and its relevance to understanding social-emotional functioning and development. In Zukow, P.G. (ed.) *Sibling Interaction Across Cultures: Theoretical and Methodological Issues*, Springer-Verlag, New York and London.

Bubeck, D. (2000) Women's difference: now you see it, now you don't. In Fricker, M. and Hornsby, J. (eds) *The Cambridge Companion to Feminism in Philosophy*, Cambridge University Press, Cambridge.

Burgoyne, J. and Clark, D. (1984) *Making a Go of It: A Study of Stepfamilies in Sheffield*, Routledge, London.

Cahill, S. (ed.) (1989) *Among Sisters: Short Stories by Women Writers*, Mentor/ Penguin, New York.

Cartmell, D. and Whelehan, I. (1998) Introduction – sisterhoods: across the litera-ture/media divide. In Cartmell, D., Hunter, I. Q., Kaye, H. and Whelehan, I. (eds) *Sisterhoods: Across the Literature/Media Divide*, Pluto, London.

Cartmell, D, Hunter, I. Q., Kaye, H. and Whelehan, I. (eds) (1998) *Sisterhoods: Across the Literature/Media Divide*, Pluto, London.

Casper, R. C. (1990) Personality features of women with good outcome from restricting anorexia nervosa, *Psychosomatic Medicine*, 52, 2: 156–70.

Chamberlain, M. (1999) Brothers and sisters, uncles and aunts: a lateral perspective on Caribbean families. In Silva, E. and Smart, C. (eds) *The New Family*, Sage, London.

Chamberlain, M. (1997a) *Narratives of Exile and Return*, Warwick University Caribbean Studies, Macmillan, London.

Chamberlain, M. (1997b) The global self: the narrative genre of Caribbean migrant women. Paper presented at *Narrating Selves and Others: Feminist Theory in Practice – An Interdisciplinary Conference on Sociocultural Critique and (Auto)biography*, Antwerp, 28–29 November.

Chappell, N. L. (1991) In-group differences among elders living with friends and family other than spouses, *Journal of Aging Studies* 5, 1: 61–76.

Cheal, D. (1991) *Family and the State of Theory*, Harvester-Wheatsheaf, New York and London.

Chernin, K. (1984) *In My Mother's House*, HarperCollins, New York.

Cicirelli, V. G. (1995) *Sibling Relationships Across the Life Span*, Plenum Press, New York.

Cicirelli, V. G. (1989) Feelings of attachment to siblings and well-being in later life, *Psychology and Aging* 4, 2: 211–16.

Cicirelli, V. G. (1982) Sibling influence throughout the life-span. In Lamb, M. E. and Sutton-Smith, B. (eds) *Sibling Relationships: Their Nature and Significance Across the Lifespan*, Lawrence Erlbaum Associates, New Jersey and London.

Clark, D. and Haldane, D. (1990) *Wedlocked? Intervention and Research in Marriage*, Polity Press, Cambridge.

Coates, J. (1996) *Women Talk*, Blackwell, Oxford.

Coates, J. (1993) *Women, Men and Language: A Sociolinguistic Account of Gender Differences in Language* (second edition), Longman, London. (First published 1986.)

Coates, J. (1988a) Introduction. In Coates, J. and Cameron, D. (eds) *Women in Their Speech Communities: New Perspectives on Language and Sex*, Longman, London.

Coates, J. (1988b) Gossip revisited: language in all-female groups. In Coates, J. and Cameron, D. (eds) (1989) *Women in Their Speech Communities: New Perspectives on Language and Sex*, Longman, London.

Coates, J. and Cameron, D. (eds) (1988) *Women in Their Speech Communities: New Perspectives on Language and Sex*, Longman, London.

Coates, K. and Silburn, R. (1970) *Poverty and the Forgotten Englishmen*, Penguin Books, Harmondsworth.

Cockburn, C. (1983) *Brothers: Male Dominance and Technological Change*, Pluto, London.

Cohler, B. J. and Grunebaum, H. U. (1981) *Mothers, Grandmothers and Daughters*, John Wiley and Sons, New York.

Collins, P. H. (1992) Black women and motherhood. In Thorne, B. and Yalom, M. (eds) *Rethinking the Family: Some Feminist Questions*, Northeastern University Press, Boston.

Connidis, I. A. (1989) Siblings as friends in later life, *American Behavioral Scientist* 33, 1: 81–93.

Cornell, D. (1991) *Beyond Accommodation: Ethical Feminism, Deconstruction and the Law*, Routledge, New York.

Cotterill, P. (1994) *Friendly Relations? A Study of Mothers-in-law and Daughters-in-law*, Taylor and Francis, London.

Cotterill, P. (1992) Interviewing women: issues of friendship, vulnerability and power, *Women's Studies International Forum* 15, 5/6: 593–606.

Cozby, J. C. (1973) Self-disclosure: a literature review, *Psychological Bulletin* 79: 73–91.

Crapanzano, V. (1984) Life histories (review article), *American Anthropologist* 86: 953–60.

Cuskelly, M. and Dadds, M. (1992) Behavioural problems in children with Down's Syndrome and their siblings, *Journal of Child Psychology and Psychiatry and Allied Disciplines* 33, 4: 749–61.

Davies, B. and Banks, C. (1992) The gender trap: a feminist post structuralist analysis of primary school children's talk about gender, *Journal of Curriculum Studies* 24, 1: 1–25.

Davies, T. (1988) *Distant Voices, Still Lives*, BFI/Channel Four/ZDF, GB and DE.

Delphy, C. (2000) Feminism at a standstill, *New Left Review* 4: 159–62.

Delphy, C. and Leonard, D. (1992) *Familiar Exploitation: A New Analysis of Marriage in Contemporary Western Societies*, Polity, Cambridge.

Department of Health (1988) *Protecting Children: A Guide for Social Workers Undertaking A Comprehensive Assessment*, HMSO, London.

Derlega, V. J., Winstead, B. A., Wang, P. T. P. and Hunter, S. (1986) Gender effects in an initial encounter: a case where men exceed women in disclosure, *Journal of Social and Personal Relationships* 2: 25–44.

Di Leonardo, M. (1992) The female world of cards and holidays: women, families and the work of kinship. In Thorne, B. and Yalom, M. (eds) *Rethinking the Family: Some Feminist Questions*, Northeastern University Press, Boston.

Dipietro, S. B. (1987) The effects of intrafamilial child sexual abuse on the adjustment and attitudes of adolescents, *Violence and Victims* 2, 1: 59–78.

Doucet, A. (1995) Gender Equality, Gender Differences and Care: Towards Understanding Gendered Labour in British Dual Earner Households. Unpublished PhD dissertation, University of Cambridge.

Doucet, A. (1993) Who remembers birthdays? Who cleans the loo? Issues of Methods and Methodology in Data Collection on Gender and Household Labour. Working Paper No. 13, Sociological Research Group, University of Cambridge.

Dowdeswell, J. (1988) *Sisters on Sisters: A Fascinating Look at their Special Relationship*, Grapevine, Northampton.

Downing, C. (2001) Reproductive Decision Making in Families at Risk for Huntingdon's Disease. Unpublished PhD dissertation, University of Cambridge.

Downing, C. (1988) *Psyche's Sisters: Re-Imagining the Meaning of Sisterhood*, Harper and Row, San Francisco.

Drummond, W. J. (1991) Adolescent relationships in a period of change: a New Zealand perspective, *International Journal of Adolescence and Youth* 2, 4: 275–86.

Duck, S. (1991) *Friends For Life: The Psychology of Personal Relationships*, Harvester-Wheatsheaf, London. (First published 1983.)

Duck, S. (1990) Relationships as unfinished business: out of the frying pan and into the 1990s, *Journal of Social and Personal Relationships* 7: 5–29.

Duck, S. and Perlman, D. (1985) The thousand islands of personal relationships: a prescriptive analysis for future explorations. In Duck, S. and Perlman, D. (eds) *Understanding Personal Relationships*, Sage, London.

Duncan, S. and Edwards, R. (1998) *Lone Mothers and Paid Work: Gendered Moral Rationalities*, Macmillan, London.

Dunn, J. (1993) *Young Children's Close Relationships: Beyond Attachment*, Sage, London.

Dunn, J. (1984) *Sisters and Brothers*, Fontana, London.

Dunn, J. and Kendrick, C. (1982) *Siblings: Love, Envy and Understanding*, Fontana, London.

Dunne, G. A. (2000) Opting into motherhood: lesbians blurring the boundaries and re-defining the meaning of parenting and kinship, *Journal of Gender and Society* 14, 1.

Dunne, G. A. (1996) *Lesbian Lifestyles: Women's Work and the Politics of Sexuality*, Macmillan – now Palgrave Macmillan, Basingstoke.

Dyke, S. (1987) Saying 'no' to psychotherapy: consultation and assessment in a case of sexual abuse, *Journal of Child Psychotherapy* 13, 2: 65–79.

East, P. and Felice, M. E. (1992) Pregnancy risk among the younger sisters of pregnant and childbearing adolescents, *Journal of Developmental and Behavioural Pediatrics* 13, 2: 128–36.

Edelman, H. (1994) *Motherless Daughters: The Legacy of Loss*, Hodder and Stoughton, London.

Edwards, R. (1993) *Mature Women Students: Separating or Connecting Family and Education*, Taylor and Francis, London.

Edwards, R. and Ribbens, J. (1998) Living on the edges: public knowledge, private lives, personal experience. In Ribbens, J. and Edwards, R. (eds) *Feminist Dilemmas in Qualitative Research: Public Knowledge and Private Lives*, Sage, London.

Edwards, R., Ribbens, J. and Gillies, V. (1999) Shifting boundaries and power in the research process: the example of researching 'step-families'. In Seymour, J. and Bagguley, P. (eds) *Relating Intimacies: Power and Resistance*, Macmillan – now Palgrave Macmillan, Basingstoke.

Epstein, D. (1993) *Changing Classroom Cultures: Anti-Racism, Politics and Schools*, Trentham Books, Stoke-on-Trent.

Ervin-Tripp, S. (1989) Sisters and brothers. In Zukow, P. G. (ed.) *Sibling Interaction across Cultures: Theoretical and Methodological Issues*, Springer-Verlag, New York and London.

Evans, M. (1993) Reading lives: how the personal might be social, *Sociology* 27, 1: 5–13.

Fabera, A. and Mazlish, E. (1987) *Siblings without Rivalry: How to Help Your Children Live Together So You Can Live Too*, Avon Books, New York.

Faderman, L. (1981) *Surpassing the Love of Men: Romantic Friendship and Love Between Women from the Renaissance to the Present*, Women's Press, London.

Fallon, I. (1988) *The Rise and Rise of Saatchi and Saatchi*, Hutchinson, London.

Farmer, P. (1999) (ed.) *Sisters: An Anthology*, Penguin, London.

Felson, R. B. and Russo, N. J. (1988) Parental punishment and sibling aggression, *Social Psychology Quarterly* 51, 1: 11–18.

Finch, J. (1989) *Family Obligations and Social Change*, Polity and Blackwell, Cambridge and Oxford.

Finch, J. and Mason, J. (1993) *Negotiating Family Responsibilities*, Routledge, London.

Finch, J. and Mason, J. (1990) Filial obligations and kin support for elderly people, *Ageing and Society* 10: 151–75.

Firth, R., Hubert, J. and Forge, A. (1969) *Families and their Relatives*, Routledge, London.

Fischer, C. (1982) *To Dwell among Friends*, University of California Press, Berkeley.

Fischer, C., Jackson, R. M., Stueve, C. A., Gerson, K., McCallister Jones, L. and Baldassare, M. (1977) *Networks and Places*, Free Press, New York.

Fischer, L. R. (1986) *Linked Lives: Adult Daughters and Their Mothers*, Harper and Row, New York.

Fishel, E. (1994) *Sisters: Shared Histories, Lifelong Ties*, Conari Press, Berkeley, California. (First published 1979.)

Flannery, D. (1997) Brothers and sisters: sibling loves in *Paris is Burning*, *Irish Journal of American Studies* 6: 171–86.

Flax, J. (1990) *Thinking Fragments*, University of California Press, Berkeley.

Fortenberry, J. D. (1986) Sister–sister incest as a manifestation of multigenerational sexual abuse, *Journal of Adolescent Health Care* 7, 3: 202–4.

Foucault, M. (1986) *The History of Sexuality*, Vol. I, Penguin Books, Harmondsworth.

Foucault, M. (1985) *The Use of Pleasure* (translated by R. Hurley), Penguin Viking, London.

Foucault, M. (1981) *The History of Sexuality*, Vol. II, Viking, London.

Foucault, M. (1980) *Power/Knowledge* (translated by C. Gordon), Harvester, Brighton.

Foucault, M. (1977) *Discipline and Punish: The Birth of the Prison* (translated by A. Sheridan), Pantheon Books, New York.

Foucault, M. (1972) *The Archeology of Knowledge* (translated by A.M. Sheridan Smith), Tavistock, London.

Fowler, H. W. and Fowler, F. G. (1964) *The Concise Dictionary of Current English* (5th edition), Claredon Press, Oxford.

Fox-Genovese, E. (1991) *Feminism without Illusions: A Critique of Individualism*, University of North Carolina Press, Chapel Hill and London.

Francis, B. J. (1996) Children's Constructions of Gender, Power, and Adult Occupation. Unpublished PhD thesis, University of North London.

Franklin, S. (1997) *Embodied Progress: A Cultural Account of Assisted Conception*, Routledge, London.

Frazer, L. (1988a) Talking about Femininity: the Concept of Ideology on Trial. Unpublished DPhil Thesis, Oxford University.

Frazer, L. (1988b) Teenage girls talking about class, *Sociology* 22, 3: 343–58.

Frecknall, P. and Luks, A. (1992) An evaluation of parental assessment of the Big Brothers/Big Sisters Program in New York City, *Adolescence* 27, 107: 715–18.

Frisby, D. and Featherstone, M. (eds) (1997) *Simmel on Culture: Selected Writings*, Sage, London.

Fulker, D. W., Cherny, S. S., Sham P. C. and Hewitt, J. K. (1999) Combined linkage and association sib-pair analysis for quantitative traits, *American Journal of Human Genetics* 64: 259–67.

Gage, J. (1989) *George Field and his Circle: From Romanticism to the Pre-Raphaelite Brotherhood*, Christie's, London.

Gallagher, P. A. and Powell, T. H. (1989) Brothers and sisters: meeting special needs, *Topics in Early Childhood Special Education* 8, 4: 24–37.

Gath, A. and Gumley, D. (1987) Retarded children and their siblings, *Journal of Child Psychology and Psychiatry and Allied Disciplines* 28, 5: 715–30.

Ghuman, P. A. S. (1991) Best or worst of two worlds? A study of Asian adolescents, *Educational Research* 33, 2: 121–32.

Giallombardo, R. (1966) *Society of Women*, Wiley, New York.

Giddens, A. (1992) *The Transformation of Intimacy: Sexuality, Love and Eroticism in Modern Societies*, Polity, Cambridge.

Gilligan, C., Lyons, N. P. and Hanmer, T. J. (eds) (1990) *Making Connections: The Relational Worlds of Adolescent Girls at Emma Willard School*, Harvard University Press, Cambridge, Mass. and London.

Gilligan, C., Ward, J. V., Taylor, J. M. and Bardige, B. (eds) (1988) *Mapping the Moral Domain: A Contribution of Women's Thinking to Psychological Theory and Education*, Centre for the Study of Gender, Education and Human Development, Harvard University Graduate School of Education, Cambridge, Mass.

Gilmore, L. (1994) The mark of autobiography: postmodernism, autobiography, and genre. In Aschley, K., Gilmore, L. and Peters, G. (eds) *Autobiography and Postmodernism*, University of Massachusetts Press, Amherst.

Gladstone, J. and Montgomery, G. (1990) The impact of a disabled child's hospitalisation on the social relationships of siblings, *Canadian Journal of Rehabilitation* 3, 4: 223–32.

Glaser, B. G. and Strauss, A. (1967) *The Discovery of Grounded Theory*, Aldine, Chicago.

Gold, D. T. (1987) Siblings in old age: something special, *Canadian Journal on Aging* 6, 3: 199–215.

Goodman, N. C. (1987) Girls with learning disabilities and their sisters: how are they faring in adulthood? *Journal of Clinical Child Psychology* 16, 4: 290–300.

Gordon, L. (1994) *Shared Lives*, Vintage, London.

Gouldner, M. and Symons Strong, M. (1987) *Speaking of Friendship: Middleclass Women and their Friends*, Greenwood Press, New York and London.

Gramsci, A. (1971) *Selections from the Prison Notebooks*, Lawrence and Wishart, London.

Grant, L. (1994) Sisters under the skin, *The Guardian* 24 October.

Green, J., Richards, M., Murton, F., Statham, H. and Hallowell, N. (1997) Family communication and genetic counselling: the case of hereditary breast and ovarian cancer, *Journal of Genetic Counselling* 6: 45–60.

Griffin, C. (1994) Absences that matter: constructions of sexuality in studies of young women's friendship groups, paper given at the *BSA Sexualities in Social Contexts* Conference, University of Central Lancashire, Preston, 28–31 March.

Griffin, C. (1992) Fear of a black (and working class) planet: young women and the racialisation of reproductive politics, *Feminism and Psychology* 2, 3: 491–4.

Griffiths, M. (1995a) Making a difference: feminism, post-modernism and the methodology of educational research, *British Educational Research Journal* 21, 2: 219–35.

Griffiths, M. (1995b) *Feminisms and the Self: The Web of Identity*, Routledge, London.

Gross, E. (1987) Feminist theory and the challenge to knowledges, *Women's Studies International Forum*, 10: 475–80.

Guba, E. G. and Lincoln, Y. S. (1994) Competing paradigms in qualitative research. In Denzin, N. K. and Lincoln, Y. S., *Handbook of Qualitative Research*, Sage, London.

Gullestad, M. (1984) *Kitchen Table Society*, Universitets Forlaget, Oslo.

Gully, K., Dengerink, H., Pepping, M. and Bergstrom, D. (1981) Research note: sibling contribution to violent behaviour, *Journal of Marriage and the Family* 43: 333–7.

Hall, S. (1992) The West and the Rest: discourse and power. In Hall, S. and Gieben, B. (eds) *Formations of Modernity: Understanding Modern Societies – An Introduction* (Book 1) Polity Press/Blackwell/The Open University, Cambridge and Oxford.

Hallett, C. and Prout, A. (eds) (2003) *Hearing the Voices of Children: Social Policy for a New Century*, Routledge Falmer, London.

Harding, S. (1987) Conclusion: epistemological questions. In Harding, S. (ed.) *Feminism and Methodology*, Open University Press, Milton Keynes.

Harrison, B. and Lyon, E. S. (1993) A note on ethical issues in the use of autobiography in sociological research, *Sociology* 27, 1: 101–9.

Hauser, R. M. and Wong, R. S. (1989) Sibling resemblance and intersibling effects in educational attainment, *Sociology of Education* 62. 3: 149–71.

Hays, R. B. (1988) Friendship. In Duck, S., Hay, D. F., Hobfoll, S. E., Ickes, W. and Montgomery, B. M. (eds) *A Handbook of Personal Relationships*, Wiley, Chichester.

Hearn, J. (1992) *Men in the Public Eye: the Construction and Deconstruction of Public Men and Public Patriarchies*, Routledge, London.

Helgeson, V. S., Shaver, P. and Dyer, M. (1987) Prototypes of intimacy and distance in same sex and opposite sex relationships, *Journal of Social and Personal Relationships* 4: 195–233.

Henriques, J., Hollway, W., Urwin, C., Venn, C. and Walkderdine, V. (eds) (1984) *Changing the Subject: Psychology, Social Regulation and Subjectivity*, Methuen, London and New York.

Henwood, K. L. (1995) Adult mother–daughter relationships: subjectivity, power and critical psychology, *Theory and Psychology* 5, 4: 483–510.

Hey, V. (1997) *The Company She Keeps: An Ethnography of Girls' Friendship*, Open University Press, Buckingham.

Hey, V. (1986) *Patriarchy and Pub Culture*, Tavistock, London.

Hochschild, A. R. (1973) *The Managed Heart: The Commercialisation of Human Feeling*, University of California Press, Berkeley.

Hochschild, A. (1983) *The Unexpected Community*, Prentice Hall, Englewood Cliffs, NJ.

Hoffmann-Riem, C. (1990) *The Adopted Child: Family Life with Double Parenthood*, Transaction Publishers, New Brunswick and London.

Hogg, C., Barker, R. and McGuire, C. (eds) (1996) *Health Promotion and the Family: Messages from Four Research Studies*, Health Education Authority, London.

Holland, J. (1996) The gender agenda in education, EU208, *Exploring Educational Issues*, Block 5 Unit 3, The Open University, Milton Keynes.

Holland, J. and Ramazanoglu, C. (1994) Coming to conclusions: power and interpretation in researching young women's sexuality. In Maynard, M. and Purvis, J. (eds) *Researching Women's Lives From a Feminist Perspective*, Taylor and Francis, London.

Holland, J., Ramazanoglu, R., Sharpe, S. and Thomson, R. (with Rhodes, T.) (1998) *The Male in the Head: Heterosexuality and Power*, Tufnell Press, London.

Holland, J., Mauthner, M. and Sharpe, S. (1996) *Family Matters: Communicating Health Messages in the Family*, Health Education Authority, London.

Holland, J., Ramazanoglu, C., Sharpe, S. and Thomson, R. (1992) *Pressured Pleasure: Young Women and the Negotiation of Sexual Boundaries*, WRAP Paper 7, Tufnell Press, London.

Holland, J., Ramazanoglu, C., Scott, S., Sharpe, S. and Thomson, R. (1991a) Between embarrassment and trust: young women and the diversity of condom use. In Aggleton, P., Hart, G. and Davies, P. (eds) *AIDS: Responses, Interventions and Care*, Falmer, Brighton.

Holland, J., Ramazanoglu, C., Scott, S., Sharpe, S. and Thomson, R. (1991b) *Pressure, Resistance, Empowerment: Young Women and the Negotiation of Safer Sex*, WRAP Paper 6, Tufnell Press, London.

Hollway, W. (1989) *Subjectivity and Method in Psychology: Gender, Meaning and Science*, Sage, London.

Hollway, W. (1984) Gender difference and the production of subjectivity. In Henriques, J., Hollway, W., Urwin, C., Venn, C. and Walkderdine, V. (eds) (1984) *Changing the Subject: Psychology, Social Regulation and Subjectivity*, Methuen, London and New York.

Hudson, G. A. (1992) *Sibling Love and Incest in Jane Austen's Fiction*, Macmillan – now Palgrave Macmillan, London.

Hughes, C. (1998) Learning to be intellectually insecure: the dis/empowering effects of reflexive practice, *International Journal of Social Research Methodology* vol. 1, 4: 281–96.

Ihinger-Tallman, M. (1986) Sibling and stepsibling bonding in stepfamilies, paper presented at the *Annual Conference of the National Council on Family Relations*, Dearborn, Michigan, 3–7 November.

Ikels, C. (1988) Delayed reciprocity and the support networks of the childless elderly, *Journal of Comparative Family Studies* 19, 1: 99–112.

Illman, J. (1993) The carnal cabaret, *The Guardian*, 30 November.

Jackson, S. (1992) The amazing deconstructing woman, *Trouble and Strife* 25: 25–31.

Jalongo, M. R. and Renck, M. A. (1985) Sibling relationships: a recurrent developmental and literary theme, *Childhood Education* 61, 5: 346–51.

Jamieson, L. (1999) Intimacy transformed? A critical look at the 'pure relationship', *Sociology* 33, 3: 477–94.

Jamieson, L. (1998) *Intimacy: Personal Relationships in Modern Societies*, Polity, Cambridge.

Jerrome, D. (1984) Good company: The sociological implications of friendship, *Sociological Review* 32: 696–718.

Jerrome, D. (1981) The significance of friendship for women in later life, *Ageing and Society* 1, 2: 175–97.

Joas, H. (1991) Mead's position in intellectual history and his early philosophical writings. In Aboulafia, M. (ed.) *Philosophy, Social Theory and the Thought of George Herbert Mead*, State University of New York Press, Albany.

Johnson, R. (1986) The story so far: and further transformations? In Punter, D. (ed.) *Introduction to Contemporary Cultural Studies*, Longman, London.

Jones, A. (1993) Becoming a 'girl': post-structuralist suggestions for educational research, *Gender and Education* 5, 2: 157–66.

Khan, V. S. (ed.) (1979) *Minority Families in Britain: Support and Stress*, Macmillan, London.

Kitzinger, J. (1994) The methodology of focus groups: the importance of interaction between research participants, *Sociology of Health and Illness* 16, 1: 103–21.

Knight, S. (1983) *The Brotherhood: The Secret World of the Freemasons*, Granada, London.

Koch-Hattem, A. (1986) Siblings' experience of pediatric cancer: interviews with children, *Health and Social Work* 11, 2: 107–17.

Komarovsky, M. (1967) *Blue Collar Marriage*, Vintage Books, New York.

Kranichfeld, M. L. (1987) Rethinking family power, *Journal of Family Issues* 8, 1: 42–56.

Kuhn, A. (1995) *Family Secrets: Acts of Memory and Imagination*, Verso, London.

Lamb, M. E. and Sutton-Smith, B. (eds) (1982) *Sibling Relationships: Their Nature and Significance across the Lifespan*, Lawrence Erlbaum Associates, Hillsdale, NJ and London.

Lapalus-Netter, G. (1989) Frères et soeurs d'enfants handicappés: la souffrance inapparente [Brothers and sisters of the handicapped child: the hidden suffering], Special Issue: Studies by the University Hospital Research Centre of Saint-Etienne, *Psychologie Médicale* 21, 2: 189–92.

Larson, S. S. (1982) The two sides of the house: identity and social organisation in Kilbroney, Northern Ireland. In Cohen, A. P. (ed.) *Belonging, Social Organisation in British Rural Studies*, Manchester University Press, Manchester.

Laslett, B. and Brenner, J. (1989) Gender and social reproduction: historical perspectives, *Annual Review of Sociology* 15: 381–404.

Lasser, C. (1988) 'Let us be sisters forever': the sororal model of nineteenth-century female friendship, *Signs: Journal of Women in Culture and Society* 14, 11: 158–81.

Lather, P. (1988) Feminist perspectives on empowering research methodologies, *Women's Studies International Forum* 11, 6: 569–81.

Lauretis, T. de (1986) Feminist studies/critical studies: issues, terms and contexts. In Lauretis, T. de (ed.) *Feminist Studies/Critical Studies*, Indiana University Press, Bloomington.

Lauretis, T. de (1984) *Alice Doesn't: Feminism, Semiotics, Cinema*, Indiana University Press, Bloomington.

Laviola, M. (1992) Effects of older brother–younger sister incest: a study of the dynamics of 17 cases, *Child Abuse and Neglect* 16, 3: 409–21.

Lawler, S. (2000) *Mothering the Self: Mothers, Daughters, Subjects*, Routledge, London.

Lees, S. (1993) *Sugar and Spice: Sexuality and Adolescent Girls*, Penguin Books, Harmondsworth.

Lees, S. (1986) *Losing Out: Sexuality and Adolescent Girls*, Hutchinson, London.

Leonard, D. and Hood-Williams, J. (1988) *Families*, Macmillan – now Palgrave Macmillan, Basingstoke.

Lessor, R. (1993) All in the family: social processes in ovarian egg donation between sisters, *Sociology of Health and Illness* 15, 3: 393–413.

Lewin, E. (1993) *Lesbian Mothers: Accouts of Gender in American Culture*, Cornell University Press, Ithaca, NY and London.

Lewis, K. (1987) Bulimia as a communication to siblings, Special Issue: Psychotherapy with families, *Psychotherapy* 24, 3: 640–5.

Leyton, E. (ed.) (1974) *The Compact: Selected Dimensions of Friendship*, Newfoundland Social and Economic Papers No. 3, Institute of Social and Economic Research, Memorial University of Newfoundland, University of Toronto Press, Toronto.

Lobato, D. J., Miller, C. T., Barbour, L., Hall, L. J. *et al.* (1991) Preschool siblings of handicapped children: interactions with mothers, *Research in Developmental Disabilities* 12, 4: 387–99.

Lugo, N. R. (1996) Empowerment education: a case study of the Resource Sisters/Compañeras Program, *Health Education Quarterly* 23, 3: 281–9.

Lugones, M. C. and Rosezelle, P. A. (1995) Sisterhood and friendship as feminist models. In Weiss, P. A. and Friedman, M. (eds) *Feminism and Community*, Temple University Press, Philadelphia.

Lynn, R., Hampson, S. and Agahi, E. (1989) Genetic and environmental mechanisms determining intelligence, neuroticism, extraversion and psychoticism: an analysis of Irish siblings, *British Journal of Psychology* 80, 4: 499–507.

Mackay, S. (ed.) (1993) *Such Devoted Sisters: An Anthology of Stories*, Virago, London.

Maltz, D. and Borker, R. (1982) A cultural approach to male-female miscommunication. In Gumperz, J. (ed.) *Language and Social Identity*, Cambridge University Press, Cambridge.

Mangold, W. and Koski, P. (1990) Gender comparisons in the relationship between parental and sibling violence and nonfamily violence, *Journal of Family Violence* 5: 225–35.

Mann, C. (1996) Girls' own story: the search for a sexual identity in times of family change. In Holland, J. and Adkins, L. (eds) *Sex, Sensibility and the Gendered Self*, Macmillan – now Palgrave Macmillan, London.

Marjoribanks, K. (1991) Sex composition of family sibships and family learning environments, *Psychological Reports* 69, 1: 97–8.

Mason, J. (1999) Deciding where to live: relational reasoning and narratives of the self. In McRae, S. (ed.) *Changing Britain: Families and Households in the 1990s*, Oxford University Press, Oxford.

Mason, J. (1996) Gender, care and sensibility in family and kin relationships. In Holland, J. and Adkins, L. (eds) *Sex, Sensibility and the Gendered Self*, Macmillan – now Palgrave Macmillan, London.

Mason, J. (1989) Reconstructing the public and the private: the home and marriage in later life. In Allan, G. and Crow, A. (eds) *Home and Family: Creating the Domestic Sphere*, Macmillan – now Palgrave Macmillan, London.

Mason, J. (1987) Gender Inequality in Long-Term Marriages. Unpublished PhD thesis, University of Kent.

Mathias, B. (1992) *Between Sisters: Secret Rivals, Intimate Friends*, Delta, New York.

Matthews, S. H. (1987) Provision of care to old parents: division of responsibility among adult children, *Research on Aging* 9, 1: 45–60.

Matthews, S. H., Werkner, J. E. and Delaney, P. J. (1989) Relative contributions of help by employed and nonemployed sisters to their elderly parents, *Journals of Gerontology* 44, 1: s36–s44.

Mauthner, M. (2001) Discourse analysis of sister life stories. Paper presented at the *Divisions and Divisions: Challenges to European Sociology*, 5th Conference of the European Sociological Association, Helsinki 28 August–1 September.

Mauthner, M. (2000) Snippets and silences: ethics and reflexivity in narratives of sistering, *International Journal of Social Research Methodology: Theory and Practice*, 3, 4: 287–306.

Mauthner, M. (1998) Bringing silent voices into a public discourse: researching accounts of sister relationships. In Ribbens, J. and Edwards, R. (eds) *Feminist Dilemmas in Qualitative Research: Public Knowledge and Private Lives*, Sage, London.

Mauthner, M. (1997) Methodological aspects of collecting data from children: lessons from three research projects, *Children and Society* 11, 1: 16–28.

May, T. (1998) Reflexivity in the age of reconstructive social science, *International Journal of Social Research Methodology* vol. 1, 1: 7–24.

Maynard, M. (1995) Beyond the 'Big Three': the development of feminist theory into the 1990s, *Women's History Review* 4, 3: 259–81.

Maynard, M. (1994) Methods, practice and epistemology: the debate about feminism and research. In Maynard, M. and Purvis, J. (eds) *Researching Women's Lives from a Feminist Perspective*, Taylor and Francis, London.

Maynard, M. (1993) Feminism and the possibilities of a postmodern research practice: extended review, *British Journal of Sociology of Education* 14, 3: 327–31.

Maynard, M. and Purvis, J. (1994) Doing feminist research. In Maynard, M. and Purvis, J. (eds) *Researching Women's Lives from a Feminist Perspective*, Taylor and Francis, London.

McCall, C. J. (1988) The organisational life cycle of relationships. In Duck, S., Hay, D. F., Hobfoll, S. E., Ickes, W. and Montgomery, B. M. (eds) *A Handbook of Personal Relationships*, Wiley, Chichester.

McFarland, M. B. (1938) *Relationships between Young Sisters as Revealed in Their Overt Responses*, Bureau of Publications, Teachers' College, Columbia University, New York.

McHale, S. M., Sloan, J. and Simeonsson, R. J. (1986) Sibling relationships of children with autistic, mentally retarded, and non-handicapped brothers and sisters, *Journal of Autism and Developmental Disorders* 16, 4: 399–413.

McNamee, S. (1997) 'I won't let her in my room' – sibling strategies of power and resistance around computer and video games. In Seymour, J. and Bagguley, P. (eds) *Relating Intimacies: Power and Resistance*, Macmillan – now Palgrave Macmillan, Basingstoke.

McNaron, T. A. H. (1985) *The Sister Bond: A Feminist View of a Timeless Connection*, Pergamon, Oxford.

McNay, L. (2000) *Gender and Agency: Reconfiguring the Subject in Feminist and Social Theory*, Polity, Cambridge.

McRae, S. (ed.) (1999) *Changing Britain: Families and Households in the 1990s*, Oxford University Press, Oxford.

McRobbie, A. (1991) *Feminism and Youth Culture: From Jackie to Just Seventeen*, Macmillan – now Palgrave Macmillan, London.

McRobbie, A. (1977) Working Class Girls and the Culture of Femininity. Unpublished MA thesis, Birmingham University.

McRobbie, A. and Nava, M. (eds) (1984) *Gender and Generation*, Macmillan – now Palgrave Macmillan, London.

Medick, H. and Sabean, D. W. (1984) *Interest and Emotion: Essays on the Study of Family and Kinship*, Cambridge University Press, Cambridge.

Mendelson, M. J. (1990) *Becoming a Brother: A Child Learns about Life, Family and Self*, MIT Press, Cambridge, Mass.

Mens-Verhulst, J. van (1993a) Introduction. In Mens-Verhulst, J. van, Schreurs, K. and Woertman, L. (eds) *Daughtering and Mothering: Female Subjectivity Reanalysed*, Routledge, London and New York.

Mens-Verhulst, J. van (1993b) Beyond daughtering and mothering. In Mens-Verhulst, J. van, Schreurs, K. and Woertman, L. (eds) *Daughtering and Mothering: Female Subjectivity Reanalysed*, Routledge, London and New York.

Mies, M. (1983) Women's research or feminist research? The debate surrounding feminist science and methodology. In Fonow, M. M. and Cook, J. A. (eds) *Beyond Methodology: Feminist Scholarship as Lived Research*, Indiana University Press, Bloomington.

Miller, D. L. (ed.) (1982) *The Individual and the Social Self: Unpublished Work of George Herbert Mead*, University of Chicago Press, Chicago.

Miller, J. (1990) *Seductions: Readings in Reading and Culture*, Virago, London.

Mirza, H. S. (1992) *Young, Female and Black*, Routledge, London.

Mogey, J. (1956) *Family and Neighbourhood*, Oxford University Press, Oxford.

Monck, E. (1991) Patterns of confiding relationships among adolescent girls, *Journal of Child Psychology and Psychiatry and Allied Disciplines* 32, 2: 333–45.

Montgomery, B. M. (1988) Quality communication in personal relationships. In Duck, S., Hay, D. F., Hobfoll, S. E., Ickes, W. and Montgomery, B. M. (eds) *A Handbook of Personal Relationships*, Wiley, Chichester.

Morgan, D. (1999) Risk and family practices: accounting for change and fluidity in family life. In Silva, E. and Smart, C. (eds) *The New Family*, Sage, London.

Morgan, D. (1996) *Family Connections: An Introduction to Family Studies*, Polity Press, Cambridge.

Morgan, D. L. (1990) Combining the strengths of social networks, social support and personal relationships. In Duck, S. with Silver, R. C. (eds) *Personal Relationships and Social Support*, Sage, London.

Morgan, R. (1984) *Sisterhood is Powerful: An Anthology of Writings From the Women's Liberation Movement*, Vintage Books, New York.

Morrison, T. (1987) *Beloved*, Pan Books, London.

Mullender, A. (ed.) (1999) *We are Family: Sibling Relationships in Placement and Beyond*, BAAF (British Agencies for Adoption and Fostering), London.

Muram, D., Speck, P. M. and Gold, S. S. (1991) Genital abnormalities in female siblings and friends of child victims of sexual abuse, *Child Abuse and Neglect* 15, 1–2: 105–10.

Murphy, L. and Della-Corte, S. (1989) Siblings, *Special Parent/Special Child* 5, 1.

Murphy, S. O. (1992) Using multiple forms of data: identifying pattern and meaning in sibling-infant relationships. In Gilgun, J. F., Daly, K. and Handel, G. (eds) *Qualitative Methods in Family Research*, Sage, London.

Nash, K. (1994) The feminist production of knowledge: is deconstruction a practice for women? *Feminist Review* 47: 65–77.

Nelson, H. L. (1996) Introduction. In Nelson, H. L. (ed.) *Feminism and Families*, Routledge, New York and London.

Nestor, P. (1985) *Female Friendships and Communities: Charlotte Brontë, George Eliot, Elizabeth Gaskell*, Clarendon, Oxford.

Nice, V. (1992) *Mothers and Daughters: The Distortion of a Relationship*, Macmillan – now Palgrave Macmillan, Basingstoke.

O'Brien, M. and Jones, D. (1996) Family and kinship in Barking and Dagenham. In Butler, T. and Rustin, M. (eds) (1996) *Rising in the East? The Regeneration of East London*, Lawrence & Wishart, London.

O'Broin, L. (1976) *Revolutionary Underground: The Story of the Irish Republican Brotherhood*, Gill and Macmillan, Dublin.

O'Connor, P. (1992) *Friendships Between Women: A Critical Review*, Harvester-Wheatsheaf, London.

O'Connor, P. (1991) Women's confidantes outside marriage: shared or competing sources of intimacy, *Sociology* 25, 2: 241–54.

O'Connor, P. (1990) The adult mother–daughter relationship: a uniquely and universally close relationship? *Sociological Review* 38, 2: 293–323.

O'Connor, P. (1987) Very Close Relationships. Unpublished PhD thesis, University of London.

Olesen, V. (1994) Feminisms and models of qualitative research. In Denzin, N. K. and Lincoln, Y. S. (eds) *Handbook of Qualitative Research*, Sage, Thousand Oaks, California.

Oliker, S. J. (1989) *Best Friends and Marriage: Exchange among Women*, University of California Press, Berkeley and Los Angeles.

Oliver, J. E. (1988) Successive generations of child maltreatment: the children, *British Journal of Psychiatry* October, 153: 543–53.

Orbach, S. and Eichenbaum, L. (1987) *Bittersweet: Facing up to Feelings of Love, Envy and Competition in Women's Friendships*, Century, London.

Ortiz, C. G. and Nuttall, E. V. (1987) Adolescent pregnancy: effects of family support, education and religion on the decision to carry or terminate among Puerto Rican teenagers, *Adolescence* 22, 88: 897–917.

Oz, S. and Fine, M. (1991) Family relationship patterns: perceptions of teenage mothers and their non-mother peers, *Journal of Adolescence* 14, 3: 293–304.

Parkin, R. (1997) *Kinship: An Introduction to the Basic Concepts*, Blackwell, Oxford.

Patton, M. Q. (1990) *Qualitative Evaluation and Research Methods*, Sage, London.

Personal Narratives Group (ed.) (1989) *Interpreting Women's Lives: Feminist Theory and Personal Narratives*, Indiana University Press, Bloomington.

Phoenix, A. (1991) *Young Mothers?*, Polity Press, Cambridge.

Phoenix, A., Woollett, A. and Lloyd, E. (eds) (1991) *Motherhood: Meanings, Practices and Ideologies*, Sage, London.

Potter, J. and Wetherell, M. (1994) Analysing discourse. In Bryman, A. and Burgess, R. G. (eds) *Analysing Qualitative Data*, Routledge, London.

Powell, B. and Steelman, L. C. (1990) Beyond sibship size: sibling density, sex composition, and educational outcomes, *Social Forces* 69, 1: 181–206.

Powers, E. A. and Bultena, G. L. (1976) Sex differences in the intimate friendships of old age, *Journal of Marriage and the Family* 38: 739–47.

Prendergast, S. (1989) Girls' experience of menstruation in school. In Holly, L. (ed.) *Girls and Sexuality: Teaching and Learning*, Open University Press, Milton Keynes.

Private Lives (1996) Such devoted sisters? *The Guardian*, 11 January.

Pulakos, J. (1987) Brothers and sisters: nature and importance of the adult bond, *Journal of Psychology* 121, 5: 521–2.

Ramazanoglu, C. (1989a) *Feminism and the Contradictions of Oppression*, Routledge, London.

Ramazanoglu, C. (1989b) Improving on sociology: the problems of taking a feminist standpoint, *Sociology* 23: 427–42.

Ramazanoglu, C. and Holland, J. (2000) Still telling it like it is: problems of feminist truth claims. In Ahmed, S., Kilby, J. and McNeil, M. *Transformations: Thinking through Feminism*, Routledge, London.

Ramazanoglu, C. and Holland, J. (1999) Tripping over experience: some problems in feminist epistemology, *Discourse*, 20 (3): 381–92.

Ramazanoglu, C. and Holland, J. (1997) Tripping over experience: some problems in feminist epistemology, paper presented at the *Transformations: Thinking through Feminisms Conference*, University of Lancaster, 17–19 July.

Rands, M. and Levinger, G. (1979) Implicit theories of relationship: an intergenerational study, *Journal of Personality and Social Psychology* 37: 645–61.

Raymond, J. (1986) *A Passion for Friends*, Women's Press, London.

Reck, A. J. (1981) *George Herbert Mead: Selected Writings*, University of Chicago Press, Chicago.

Reinharz, S. (1992) *Feminist Methods in Social Research*, Oxford University Press, Oxford.

Reis, H. T. and Shaver, P. (1988) Intimacy as an interpersonal process. In Duck, S., Hay, D. F., Hobfoll, S. E., Ickes, W. and Montgomery, B. M. (eds) *A Handbook of Personal Relationships*, Wiley, Chichester.

Reisman, J. M. (1981) Adult friendships. In Duck, S. and Gilmour, R. (eds) *Personal Relationships vol. 2: Developing Personal Relationships*, Academic Press, London and New York.

Reit, S. V. (1985) *Sibling Rivalry – The Bank Street College of Education Child Development Series*, Ballantine, New York.

Ribbens, J. (1994) *Mothers and Their Children: A Feminist Sociology of Childrearing*, Sage, London.

Ribbens, J. and Edwards, R. (1995) Introducing qualitative research on women in families and households, *Women's Studies International Forum* 18, 3: 247–58.

Rich, A. (1995) *What is Found There – Notebooks on Poetry and Politics*, Virago, London.

Rich, A. (1984) *Of Woman Born: Motherhood and Experience and Institution*, Virago, London.

Ricoeur, P. (1981) *Hermeneutics and the Human Sciences*, ed., trans. and intro. John B. Thompson, Cambridge University Press, Cambridge.

Riessman, C. K. (1989) Life events, meaning and narrative: the case of infidelity and divorce, *Social Science and Medicine* 29, 6: 743–51.

Rogers, A. (1993) Voice, play, and a practice of ordinary courage in girls' and women's lives, *Harvard Educational Review* 63: 265–95.

Rose, N. (1996) *Inventing Our Selves: Psychology, Power and Personhood*, Cambridge University Press, Cambridge.

Ross, H. G. and Milgram, J. I. (1982) Important variables in adult sibling relationships: A qualitative study. In Lamb, M. E. and Sutton-Smith, B. (eds) *Sibling Relationships: Their Nature and Significance Across the Lifespan*, Lawrence Erlbaum Associates, New Jersey and London.

Rossiter, A. B. (1994) Chips, coke and rock-'n'-roll: children's mediation of an invitation to a first dance party, *Feminist Review* 46: 1–20.

Rowe, D. C., Rodgers, J. L. and Meseck-Bushey, S. (1992) Sibling delinquency and the family environment: shared and unshared influences, *Child Development* 63, 1: 59–67.

Rubenfeld, M. I. and Gilroy, F. D. (1991) Relationship between college women's occupational interests and a single-sex environment, *Career Development Quarterly* 40, 1: 64–70.

Salvi, F., Michelucci, R., Plasmati, R., Parmeggiani, L., Zonari, P., Mascalchi, M. and Tassinari, C. A. (1992) Slowly progressive familial dementia with recurrent strokes and white matter hypodensities on CT scan, *Italian Journal of Neurological Sciences*, 13, 2: 135–40.

Sandmaier, M. (1995) *Original Kin: The Search for Connection Among Adult Sisters and Brothers*, Plume/Penguin, New York.

Schachter, F. F. and Stone, R. K. (eds) (1987) *Practical Concerns about Siblings: Bridging the Research–Practice Gap*, Haworth Press, New York and London.

Schutz, A. (1972) *The Phenomenology of the Social World*, (translated by Walsh, G. and Lehnert, F.) Heinemann, London. (First published 1967 and 1932.)

Schutz, A. and Luckmann, T. (1973) *The Structures of the Life-World*, (translated by Zaner, R. M. and Gengelhardt, H. T.), Northwestern University Press, Evanston, Ill.

Schutz, I. (ed.) (1966) *Three Studies in Phenomenological Philosophy – Collected Papers of Alfred Schutz*, Volume III, Martinus Nijhoff, The Hague.

Sedgwick, E. K. (ed.) (1997) *Novel Gazing: Queer Readings in Fiction*, Duke University Press, Durham, NC and London.

Segal, L. (1983) *What is to be Done about the Family?*, Penguin, London.

Seginer, R. (1992) Sibling relationships in early adolescence: a study of Israeli Arab sisters, *Journal of Early Adolescence* 12, 1: 96–110.

Seidl, F. W. (1982) Big sisters: an experimental evaluation, *Adolescence* 17, 65: 117–28.

Senapati, R. and Hayes, A. (1988) Sibling relationships of handicapped children: a review of conceptual and methodological issues, *International Journal of Behavioural Development* 11, 1: 89–115.

Serfontein, J. H. P (1979) *Brotherhood of Power: an Exposé of the Secret Afrikaner Broederbond*, Collings, London.

Sharpe, S. (1994) *Fathers and Daughters*, Routledge, London.

Shaw, A. (1988) *A Pakistani Community in Britain*, Blackwell, Oxford.

Side, K. (1999) Making and breaking women's friendships in feminist theory. In Symes, R. A., Kaloski, A. and Brown, H. (eds) *Celebrating Women's Friendship: Past, Present and Future*, Raw Nerve Books, York.

Silva, E. and Smart, C. (1999) The 'new' practices and politics of family life. In Silva, E. and Smart, C. (eds) *The New Family*, Sage, London.

Skeggs, B. (1997) *Formations of Class and Gender: Becoming Respectable*, Sage, London.

Smart, C. and Neale, B. (1999) *Family Fragments?*, Polity Press, Cambridge; Blackwell, Malden, Mass.

Smiley, J. (1991) *A Thousand Acres*, Fawcett Columbine, New York.

Smith, D. (1988) *The Everyday World as Problematic: A Feminist Sociology*, Open University Press, Milton Keynes. (First published 1987.)

Smith, D. (1974) Women's perspective as a radical critique of sociology, *Sociological Quarterly* 44: 7–13.

Smith-Rosenberg, C. (1975) The female world of love and ritual: relations between women in nineteenth-century America, *Signs* 1, 1: 1–29.

Song, M. (1999) *Helping Out: Children's Labour in Ethnic Businesses*, Temple University Press, Philadelphia.

Southall Black Sisters (1990) *Against the Grain: A Celebration of Survival and Struggle*, Southall Black Sisters, Southall, Middlesex.

Spender, D. and Spender, L. (1984) *Scribbling Sisters*, Hale and Iremonger, Sydney.

Stacey, J. (1992) Backward toward the postmodern family: reflections on gender, kinship and class in the Silicon Valley. In Thorne, B. and Yalom, M. (eds) *Rethinking the Family: Some Feminist Questions*, Northeastern University Press, Boston.

Stack, C. (1974) *All Our Kin*, Harper and Row, New York.

Stake, R. E. (1994) Case studies. In Denzin, N. K. and Lincoln, Y. S. (eds) *Handbook of Qualitative Research*, Sage, Thousand Oaks, California.

Stanley, L. (1993) On auto/biography in sociology, *Sociology* 27, 1: 41–52.

Stanley, L. (1992) *The Auto/biographical I: The Theory and Practice of Feminist Auto/biography*, Manchester University Press, Manchester.

Stanley, L. (1987) Biography as microscope or kaleidoscope? The case of 'power' in Hannah Cullwick's relationship with Arthur Munby, *Women's Studies International Forum* 10: 19–37.

Stanley, L. and Morgan, D. (eds) (1993) Special Issue: Auto/biography in Sociology, *Sociology* 27, 1.

Stanley, L. and Wise, S. (1990) Method, methodology and epistemology in feminist research processes. In Stanley, L. (ed.) *Feminist Praxis: Research, Theory and Epistemology in Feminist Sociology*, Routledge, London.

Steedman, C. (1986) *Landscape for a Good Woman: A Story of Two Lives*, Virago, London.

Stoneman, Z., Brody, G. H., Davis, C. H. and Crapps, J. M. (1988) Childcare responsibilities, peer relations, and sibling conflict: older siblings of mentally retarded children, *American Journal on Mental Retardation* 93, 2: 174–83.

Stoneman, Z., Brody, G. H. and MacKinnon, C. E. (1986) Same-sex and cross-sex siblings: activity choices, roles, behavior and gender stereotypes, *Sex Roles* 15, 9–10: 495–511.

Straus, M., Gelles, R. and Steinmetz, S. (1980) *Behind Closed Doors: Family Violence in the American Family*, Anchor Press/Doubleday, New York.

Strauss, A. (1987) *Qualitative Analysis for Social Scientists*, Cambridge University Press, Cambridge.

Sulloway, F. J. (1996) *Born to Rebel: Birth Order, Family Dynamics, and Creative Lives*, Little, Brown and Company, London.

Tannen, D. (1991) *You Just Don't Understand: Women and Men in Conversation*, Virago, London.

Taylor, L. (1982) The effects of a non-related adult friend on children of divorce, *Journal of Divorce* 5, 4: 67–76.

Thompson, B., MacGillivray, I. and Fraser, C. (1991) Some factors in the choice of male or female sterilisation in Aberdeen, *Journal of Biosocial Science* 23, 3: 359–63.

Thomson, R. and Scott, S. (1991) *Learning about Sex: Young Women and the Social Construction of Sexual Identity*, WRAP Paper 4, Tufnell Press, London.

Thorne, B. (1992) Feminism and the family: two decades of thought. In Thorne, B. and Yalom, M. (eds) *Rethinking the Family: Some Feminist Questions*, Northeastern University Press, Boston.

Tong, R. (1992) *Feminist Thought: A Comprehensive Introduction*, Routledge, London.

Usher, P. (1996) Feminist approaches to research. In Scott, D. and Usher, R. (eds) *Understanding Educational Research*, Routledge, London.

Vandereycken, W. and Vrecken, E. van (1992) Siblings as co-patients and co-therapists in eating disorders. In Boer, F. and Dunn, J. (eds) *Children's Sibling Relationships: Developmental and Clinical Issues*, Lawrence Erlbaum Associates, Hove and London.

VanEvery, J. (1999) From modern nuclear family households to postmodern diversity? The sociological construction of 'families'. In Jagger, G. and Wright, C. (eds) *Changing Family Values*, Routledge, London.

VanEvery, J. (1995) *Heterosexual Women Changing the Family: Refusing to be a 'Wife'!*, Taylor and Francis, London.

Vaughan, D. (1987) *Uncoupling: Turning-Points in Intimate Relationships*, Methuen, London.

Walby, S. (1990) *Theorising Patriarchy*, Blackwell, Oxford.

Walkerdine, V. (1994) Femininity as performance. In Stone L. (ed.) *The Education Feminism Reader*, Routledge, London.

Walkerdine, V. (1990) *Schoolgirl Fictions*, Verso, London.

Walkerdine, V. (1986) Post-structuralist theory and everyday social practices: the family and the school. In Wilkinson, S. (ed.) *Feminist Social Psychology: Developing Theory and Practice*, Open University Press, Milton Keynes.

Walkerdine, V. (1985) On the regulation of speaking and silence: subjectivity, class and gender in contemporary schooling. In Steedman, C., Urwin, C. and Walkerdine, V. (eds) *Language, Gender and Childhood*, Routledge, London.

Wallinga, C., Paguio, L. and Skeen, P. (1987) When a brother or a sister is ill, *Psychology Today* 21, 8: 42–3.

Warman, D. W. (1986) Father-Adolescent Son Communication about Sexuality. Unpublished PhD dissertation, Syracuse University, New York.

Waters, B. G., Beumont, P. J., Touyz, S. and Kennedy, M. (1990) Behavioural differences between twin and non-twin female sibling pairs discordant for anorexia nervosa, *International Journal of Eating Disorders* 9, 3: 265–73.

Watson, M. (1997) The Eldest/Oldest Sister: a Feminised Role for Life? Unpublished MA dissertation, Institute of Education, University of London.

Weedon, C. (1987) *Feminist Practice and Poststructuralist Theory*, Blackwell, Oxford.

Weeks, J. (1995) *Invented Moralities: Sexual Values in an Age of Uncertainty*, Polity Press, Cambridge.

Weeks, J., Donovan, C. and Heaphy, B. (1999a) Everyday experiments: narratives of non-heterosexual relationships. In Silva, E. B. and Smart, C. (eds) *The New Family?*, Sage, London.

Weeks, J., Heaphy, B. and Donovan, C. (1999b) Partners by choice: equality, power and commitment in non-heterosexual relationships. In Allan, G. (ed.) *The Sociology of the Family: A Reader*, Blackwell, Oxford.

Weeks, J., Donovan, C. and Heaphy, B. (1999c) Families of choice. In McRae, S. (ed.) *Changing Britain: Families and Households in the 1990s*, Oxford University Press, Oxford.

Weeks, J., Heaphy, B. and Donovan, C. (1999d) Partnership rites: commitment and ritual in non-heterosexual relationships. In Seymour, J. and Bagguley, P. (eds) *Relating Intimacies: Power and Resistance*, Macmillan – now Palgrave Macmillan, Basingstoke.

Weiss, L. and Lowenthal, M. F. (1975) Life courses perspectives on friendship. In Lowenthal, M. F., Thurnher, M., Chiriboga, D. (eds) *Four Stages of Life*, Jossey-Bass, San Francisco and London.

Wellman, B. (1990) The place of kinfold in personal community networks, *Marriage and Family Review* 15: 195–221.

Weston, K. (1991) *Families We Choose: Lesbians, Gays, Kinship*, Columbia University Press, New York.

Wetherell, M. (1995) Social structures, ideology and family dynamics: the case of parenting. In Muncie, J., Wetherell, M., Langan, M., Dallos, R. and Cochrane, A. (eds) *Understanding the Family*, Sage/The Open University Press, London.

Whitehead, M. M. and Nokes, K. M. (1990) An examination of demographic variables, nurturance and empathy among homosexual and heterosexual Big Brother/Big Sister volunteers, *Journal of Homosexuality* 19, 4: 89–101.

Williams, S. and Bendelow, G. (1998) Emotions in social life: mapping the sociological terrain. In Bendelow, G. and Williams, S. (eds) *Emotions in Social Life: Critical Themes and Contemporary Issues*, Routledge, London.

Williams, T., Wetton, N. and Moon, A. (1989) *A Picture of Health: What Do You Do That Makes You Healthy and Keeps You Healthy?*, Health Education Authority, London.

Willmott, P. and Young, M. (1960) *Family and Class in a London Suburb*, Routledge, London.

Wilson, S. A. (1992) The family as caregivers: Hospice home care, *Family and Community Health* 15, 2: 71–80.

Woollett, A. and Dosanjh-Matwala, N. (1990) Asian women's experience of childbirth in East London: the support of fathers and female relatives, *Journal of Reproductive and Infant Psychology* 8, 1: 11–22.

Wright, P. H. (1982) Men's friendships, women's friendships and the alleged inferiority of the latter, *Sex Roles* 8, 1: 1–20.

Yeatman, J. and Reifel, S. (1992) Sibling play and learning, *Play and Culture* 5, 2: 141–58.

Young, M. and Willmott, P. (1962) *Family and Kinship in East London*, Penguin Books, Harmondsworth. (First published 1957.)

Index